REHRAS SAHIB & SOHILA

MANESHWAR S. CHAHAL

FiNGERPRINT!

Published 2025

FINGERPRINT!
Prakash Books

Fingerprint Publishing
@FingerprintP
@fingerprintpublishingbooks
www.fingerprintpublishing.com

ISBN: 978 93 5856 761 8

Praise for the series- *Way to God in Sikhism*

Japji Sahib

"Chahal's objective is to present easily understandable exposition of the lofty spiritual grandeur of Japuji to the English-knowing people. The treatise contains perceptive commentaries and closely reasoned critiques. The writing is crisp, research impressive, inferences adroit and conclusions sound—an accomplishment of sound merit and scholarship."

(Abstracts of Sikh Studies, Chandigarh)

"The author uses abundant imagery—the annotation creates a cascading effect. References intersperse freely with the author's version of the text and updates on other learned men's versions of the same phrase—this book is a labour of love—painstaking research has gone into it."

(The Tribune, Chandigarh)

"Very little work has been done on the Banis in English. Japji Sahib, Way to God in Sikhism is a praiseworthy effort in this direction. "

(The Ajit, Jullundur, in Punjabi.)

"Japji Sahib – Way to God in Sikhism", is an in-depth study of the Guru's revelatory message. The Japji encapsulated into thirty eight pauṛis (steps) has been brilliantly captured by the author. His familiarity with the earlier interpretations, combined with his profound insight into the scripture and keen mental perception animate his exposition with a charm and dignity. Chahal's exposition deserves to be ranked as one of the best."

(The Sikh Review, Calcutta)

"The author has put in a lot of hard work. It is well written and both the language employed and the idiom used flow easily. Chahal has collated an extensive array of explanations, views and interpretations on the Japji."

(Studies in Sikhism and Comparative Religion, New Delhi)

Āsa di Vār

"The intense exploration and research by the author is visible from page one—a remarkable thesis, well studied and argued in all subtle details—deserves all praise—strongly recommended as a must for all public libraries and private collections for regular perusal.

(Abstract of Ṣikh Studies, Chandigarh)

"The translation and explanations are detailed—it should help readers grasp the textual meaning of the Vār. Enjoy the book. It should deepen the ras of Āsa di Vār Kirtan next time you hear it."

(Studies in Sikhism and Comparative Religion, New Delhi)

Jāp Sahib

Third in the series 'Way to God in Sikhism', the first two being Japji Sahib and Āsa diVār, it is a beautiful production, perhaps the first of its kind in English. Shows the depth to which the author has gone in his study. The book is valuable for the English reading public—a valuable addition to the Gurbāṇi literature in English.

(Abstract of Sikh Studies, Chandigarh)

Dedicated to all those who see the Oneness in all His Creation

ACKNOWLEDGEMENTS

‘Way to God in Sikhism’ was conceptualised more than a decade ago, and the first book in the series, *Japji Sahib*, was published by Prakash Books in 2006, in hardcover and softcover simultaneously. It was reprinted and then brought out by them in an improved 2nd edition in 2013. The *Āsa di Vār* and the *Jāp Sahib* that followed have also both been well received. The reviews for the entire series have been kind; even more gratifying has been the feedback from individual readers who found the books useful and felt that it has improved their comprehension of the Guru’s word

This, the fourth book in the series ‘Way to God in Sikhism’, is presented to you in the hope that it will be of equal benefit to the lay seeker, in which category the author squarely places himself.

As with the earlier books, my work on this book has been greatly facilitated by the constant and sincere help from Sardar Darshan Singh, Chief Engineer (Retd) and Sardar Mohinder Pal Singh, Assitant General Manger (Retd). The many valuable suggestions from them have been immensely helpful. Sardar Darshan Singh went over the original text with a fine-tooth comb and Sardar MP Singh did the same at the publishing stage. I am greatly indebted to both these men of God.

My thanks are equally due to Prakash Books for the rigorous scrutiny of the text, which I hope will have made the book error free. Thank you Ashwaniji and Shikhaji. Thanks also to the editor and the proofreader who put in so much effort.

CONTENTS

1

INTRODUCTION

The prescription of precisely defined prayers, and the time and frequency for reciting these, is an inevitable part of any organised religion. Thus, the Hindu has his morning and evening rituals, along with numerous observances of eating restrictions and dress prescriptions. The Muslim has his five daily prayers, or *Namāz,* to be recited at prescribed times and in a specific fashion, facing the Mecca, which is to the West for the Muslims in most of Asia. In the same way, the Sikh is required to follow a certain discipline with regard to his prayer regimen. It is commanded of a Sikh, as part of the daily code of conduct, to follow the *Nitnem*, which literally translates as 'daily routine'. The *Ardās* is treated as an integral part of this routine and recited at the conclusion of the prayers both in the morning and in the evening. The Rehrās Sahib is the first of the two evening prayers, the other being the Sohila, which is often called Kirtan Sohila; probably because it is usually sung to music and not merely recited.

It would be relevant here to see how the presently prescribed code of conduct came into existence. There are numerous *Rehatnāmas* written at various times in Sikh history; many dated from soon after the passing of Guru

Gobind Singh. These lay down various prescriptions, some extremely detailed, a few more general in nature. As a result, the question of what should be the code of conduct, or *Rehat*, for a true Sikh had become a matter of convention and custom, and there inevitably was scope for different interpretations of what was required of a Sikh in his daily life, both in observance of his religious customs as also in his social interaction. The leaders of the community wisely decided, therefore, to take steps to standardise the practices and provide a uniform code to leave no doubt as to what every Sikh was required to do as a member of the Sikh *Panth*. The result of this initiative was the code, called the *Rehat Maryāda* that currently governs the daily life of a practising Sikh.

For this purpose the representative elected body of the community, the Shiromani Gurdwāra Prabandhak Committee (SGPC), set in motion, in 1931, a comprehensive process of consultation with eminent Sikh scholars and other persons who were important in the religious and social fields among the Sikhs. As we have noted above there were prevalent at that time many *Rehatnāmas,* guidelines for conduct, but there was no single document that could be seen as authoritatively laying down the code of conduct for the Sikh nation. The consultative process was intended to synthesise and standardise these practices based on the existing *Rehatnāmas,* as also the then existing practices, to achieve as much uniformity of opinion as was possible. The process was, inevitably, long and there were many references back and forth between various Sikh organisations. At the end of it, after nearly 15 years of hard work, there emerged the present *Rehat Maryāda,* a document that neatly synthesised the various viewpoints. This *Rehat Maryāda* was adopted formally in 1946. It prescribed various practices for guiding the Sikh through his daily interactions, and laid down, inter alia, the form of prayers, to be followed uniformly by all practising Sikhs. For a body of men that aspires to be called a nation homogeneity in this respect is as essential as any other social prescription.

This set of prayers thus prescribed is called the *Nitnem*. Article IV of the *Rehat Maryāda*, reproduced verbatim below, tells us precisely the time and mode of the prayers to be recited.

Article IV:-

(1) A Sikh should wake up in the ambrosial hours (three hours before dawn), take bath, and, concentrating his/her thoughts on One Immortal Being, repeat the name *Waheguru* (Wondrous Destroyer of Darkness).

(2) He/she should recite the following scriptural compositions every day:

a) The Japu, the Jaapu and the Ten Sawayyas–beginning *Sarawag Sudh*–in the morning

b) Sodar Rehrās comprising the following compositions:

(i) The nine hymns of the Guru Granth Sahib, occurring in the holy book after the Japji Sahib, the first of which begins with "*Sodar*" and the last of which ends with "*saran pare ki rakho sarma*",

(ii) The Benti Chaupayi of the tenth Guru, beginning "*hamri karo hath dai rachha*" and ending with "*dushtt dokh te leho bachai*",

(iii) The Sawayya beginning with the words "*pāe gahe jab te tumre*",

(iv) The Dohira beginning with the words "*sagal duār kau chhādd kai*",

(v) The first five and the last *pauṛi* (stanzas) of Anand Sahib and

(vi) The Mundawani and the Slok Mahla 5 beginning with "*tera kita jato nahi*" –in the evening after sunset.

c) The Sohila–to be recited at night before going to bed.

d) The morning and evening recitations should be concluded with the *Ardās* (formal supplication litany).

It will be seen that the three *Bāṇīs* that are prescribed for the morning are each the composition of a single author, Japji Sahib of Guru Nanak, and the Jap Sahib and Sawayyas of the tenth Nanak Guru Gobind Singh. On the other hand the two *Bāṇīs* prescribed for the evening prayers are composites, comprising hymns from the *Bāṇīs* of the later Gurus also. Thus, the Rehrās Sahib as spelt out in the *Rehat Maryāda* has hymns not only by Guru Nanak himself but also by the third, the fourth, and the fifth Nanak. It also, in addition, incorporates the *Chaupayi* composed by the tenth Nanak, the text of which is to be found from page 1386 to page 1388 of the Dasam Granth. After the recitation of the *Chaupayi*, the *Rehat Maryāda* prescribes that there will be recited six *pauṛis*, the first five and the fortieth of the Anand Sahib, a composition by the third Nanak. The Rehrās is then concluded with some more hymns composed by the fifth Nanak

It will also be noted that the Rehrās Sahib comprises not only the Sodar consisting of the hymns mentioned at pages 8 to 12 of the Sri Guru Granth Sahib (SGGS), but also the additional hymns as recounted above. It can safely be concluded that the Rehrās Sahib had at one time consisted only of the hymns from pages 8 to 12 of the SGGS, but has evolved over time into its present form, as evident from the fact that the committee of learned men included this expanded form into the Nitnem while formulating the *Rehat Maryāda.*

There is clear evidence that some of the *Bāṇīs* had been part of the daily prayer routine since the earliest days of this young religion. Referring to the earliest days of this new religion, Bhai Gurdas, that revered savant and great soul, says in *Pauṛi* 38 of the first of his *Vārs*–

So dar Ārti gāviai amrit velay jāp uchāra.

Why need we give so much credence to what Bhai Gurdas may have said? Who was he? It is useful here to take a brief look at this great man. When Guru Arjan Dev, the fifth Nanak, undertook the enormous, and most vital, task of compiling the compositions of the preceding Gurus and many Bhagats, he had Bhai Gurdas assisting him. The Guru collected, scrutinised, selected and then started the actual process of scribing these hymns and compositions into the form of a book. He consciously decided to include not only the hymns of the Gurus but also those of other saints. At the invitation of the Guru, followers of different sects, both Hindu and Muslim, came to the Guru and recited the hymns of their teachers. Guru Arjan then put his seal of approval on such hymns as closely echoed the philosophy enunciated by Guru Nanak, the philososphy he wanted to place before all mankind and to inculcate in his community. It is said that after the selections had been made, the Guru dictated the hymns to Bhai Gurdas, who did the actual scribing of the Granth Sahib. Learned ones say that not only did Bhai Gurdas himself do much of the scribing; he also supervised the team assembled by the fifth Nanak, consisting of four other scribes, namely Bhai Haria, Bhai Sant Das, Bhai Sukha and Bhai Mansa Ram. The task was completed, the index prepared and the book was then reverently bound and formally installed in the Harmandir Sahib on 16 August 1604 AD. It has become since that day, and for all times to come, the living Guru, the ever-present guide for a Sikh's spiritual as well as his mundane life.

There is some lack of unanimity among learned ones about the details of the early life of the remarkable Bhai Gurdas. The encyclopedia of Sikhism tells us that he was born in 1551 in a Bhalla Khatri family at Goindwal, a village on the banks of the river Beas, located in the present day district of Amritsar in the state of Punjab. His father, Bhai Ishar Das was a first cousin of the third Nanak, Guru Amar Das. Bhai Gurdas lost his mother, Bibi Jivani, in 1554 AD when he was barely three years old. His father passed away in 1563 AD, leaving him orphaned at the tender age of nine. The Guru Granth Vishvakosh (Ed: Dr. Rattan Singh Jaggi), on the other hand says the year of his birth could be anywhere between 1543–1553 AD, and that he was born in village Gillwali. Quoting the *Bansāwali Dasā(n) Pātshāhian ka* by Kesar Singh Chhibber the Vishvakosh says that his father died in 1554 AD and then in 1563 AD he also lost his mother, leaving him orphaned, and that when Guru Amar Das settled the town of Goindwal the entire family of Bhai Gurdas also shifted there.

In either case, the fact remains that Bhai Gurdas spent his tender years in Goindwal and acquired great knowledge of the scriptures, and also became proficient in all the then prevalent languages–Sanskrit, Persian, as also Punjabi in the Gurumukhi script and Brajbhāsha.

The innate brilliance of the young Gurdas reached fruition here as his early years at Goindwal gave him opportunity to interact with the many scholars and holy men who would often stop in the town that lay squarely on road between the two most important towns of the Mughal Empire–Lahore and Delhi. He was also, later, to spend time at that great and ancient centre of learning, Varanasi, where he studied Hindu scriptures even as he learnt Sanskrit.

The learned ones say that Guru Ram Das initiated him into Sikhism in 1579 AD. The Guru assigned to him the important office of the Sikh missionary in charge at Agra. He travelled extensively, visiting Agra, Lucknow, Rajasthan, as also the hill areas of Jammu and Chamba preaching the philosophy of Guru Nanak.

He was to become a highly respected scholar and an extremely influential preacher of the new and dynamic religion, Sikhism. There is some difference of opinion on his compositions also. The Vishvakosh tells us that though some learned ones say he composed 39*Vārs*, but most agree that there is also a 40th *Vār.* He also authored many *Kabits* in Brajbhāsha, the number of which is generally believed to be 556, though the Vishvakosh speaks of another 119 *Kabits* located through the efforts of the great saint-poet Bhai Vir Singh. In addition to these, there are six *sloks* in Sanskrit by him. Though none of his compositions is included in the Granth Sahib, but these are yet accorded semi-canonical status. These are among the hymns allowed to be sung as Kirtan in the Harmandir Sahib at Amritsar, along with the verses from the SGGS and the Dasam Granth, and of course from the works of Bhai Nand Lal.

Bhai Gurdas remained prominent in the affairs of the new community, also participating in the momentous event of the excavation of the pool at the Harmandir Sahib, which was commenced in 1577AD. Such was the renown of his scholarship that he was chosen to recite and explain hymns from the SGGS to Emperor Akbar when the Emperor visited Kartarpur Sahib in 1596-97 AD. This was the place where Guru Nanak had finally settled after he had completed his extensive travels to the four corners of the land, and countries beyond. It was in Kartarpur Sahib that Guru Nanak himself installed the second Nanak, Guru Angad.

Succession issues had caused some tension at that time and Guru Nanak's sons, Sri Chand and Lakhmi Das had not thereafter actively participated in the activities of the *Panth*, apparently losing all interest after they had been overlooked for the Guruship. Similar trouble surfaced briefly again when the third Nanak installed his son-in-law, Ram Das as the fourth Nanak in preference to his own sons, Mohri and Mohan. When the fifth Nanak was installed in 1581 AD, his elder brothers Prithi Chand and Mahadev opposed him. This was also the time when many were becoming alarmed at the growing strength of the new faith. Efforts were made to harm it by falsely accusing the Sikh philosophy of being anti-Muslim in tone. The situation was aggravated further by the family feuds within the Gurus' family.

There were thus attacks from outside as well as within and circumstances were so evolving that Sikhism was in real danger of facing official opposition from the rulers in its nascent stages. Akbar's visit is said to have arisen from the misinformation which the Guru's brother Prithi Chand was assiduously spreading as a result of his desire to be installed Guru himself. It is said that Bhai Gurdas's exposition so abundantly made clear to the Emperor that the thrust of the scripture of this new religion was purely spiritual, that the dark clouds of danger were soon dispelled. Akbar was a very secular ruler in any case and he seems to have readily comprehended the essentially egalitarian and humanistic spirit of Sikhism.

After the death of the fourth Nanak, Guru Ram Das, Bhai Gurdas had formed an equally close relationship with the fifth Nanak, Guru Arjan Dev. There was, of course, also the familial connection with the third Nanak. However, much beyond any family kinship the Guru had great respect for Bhai Gurdas's brilliant scholarship, deeply spiritual nature and his deep understanding of the Sikh tenets. It was in this background that the Guru chose him to be the scribe for the compilation of the Adi Granth, where the learned ones say that he was not only the scribe for but he also supervised the four other scribes.

He was a deeply gifted seer and his poetry is redolent of his devotion and love for the Lord. As we have noted earlier he has many poetical works to his credit and his literary work has rightly been called the "Key to the *Bāṇi*". It has historical importance apart from its spiritual merit and is for this reason frequently referred to and used in explaining and understanding the hymns of the Gurus. His most well known work is the *Vārs*. It is in the 1st *Vār*, the 38th *pauṛi,* where he says *Sodar Ārti gāviai amrit velay jāp uchāra,* thus providing historical confirmation for what constituted the daily prayers in those earliest days of this new religion.

Bhai Gurdas is telling us here that the *Bāṇis* titled *So dar* and *Ārti,* were recited daily, and further, that, in the ambrosial hours, the early morning, the Japji was recited. This confirms that in the evening the prayers recited were the *So dar* and the *Ārti*. Today the *So dar* is a major part of the Rehrās Sahib, and the *Ārti* is part of the Sohila as prescribed in the *Rehat Maryāda.*

So dar is the first word inscribed in the SGGS at page 8, in the text just where the Japji Sahib concludes. It is easy to conclude that this was meant to be the first *Bāṇi* of the evening prayers. The fifth Nanak, when compiling the SGGS, has given further strength to this view by inscribing from pages 8 to 12 some of the *Bāṇis* of Guru Nanak commencing with *So dar*; and including thereafter the composition of the fourth Nanak titled *So Purakh,* along with some of his own compositions. These, and the Japji Sahib, are placed before the main body of the prayers, listed under the various *Rāgs*, which starts with *Sri Rāg* at page 14. The Japji Sahib and the *Bāṇis* inscribed thereafter from page 8 to 12, followed by the Sohila at pages 12–13, must therefore have been the prayers forming part of the evening prayers at that time.

As we know, the Rehrās Sahib includes many other hymns in addition to the hymns inscribed from pages 8 to 12. It would seem that while in the early days of Sikhism, the evening prayers were limited to these hymns commencing with *So dar* at the time of Bhai Gurdas, but the practice arose subsequently of many more *Bāṇis,* of different Gurus being recited and as a result, the Rehrās assumed a longer form.

Since this prayer has obviously evolved as a composite, its exact form and content could possibly have become a matter of debate within the community. It must have been in this background that the *Rehat Maryāda* spells out in such precise detail the compositions to be included in this *Bāṇi* and be recited as part of the evening liturgy.

Though the evening prayers in the time of Bhai Gurdas consisted of the *Bāṇi* called *So dar*, it had attained a different form and was called the Rehrās even in those early days This is evident from the following extract from the *Tankhāh Nāma* of Bhai Nand Lal:

ਬਿਨ ਰਹਿਰਾਸ ਸੰਧਿਆ ਜੋ ਖੋਵਹਿ। ਕੀਰਤਨ ਪੜ੍ਹੇ ਬਿਨੁ ਰੈਣ ਜੋ ਸੋਵਹਿ॥

Bin rehrās sandhya jo khoveh. Kīrtan paṛay bin
raiṇe jo soveh.

This translates as, 'He, who wastes his evening without reciting the Rehrās prayer, and goes to bed without singing His praises'. The *Tankhah Nāma* then goes on to say that such a Sikh will find no recognition.

Further, the *Rehatnāma* of Bhai Prahlad Singh says:

ਪ੍ਰਾਤਾ ਕਾਲ ਗੁਰ ਗੀਤ ਨਾ ਗਾਵੈ । ਰਹਿਰਾਸ ਬਿਨਾ ਪ੍ਰਸਾਦਿ ਜੋ ਖਾਵੈ ॥
ਬਾਹਰਮੁਖੀ ਸਿਖ ਤਿਨ ਜਾਨੋ । ਸਭ ਬਰਤਨ ਮਿਥਿਆ ਤਿਨ ਮਾਨੋ ॥
Prāta kāl gur gīt na gāvai. Rehrās bina prasād jo pāvai.
Bāhar mukhi sikh tin jāno. Sabh bartan mithhiya tin māno.

This translates as, 'He who does not sing the Guru's hymns in the morning and partakes of food without reciting the Rehrās, deem him a Sikh only in name, and treat all his dealings as false'. Thus, we can see that within the span of about a century between Bhai Gurdas and Bhai Nand Lal the evening prayer had come to be called not *So dar* but Rehrās. Bhai Nand Lal was a contemporary of the tenth Nanak and lived from 1633 to 1713AD. The change in nomenclature had apparently already taken place during that period. Possibly, because of this circumstance the present day title of this *Bāṇi* has come to be known as the *So dar Rehrās.*

The term *So dar* as used here derives from '*So*' meaning 'that', and '*Dar*' meaning door, threshold or entrance, though sometimes also used to denote an abode. However, the derivation of the word Rehrās can be viewed in different ways. It will also be seen that this word has been employed to convey various meanings in the SGGS. Bhai Kahn Singh in his Mahan Kosh lists the various number connotations in which this word has been used. These are:

1. Prayer or Request, as in "*Tis āgay Rehrās hamāri sacha apar apāro*". (Sidh Goshtt, Rāg Ramkali Mahla 1, SGGS page 938)
2. Tradition or Practice, as in "*Har kīrat hamari Rehrās"*. (Gūjri Mahla 4, SGGS page 10)
3. Welcome, greetings, good wishes, as in "*Sabh jan kau āye kraih Rehrās*". (Gauṛi ki Vār Mahla 4, SGGS, page 305)
4. Deriving from the Persian phrase "*Rāh e Rāst*", meaning the right path.
5. The *Bāṇi* prescribed for evening recitation, in which sense it includes the recitation of *So dar, So purakh, Benti Chaupayi, Anand,* and *Mundāvaṇi*.

Some learned ones also interpret it as derived from *Rāh* meaning path, and *Rās* meaning provisions. Thus, they take it to mean that the prayer is a provision for our journey from this world of mortals to the Lord. All these renderings have their own validity, in their own context. The more appealing rendering in the present context seems to be as 'prayer', the sense in which it has been used in the *Sidh Goshtt*, even though the *Mahan Kosh* seems to prefer the rendering as 'tradition or practice'.

This composition, the *So dar* is by Guru Nanak and it has been inscribed at three different places in the Sri Guru Granth Sahib. It occurs firstly as *Pauṛi* 27 of the Japji Sahib, at page 6 of the SGGS, the first Morning Prayer, where it is not set to any specific metrical measure. It occurs again at page 8, as the first hymn of the Rehrās, recited at sunset. Here it is required to be sung in the musical measure known as *Rāg Āsa*. Finally, it will be found again at page 348 of the SGGS, as part of the compositions under *Rāg Āsa*. The three versions are not exactly identical, there being some minor differences with a word spelt differently or changed slightly, possibly because setting it to the musical meter would require the syllables to scan true. Thus, in the opening lines of the hymn the words in the Japji Sahib are-

ਸੋ ਦਰੁ ਕੇਹਾ ਸੋ ਘਰੁ ਕੇਹਾ ਜਿਤੁ ਬਹਿ ਸਰਬ ਸਮਾਲੇ॥	So dar keha so ghar keha jit baih sarab samālay.
ਵਾਜੇ ਨਾਦ ਅਨੇਕ ਅਸੰਖਾ ਕੇਤੇ ਵਾਵਣਹਾਰੇ ॥	Vājay nād anek asankha ketay vāvaṇhāray

These two lines are slightly differently worded in the Rehrās Sahib, where these read as follows:-

ਸੋ ਦਰੁ ਤੇਰਾ ਕੇਹਾ ਸੋ ਘਰੁ ਕੇਹਾ ਜਿਤੁ ਬਹਿਸਰਬ ਸਮਾਲੇ॥	So dar tera keha so ghar keha jit baih sarab samālay.
ਵਾਜੇ ਤੇਰੇ ਨਾਦ ਅਨੇਕ ਅਸੰਖਾ ਕੇਤੇ ਤੇਰੇ ਵਾਵਣਹਾਰੇ ॥	Vājay teray nād anek asankha ketay teray vāvaṇhāray

It will be noted that the word 'teray' has been added in each line in the second case. There are other similar examples of a different word being used; thus *Tudhno* for *Tuhno*, or *Brahmandda* for *Varbhandda.* Other minor differences will be seen in the versions at page 8 and at page 348 of the SGGS, though both are set to the same musical meter. It will however, be equally clear from a simple reading of the two versions that there is no change whatsoever in the essence of the hymn and in each version they carry exactly the same meaning.

2

WHERE IS THAT ABODE?

The evening prayers commence with the query, *so dar keha*– 'whither that gate'. The Guru is here articulating the question that frequently arises in the mind of the ordinary devotee. So vast and mysterious is the Universe, so unfathomable to the human mind its intricacies that we are bound to ask in awe and wonder as to how it is all managed. Where is the creator? In what abode does He reside, in what surroundings?

Having in this opening hymn voiced this question, the Guru proceeds to provide the only possible answer to these questions, that the Lord is all-pervading and omni present. In the process of giving us this answer, he paints the picture of a magnificent Lord presiding over the entire creation, and being worshipped by all His creatures big or small. He says:

ਸੋ ਦਰੁ ਰਾਗੁ ਆਸਾ ਮਹਲਾ ੧	*So dar Rāg Āsa Mahla 1*
੧ ੳ ਸਤਿਗੁਰ ਪ੍ਰਸਾਦਿ	Ek onkār satgur prasad
ਸੋ ਦਰੁ ਤੇਰਾ ਕੇਹਾ ਸੋ ਘਰੁ ਕੇਹਾ ਜਿਤੁ	So dar tera keha so ghar
ਬਹਿ ਸਰਬ ਸਮਾਲੇ॥	keha jit baih sarab samālay.
ਵਾਜੇ ਤੇਰੇ ਨਾਦ ਅਨੇਕ ਅਸੰਖਾ ਕੇਤੇ	Vājay teray nād anek asankha

ਤੇਰੇ ਵਾਵਣਹਾਰੇ ॥	ketay teray vāvaṇharay.
ਕੇਤੇ ਤੇਰੇ ਰਾਗ ਪਰੀ ਸਿਉ	Ketay teray rāg pari siu kahiai
ਕਹੀਅਹਿ ਕੇਤੇ ਤੇਰੇ ਗਾਵਣਹਾਰੇ ॥	ketay teray gāvaṇhāray.
ਗਾਵਨਿ ਤੁਧਨੋ ਪਵਣੁ ਪਾਣੀ ਬੈਸੰਤਰੁ	Gāvan tudhno pavaṇ pāṇi
ਗਾਵੈ ਰਾਜਾ ਧਰਮੁ ਦੁਆਰੇ ॥	baisantar gāvai raja dharam duāray.
ਗਾਵਨਿ ਤੁਧਨੋ ਚਿਤੁ ਗੁਪਤੁ ਲਿਖਿ	Gāvan tudhno chit gupt likh
ਜਾਣਨਿ ਲਿਖਿ ਲਿਖਿ ਧਰਮੁ ਬੀਚਾਰੇ ॥	jāṇan likh likh dharam bīchāray.
ਗਾਵਨਿ ਤੁਧਨੋ ਈਸਰੁ ਬ੍ਰਹਮਾ	Gāvan tudhno īssar brahma
ਦੇਵੀ ਸੋਹਨਿ ਤੇਰੇ ਸਦਾ ਸਵਾਰੇ ॥	devi sohan teray sada sawāray.
ਗਾਵਨਿ ਤੁਧਨੋ ਇੰਦ੍ਰ ਇੰਦ੍ਰਾਸਣਿ	Gāvan tudhno indra indrāsaṇ
ਬੈਠੇ ਦੇਵਤਿਆ ਦਰਿ ਨਾਲੇ ॥	baitthay devtia dar nālay.
ਗਾਵਨਿ ਤੁਧਨੋ ਸਿਧ ਸਮਾਧੀ	Gāvan tudhno sidh samādhi
ਅੰਦਰਿ ਗਾਵਨਿ ਤੁਧਨੋ ਸਾਧ ਬੀਚਾਰੇ ॥	andar gāvan studhno sādh bīchāray.
ਗਾਵਨਿ ਤੁਧਨੋ ਜਤੀ ਸਤੀ ਸੰਤੋਖੀ	Gāvan tudhno jati sati santokhi
ਗਾਵਨਿ ਤੁਧਨੋ ਵੀਰ ਕਰਾਰੇ ॥	gāvan tudhno vīr karāray.
ਗਾਵਨਿ ਤੁਧਨੋ ਪੰਡਿਤ ਪੜਨਿ	Gāvan tudhno pandit paṛan
ਰਖੀਸਰ ਜੁਗੁ ਜੁਗੁ ਵੇਦਾ ਨਾਲੇ ॥	rakhīsar jugu jug veda nālay.
ਗਾਵਨਿ ਤੁਧਨੋ ਮੋਹਣੀਆ ਮਨੁ	Gāvan tudhno mohṇīa
ਮੋਹਨਿ ਸੁਰਗੁ ਮਛੁ ਪਇਆਲੇ ॥	man mohan surg machh paiālay.
ਗਾਵਨਿ ਤੁਧਨੋ ਰਤਨ ਉਪਾਏ	Gāvan tudhno ratan upāye
ਤੇਰੇ ਅਠਸਠਿ ਤੀਰਥ ਨਾਲੇ ॥	teray atthsatth tīrath nālay.
ਗਾਵਨਿ ਤੁਧਨੋ ਜੋਧ ਮਹਾਬਲ ਸੂਰਾ	Gāvan tudhno jodh mahabal
ਗਾਵਨਿ ਤੁਧਨੋ ਖਾਣੀ ਚਾਰੇ ॥	sūra gāvan tudhno khāṇi chāray.
ਗਾਵਨਿ ਤੁਧਨੋ ਖੰਡ ਮੰਡਲ ਬ੍ਰਹਮੰਡਾ	Gāvan tudhno khandd manddal
ਕਰਿ ਕਰਿ ਰਖੇ ਤੇਰੇ ਧਾਰੇ ॥	brahmandda kar kar rakhay teray dhāray.
ਸੇਈ ਤੁਧਨੋ ਗਾਵਨਿ ਜੋ ਤੁਧੁ	Seyi tudhno gāvan jo tudh

ਭਾਵਨਿ ਰਤੇ ਤੇਰੇ ਭਗਤ ਰਸਾਲੇ ॥	bhāvan ratay teray bhagat rasālay.
ਹੋਰਿ ਕੇਤੇ ਤੁਧਨੋ ਗਾਵਨਿ ਸੇ ਮੈ ਚਿਤਿ ਨ ਆਵਨਿ ਨਾਨਕੁ ਕਿਆ ਬੀਚਾਰੇ॥	Hor ketay tudhno gāvan se mai chit na āvan Nanak kia bichāray.
ਸੋਈ ਸੋਈ ਸਦਾ ਸਚੁ ਸਾਹਿਬੁ ਸਾਚਾ ਸਾਚੀ ਨਾਈ ॥	Soyi soyi sada sach sahib sācha sāchi nāyi.
ਹੈ ਭੀ ਹੋਸੀ ਜਾਇ ਨ ਜਾਸੀ ਰਚਨਾ ਜਿਨਿ ਰਚਾਈ ॥	Hai bhi hosi jāye na jāsi rachna jin rachāyi.
ਰੰਗੀ ਰੰਗੀ ਭਾਤੀ ਕਰਿ ਕਰਿ ਜਿਨਸੀ ਮਾਇਆ ਜਿਨਿ ਉਪਾਈ ॥	Rangi rangi bhāti kar kar jinsi maya jin upāyee.
ਕਰਿ ਕਰਿ ਦੇਖੈ ਕੀਤਾ ਆਪਣਾ ਜਿਉ ਤਿਸ ਦੀ ਵਡਿਆਈ ॥	Kar kar dekhai kīta āpna jiu tis di vaddiāyi.
ਜੋ ਤਿਸੁ ਭਾਵੈ ਸੋਈ ਕਰਸੀ ਫਿਰਿ ਹੁਕਮੁ ਨ ਕਰਣਾ ਜਾਈ ॥	Jo tis bhāvai soyi karsi phir hukam na karṇa jāyi.
ਸੋ ਪਾਤਿਸਾਹੁ ਸਾਹਾ ਪਤਿਸਾਹਿਬੁ ਨਾਨਕ ਰਹਣੁ ਰਜਾਈ ॥	So patsāh sāha pātsahib Nanak rahaṇ rajāyi.

Glossary:

ਦਰੁ	Dar	Gate (abode)
ਸਮਾਲੇ	Samālay	Taking care
ਰਾਗ ਪਰੀ	Rāg pari	The Rāginis
ਵਾਵਣਹਾਰੇ	Vāvaṇhāray	Players of music
ਪੰਡਿਤ	Pandit	Learned, knowledgeable
ਬੈਸੰਤਰੁ	Baisantar	Fire
ਚਿਤੁ ਗੁਪਤੁ	Chitgupt	Recording angel. The Chitragupt of Hindu mythology
ਦੇਵੀ	Devi	Consort of Shiva, the female Divine principle
ਇੰਦ੍ਰਾਸਣਿ	Indrāsaṇ	Indra's throne

ਰਖੀਸਰ	Rakhīsar	Great Rishi (Literally god of Rishis)
ਮੋਹਣੀਆ	Mohṇīa	Enchantresses, Celestial beauties in Indra's court
ਸੁਰਗੁ	Surg	Heaven
ਮਛੁ	Machh	Earth, The middle region
ਪਇਆਲੇ	Paiālay	Nether worlds
ਰਤਨ ਉਪਾਏ	Ratan upāye	Jewels created
ਖਾਣੀ ਚਾਰੇ	Khāṇi chāray	The four Sources of birth
ਖੰਡ ਮੰਡਲ	Khandd manddal	Continents and worlds
ਬ੍ਰਹਮੰਡਾ	Brahmandda	The Universe
ਧਾਰੇ	Dhāray	Supported, sustained
ਭਗਤ ਰਸਾਲੇ	Bhagat rasālay	Devotees absorbed in Him
ਜਿਨਸੀ	Jinsi	Species
ਮਾਇਆ	Maya	Illusion, here entire Creation
ਪਤਿਸਾਹਿਬੁ	Pātsahib	Emperor
ਰਜਾਈ	Rajāyi	According to His Will

The Guru here sings a truly magnificent paean to the Divine encompassing in one vision a vast Universe consisting of the biggest and the small eternally singing to Him. As is usual he begins the composition with an invocation to the Lord, which is usually the *Mool Mantra*. Here, the shortest form of this invocation has been employed. The Guru is telling us that the Lord Creator is uniquely one and that we can reach him only through the help and blessing of the true Guru.

The Guru then begins the hymn by asking in awe and wonder, "Where is that Divine Portal, that Abode where thy seat, from where you sit and tend to this entire Creation". The word ਦਰੁ–*dar*–literally means door or gate. It is however also used as a metaphor for the house or the abode itself. The term ਸਰਬ ਸਮਾਲੇ–*sarb samālay* literally means 'support all'. Here, the reference is to the entire Creation which is not only supported but has been brought into existence, placed within its framework and endowed with the laws for its functioning. The Guru is referring also to the complex interplay of massive forces, as well as the human interactions, which the Lord has set in motion. The Guru expresses his awe and wonder by asking where does the Lord sit and perform these wonders. The Guru as an achieved, a realised soul is obviously aware of the answer. He knows better than any of us that there can be no single such abode, because he tells us repeatedly throughout the SGGS that the Transcendent Lord is immanent in His creation. This creation is sustained and nurtured by the all-pervading will of the Lord, and there is no single spot where we can say He resides. The Guru here articulates, in love and wonder, a very human thought as he sketches out for us a picture of the Lord. He visualises for Him the characteristics of an earthly ruler with an abode. He then proceeds to answer the question by describing in sublime poetical imagery that infinite abode where His vast Creation, each part of it, is paying homage to the Lord eternally.

In the second and third lines, the Guru says that within His domain, and singing of His wonders are the uncountable *nād*–musical instruments, and that there are innumerable *Vāvaṇharay*–musicians, who play these. Innumerable also are the *Rāgs* and *Rāginis*. The term *Rāg* refers to the Indian classical measure of musical notes and *Rāgini* is used to describe a minor variant of a *Rāg*. *Rāg Pari* here means the same as *Rāgini*. The term ਪਰੀ–*pari*–literally means a fairy, a celestial nymph, or a beautiful woman, but the phrase here is used for *Rāgini*. The Guru is here using the term *Rāg* not merely to refer to the system of musical notes, but as melody personified. Each *Rāg* and *Rāgini* in the common Indian belief is given specific characteristics, and often there are paintings depicting these in human form. The Guru here refers to these *Rāgs* personified singing hymns to the Lord Creator. Similarly, the musical instruments personified as *nād*–the Divine Sound resound in eternal paeans to Him.

In the 4th and 5th lines, as also later, the Guru lists the many gods of the Hindu pantheon, and many forces of nature, as sitting in the Lord's court and singing praises to Him. Here he says among those who sing to Him are ਪਾਣੀ–*Pāni*, Water, ਪਵਨ–*Pavan*, Wind; and ਬੈਸੰਤਰ–*Baisantar*, Fire. He says *Dharamraj* also sits at this portal and sings eulogies. *Chitragupt*, who records human actions for *Dharamraj* to judge, also sings to Him. In the Hindu cosmology, *Dharamraj* is the Divine power vested by the Lord with authority to judge human beings. *Chitragupt* is the watcher who does the actual recording. He is supposed to have been born from Brahma's body when he was in deep meditation, and Brahma himself assigned him the task of recording human deeds. It may be of interest here to note that while in Hindu mythological references *Chitragupt* is definitely one person, some learned commentators take *Chitra* and *Gupt* as two separate entities; *Chitra* means picture or image, or something visible, and *Gupt* means secret. So, they say *Chitra* sees and records the overt actions and deeds, while *Gupt* sees and records their secret thoughts and the evils, including their unworthy thought. This view may have been influenced by the similar concept in Islam that there are two recording angels, one on our right recording our good deeds and the other on the left, noting down all the bad deeds. The reference in the *Quran Sharif* is in chapter 50, *Surah Qāf,* lines 16-18.J. M. Rodwell translates the lines in the *surah* as,

"When the two angels charged with taking account shall take it, one sitting on the right hand, the other on the left:

Not a word doth he utter, but there is a watcher with him ready to note it down:"

Abdullah Yusuf Ali in his translation titled *The Illustrious Qur'an* renders these lines as, "Behold, two (guardian angels) appointed to learn (his doings) learn (and note them), one sitting on the right and one on the left."

Of course, whether *Chitragupt* is one or two entities does not in the least alter the Guru's message here, that the Lord creates all these supposedly great entities and they pay Him homage. The Guru says in these lines that the mighty *Dharamraj*, along with *Chitragupt* are singing to Him.

The precise point the Guru is stressing in this magnificent hymn is that our very existence in full accord with the Divine will of the Lord is our song of praise to Him. All created entities big or small, human or superhuman, are in total obedience to His will and this is the celestial song that resonates through the firmament.

In the sixth and seventh lines, the Guru lists the other mighty powers that, in Hindu mythology, can be called the guardian powers, the super entities created by Him to manage the operation of His created Universe in accordance with His laws. The Guru says singing to Him are *Issar, Brahma* and *Devi*, who shine with the effulgence granted by the Lord. In addition, singing is *Indra* sitting on his throne, and his attendant *Devtas*. *Issar* is another name for Lord Shiva, who personifies the destructive principle in the Holy Trinity. Brahma is a part of that Trinity and he is charged with the duty of Creation, the preservation of which is then the charge of Lord Vishnu the third component, not listed here but implicit; all in accordance with His will. The divine powers called *devtas,* in Hindu mythology, are believed to have power over a particular element. Their ruler is called Lord Indra, known also as the Rain god, and the wielder of the thunderbolt. The similarity in this aspect to the Norse Odin and the Greek Zeus will be noted, both of whom the rulers of the gods in their respective pantheons and who are also wielders of thunderbolts. The Guru says that this Indra along with the gods and godlings in his court are also engaged in eternal eulogies to Him. The word *Devi* seems to have been used here for the goddesses who are consorts of the gods in the Hindu pantheon. This term is sometimes used to refer to the Female Principle of the Divine. It is also one of the names for the consort of Lord Shiva, *Pārvati* who is known by various names such as *Sati* or *Devi* or *Durga*. In Hindu mythology the *Devi* is often depicted as being more powerful than the gods, often coming to their aid against especially powerful foes. All these mighty ones, says the Guru, sing His praises, sitting at His portals.

In the eighth and ninth lines, the Guru lists those who are not among the great powers or *devtas* but are no less revered. These are humans, who have acquired great spiritual status and are to be counted as no less than the divine ones whose list we enumerated above. Among these humans are, the Guru says, the *Sidh*–adepts, the *Sādh*—saintly men, with minds fixed on Him. There are also the great souls, *Jati*—men who have achieved continence, the *Sati*—those who give with an open heart and the *Santokhi*—those who are ever content with what the Lord bestows on them. Also listed by the Guru in the ninth line are the *Vīr Karāray*—redoubtable heroes and warriors. Let us discuss what extraordinary qualities these special humans have.

The *Sidh,* or *Sidha,* is a class of humans who through great austerity and self-discipline to acquire mystical powers, called *sidhis*, which enable the wielder to perform miracles. It may be of interest here that there are said to be eight primary and ten secondary *sidhis* according to the Puranas. The eight primary ones are,

Aṇima:	reducing one's body to any size
Mahima:	expanding one's body to an infinitely large size
Garima:	becoming infinitely heavy
Laghima:	becoming almost weightless
Prāpti:	having unrestricted access to all places
Prākāmya:	realising whatever one desires
Ishttva:	possessing absolute lordship
Vaśtva:	the power to subjugate all.

It needs to be understood, however, that in Sikhism the pursuit of any such practices or goals is strictly discouraged. As *pauṛi* 29 of the Japji Sahib says, *ridh sidh avra sād*. The Guru is expressing his disapproval of this fascination for *ridhis* and *sidhis* by using the term *avra sād* literally meaning different taste or enjoyment, suggesting that it is not the real thing. The implied message is that these pursuits are not the way to the Lord, that these will give only a false sense of fulfillment. The right method is the constant fixing of ones mind on Him and living in a state of total surrender to His will. Nevertheless, the *Sidha* is regarded as a man who has sought to discipline his own inner self and is therefore to be respected.

The *Sādh* is a seeker who has control over the senses and is able to fix his mind on the Lord. The *Jati* are those with super human control over their weaker urges–the men of complete continence. The *Sati* are those free from greed who give from the largeness of their heart without expectation of return and the *Santokhi* are the contented ones. The Guru's prescription stresses this particular quality, contentment, repeatedly. It is throughout the SGGS treated as a highly desired quality without which the hunger for material goods will keep eroding our efforts towards uplifting ourselves on the path to godliness.

Lastly, he lists the righteous heroes and the warriors. We all know that the qualities of bravery and valour are valued in this world. The Guru has recognised this fact and has in his world view given it high value. We will find him lauding at more place than one in the SGGS, the warrior who fights the just battle. Thus, we have Bhagat Kabir telling us,

ਗਗਨ ਦਮਾਮਾ ਬਾਜਿਓ ਪਰਿਓ ਨੀਸਾਨੈ ਘਾਉ॥	Gagan damāma bājiyo pariyo nisānai ghāo.
ਖੇਤੁ ਜੁ ਮਾਂਡਿਓ ਸੂਰਮਾ ਅਬ ਜੂਝਨ ਕੋ ਦਾਓ॥	Khet(u) ju mānddiyo sūrma ab jūjhan ko dāo.
ਸੂਰਾ ਸੋ ਪਹਿਚਾਨੀਐ ਜੁ ਲਰੈ ਦੀਨ ਕੇ ਹੇਤ॥	Sūra so pahchāniai ju larai dīn kay hait.
ਪੁਰਜਾ ਪੁਰਜਾ ਕਟਿ ਮਰੈ ਕਬਹੂ ਨ ਛਾਡੈ ਖੇਤੁ॥	Purja purja katt(i) marai kabhoo na chhāddai khait.

Kabir *ji* is saying that this life we have been granted is our field of action. When the tocsin rang in the form of the Guru's word, it hit home, or in other words the heart was moved. In the second line he says the warrior has now taken position in this battle and the time for struggle is upon us. In the third and fourth lines he says the true warrior is he who fights against evil and sustains the downtrodden, the meek, and when he takes up this battle, he may be cut to pieces but will not abandon the battle. The message is that this world is our arena and in accordance with the Guru's message we have to follow the path of taking up cudgels against the evil within us and around us. In doing so we have to fight the righteous battle and stand up for the weak at any cost.

It would be clear from this that the term warrior here does not refer to just any strong fighter, but only those warriors whose cause is righteous, the redoubtable hero who brings succor to the weak and the oppressed. These *Vīr karāray* are worthy of respect as much as the *Sidh,* the *Sādh* and the *Jati, Sati, Santokhi*. All these worthy ones, says the Guru, are singing His praises at His portal.

In the 10th and 11th lines, the Guru lists some more categories of great humans, who are ever singing of Him, through the ages. Among these, he lists the *Pandits*–learned ones, and the *Rakhīsar*– the highest among *rishis*, along with their Vedas–scriptures, who sing to Him throughout all creation. Then there are the *Mohṇīa*–enchanting beauties of the *surg machh paiālay*–Heavens, Earth and the Netherworlds. They also sing to the Lord.

The Guru is telling us that all of these great ones worship Him in their own individual way, by living in accordance with the Lord's will performing the tasks He has assigned to each. The *pandits* worship through their knowledge, as do the great *rishis*, whose mode of singing to Him is through the Vedas, the holy books of knowledge, from age to age. The *mohṇīa* sing to Him through their devotion to beauty. Dr. Gopal Singh renders this line to mean that earth, underworlds and the heavens sing to Him. However, other learned ones, like Prof. Sahib Singh, Bhai Vir Singh, T. S. Doabia and Prof. Talib have construed it to mean that the *mohṇīa* of all created regions are worshipping Him, and this is the more appealing view.

In the 12th and 13th lines, the Guru lists other great ones as also some wondrous things, and indeed the entire gamut of created beings. He says, "Singing to thee, are the *ratan*–jewels created by you, and the sixty eight holy *tīraths*. Supreme heroes and all the four sources of created beings sing to thee". Some commentators take the reference to jewels here to mean the entire wealth in the Universe. Most learned ones, however, and the *Shabdarth*, take it as referring to the fourteen jewels that emerged from the churning of the Primal Ocean. This myth says that the gods and the demons once churned this Ocean with the mountain, *Mandira* as the churning stick and the Primal Serpent, *Vāsuki,* as the churning cord. The Primal Serpent is also called *Ananta,* and has been identified with *Shesha* on whose back Lord Vishnu reclines in the Primal Ocean. The myth says that Lord Vishnu assumed the *Kurma,* or the Tortoise, form that is counted as the second of his Ten Avatars. On the back of this divine Tortoise was placed the Primal Mount *Mandira*. The Primal Serpent *Vāsuki* having accepted their request, since he was the only 'cord' long enough and strong enough, was twined around the churning stick and the churning commenced. From that mighty churning, invaluable jewels–numbering fourteen–emerged. These are usually considered to have included the miraculous cow *Kāmdhenu* that can grant any wish, *Amrita* the nectar of immortality, and the divine physician *Dhanwantri* who brought the great healing science of *Ayurveda* to this world. These wondrous creations, says the Guru, sing to Him, as do the sixty-eight *tīraths*. These are the special places of pilgrimage in Hinduism, a visit to which will wash away all sins.

The Gurus of course did not sanction such beliefs and in fact deprecated such ritual visits to *tīraths* as a futile exercise. The Guru's message is that we need to live in total surrender to and total acceptance of the Lord's Will, which would bring an exaltation of the spirit within us, making such pilgrimages quite redundant.

The Guru then says the supreme warriors through their valour, and the four *khāṇis* are singing to Him. This term comes from the term *khān* meaning a mine or source. It was the common belief that these are four such sources of life, these being *anddaj, jeraj, setaj, utbhuj*–literally egg born, placenta born, sweat born and earth born. This is really meant to convey that the entire created world of living things sing to Him.

In the 14th and 15th lines the Guru, having listed many living and non-living things and objects and beings of great worth, now sums it up. He says, "The lands, the continents, and the entire universe which You have created and are supporting, sing to Thee". He then enters a caveat and says, "Only those sing to Thee however, on whom You bestow Your acceptance and are immersed totally in You". Commentators have variously explained the terms *khandd* and *manddal*. Some learned ones render the term *khandd* as meaning continents, and *manddal* as meaning the world. Thus, Dr. Sangat Singh renders *khandd manddal brahmandda* as 'the continents, the solar system and the galaxies'. Prof Talib renders the phrase as 'region, continents and the universe', Prof Sahib Singh translates *khandd* to mean part of the universe i.e. each world, *manddal* as *chakar*, meaning a circle of the universe comprising one sun and its attached worlds, and *brahmandda* as the entire universe. *Khandd* of course literally means portion and *Manddal* is used as another word for the mystical *chakras,* as also for division. *Brahmandda* means the entire created Universe, each part of which sings to Him. Whichever rendering we choose the real meaning is that every part of the created Universe is in homage to the Lord. The Guru in the Āsa di Vār has put the same concept in a slightly different way, where he says "*Bhai vich sūraj bhai vich chand. Koh karori chalt na unt"*. This means the Sun and the Moon endlessly move in awe and fear of Him. And, what keeps them moving is nothing but their obedience to His divine laws.

The Guru then adds that only those are able to sing whom He grants this grace. In other words, even devotion to Him is contingent upon the Lord bestowing His blessing on the devotee. On our own strength, we cannot even worship Him. The entire message centres on the Lord's vast magnificence and the total compliance with His divine will by all creation.

In line 16, the Guru now speaks of the many beyond this list who also sing to Him. He says there are others too, whose details he cannot even recall. This is a remarkably humble admission for a great seer who was a truly achieved, a realised soul. He is in this way telling us to remember that the created universe is infinite; the created beings are beyond count and the Lord's mysteries not within human ken. There may be many others singing the Lord's glory beyond what even a great, realised soul like the Guru can recall or enumerate. When the Guru says that only those can sing of Him upon whom He has bestowed His grace; he is telling us that the rest are in oblivion and are lost to Him. They will thus remain until they can raise themselves to such a level and become worthy of that grace and be worthy of meditating on the Lord. Remember, though, that this grace is always at the Lord's will, and not based on our worth, our merit or the lack of it. The ones who are fortunately blessed with His grace are devotees rapt in devotion to Him, he says, and they all sing of Him, by living in full accord with the Lord's will, His immutable divine laws.

Having completed his delineation of this vast Cosmos and its creatures singing to Him in total harmony, the Guru now in lines 17 and 18 speaks directly of Him. He says that the Lord is the One Eternal Reality. As he puts it, the Lord is ਸਦਾ ਸਚ–*sada sach*, meaning forever the Truth. All else is mere illusion or but a reflection of Him. Then he adds that the Lord is the True Master and true is His greatness. The word ਨਾਈ–*nāyi* used in ਸਾਚੀ ਨਾਈ–*sāchi nāyi* is explained by some as Name, thus rendering this phrase, as 'His Name is True'. However, other learned ones such as Prof Sahib Singh and some others like Narain Singh, explain the term *Nāyi* as 'greatness', which seems here the more appealing interpretation. The line would, thus, be interpreted as meaning that only the Eternal Lord, the True Master has true Greatness. Very often Humans who may achieve small measure of power, or wealth or stature will foolishly flaunt their puny status. The Guru here reminds us, and all such poseurs, that real greatness belongs only to the Lord Himself, because His greatness is everlasting. The Guru, to underline further this point, tells us that the Lord will forever exist. He says, ਹੈਭੀ ਹੋਸੀ ਜਾਏ ਨਾ ਜਾਸੀ–*Haibhi hosi jāye na jāsi,* meaning that He is today and He will forever continue to be. He is not born nor will He die. *Jāye* derives from *janam*–birth, and *jāsi* means departs. The Guru then adds that the Lord is the one who has brought all creation into existence, ਰਚਨਾ ਜਿਨ ਰਚਾਈ–*rachna jin rachāyi.*

In the 19th and 20th lines, the Guru says that of multifarious hues and types are the species that the Lord has through His *Maya* manifested. It is His pleasure that He thus acts and then in His greatness watches over it all. ਰੰਗ–rung means colour, and ਭਾਤੀ–*bhāti* means type and ਜਿਨਸੀ–*jinsi* means species. The Lord in His wisdom, and at His divine pleasure, has chosen to bring into existence species, each different from the other in size, shape, type and nature. He has chosen thus to use His *Maya* to manifest all these. Having brought this great and diverse universe into existence, the Lord now ਵੇਖੈ–*vekhai,* watches over and cares for His Creation. Why does He choose to do it? Because, says the Guru, such is His *vaddiāyi*–Greatness. In other words, it is all a complete mystery to us mortals, and the only thing we can say is that such is His pleasure.

In the last two lines, the 21st and 22nd, the Guru adds further to this thought. He says the Lord has wrought all this because it so *bhāvai*—pleases Him. His actions are not subject to *hukam*–no outside direction or command. While the entire creation moves in accordance with His *hukam*, He is not subject to any binding force Himself. There is none in existence who could control what the Lord may choose to do, or how He should manifest His will in His creation. Whatever happens is at the sole and exclusive pleasure of the Lord alone. There is none to command Him. He is *Pātsahib*–the King of kings, the Emperor over all. Total and unquestioned is His sovereignty. He will command what He will, as He wills and when He wills. Therefore, says the Guru, *Nanak rahaṇ rajāyi*—live in total concord with His will. The lesson of this hymn is here in these words summed up, surrender yourself completely and mould your existence in accordance with the Lord's Will. Accept Him, Love Him and do not question what or why He does what He is doing.

In this beautiful piece of inspired poetry, the Guru has sketched out for us his vision of the divine abode. An abode that comprises the entire universe, an abode where His created beings big or small, mean or divine, and His created things, the world and the wondrous things there in are all existing in total harmony entirely in character with their own given nature treating it as the Lord's gift. Each creature, each godling and the mightiest super gods–The Holy Trinity, are all in tune with the Creator. The song of their existence is sung in complete harmony without any discordant or dissenting note. And, this song is to His greatness. These are all, therefore existing in total acceptance and surrender to the Lord. The Guru has used this to tell the egoistic human to see the grandeur that exists around him, to experience the awe that this mighty and wonderful picturisation should evoke and to learn to emulate this great example. Live in harmony with His way, accept what He has chosen to bestow on you, and attune yourself to His Will. This is the path all the mighty and the great, all the achieved souls in this universe have followed since the day of creation. We have, therefore, to learn to follow the footsteps of these lucky ones, and, by adopting the path the Guru has delineated we will move towards self-realisation, towards *Moksha, Nirvāṇa*. The key, the secret is just one–live according to His will, in total surrender to Him.

We will have noted that in these last four lines, the 16th through 19th, the Guru repeats his oft-stressed message, his theme that the Lord is beyond comprehension. The Lord Creator is eternally the Truth. His Creation has innumerable aspects, many categories and multifarious species that He has been pleased to create. His actions are as He pleases and there is no power whose command can work on Him.

There is a belief among some that this hymn, the *So dar*, was the first utterance of the Guru after he emerged from his three-day absence in the *Bein* River, during which time he is believed to have visited with the Lord. Most learned ones, however, believe that actually the words the Guru uttered at that momentous time were 'There is no Hindu, There is no Mussulman'. In effect, he was encapsulating his message of Humanism and of Spirituality beyond religion. When exactly this hymn was composed, is not accurately known. We must also bear in mind that the words here should not be taken to mean an actual scene in an actual throne room of the

Creator. That interpretation would run counter to the Guru's message, because the Lord permeates all and is immanent in the entire creation.

The Guru has made no secret of the impossibility of ever describing or measuring the Lord. The Lord does not have dimensions or a shape; nor can He ever be described as exclusively residing at any one particular place. No one can therefore claim to have seen Him, because such a claim would mean the Lord has shape, or form, or identifying marks, all impossibilities, as the Guru himself has repeatedly said. As the Guru has made clear, even Brahma, Vishnu, Mahesh have been unable to find His limits. To say that the Guru was describing an actual encounter would thus be negating the Guru's clear and repeated message. The real message is therefore one of describing in awe and wonder the entire gamut of Creation including both the living and the inorganic, the mortal as well as the divinities of ascending power who supervise the mortal world. The description includes places as also unseen planes of existence. The Guru is telling us that all these exist in total accordance with His will and in doing so are in a state of continuing homage to the Creator. The only way we can take this to be an actual encounter is by assuming that the omnipotent Lord in His pleasure chose so to manifest Himself to the Guru. This assumption is however not essential to an understanding of the real message here.

To sum up this great piece of divine poetry, the Guru has drawn for us a magnificent picture of how the entire universe of created beings, men, gods, fauna and flora, the great sages, the redoubtable warriors and all the innumerable types of living beings and powers are in homage and supplication to the Lord. The Guru has, in his vision, included the created worlds, the nether regions and the heavenly regions as joining in this cosmic prayer and eulogy, thus leaving none uncovered. The Lord's transcendent form is described by saying that He is the Eternal and the Real Truth, and that he is the only Master of this cosmic show. His immanent form is also described in the form of the material world with its multitude of beings created in a vast variety of forms and shapes as it pleased Him.

In the end, the Guru has repeated his constant refrain *Nanak rahaṇ rajāyi*–stay ever content in His will. This is the crux of the Guru's message, occurring throughout the *Gurbāṇi,* starting with the very first *Pauṛi*, which ended with this magic formula *hukam rajāyi chalṇa Nanak likhiya nāl.*

3

THE UNFATHOMABLE MYSTERY

In this hymn, Guru Nanak speaks to us of the impossibility of ever being able to accurately describe the Unknowable One, the Lord Creator. This hymn is at page nine of the SGGS and repeats again at page 348 of the SGGS in exactly the same form. The Guru says:

ਆਸਾ ਮਹਲਾ ੧	Āsa Mahla 1
ਸੁਣਿ ਵਡਾ ਆਖੈ ਸਭੁ ਕੋਇ ॥	Suṇ vadda ākhai sabh koye.
ਕੇਵਡੁ ਵਡਾ ਡੀਠਾ ਹੋਇ ॥	Kevadd vadda ddīttha hoye.
ਕੀਮਤਿ ਪਾਇ ਨ ਕਹਿਆ ਜਾਇ ॥	Kīmat pāye na kaheya jāye.
ਕਹਣੈ ਵਾਲੇ ਤੇਰੇ ਰਹੇ ਸਮਾਇ॥੧॥	Kahṇai vālay teray rahay samāye. 1.
ਵਡੇ ਮੇਰੇ ਸਾਹਿਬਾ ਗਹਿਰ ਗੰਭੀਰਾ ਗੁਣੀ ਗਹੀਰਾ ॥	Vadday meray sahiba gahar gambhīra guṇi gahīra.
ਕੋਇ ਨ ਜਾਣੈ ਤੇਰਾ ਕੇਤਾ ਕੇਵਡੁ ਚੀਰਾ॥ ੧॥ ਰਹਾਉ ॥	Koye na jaṇai tera keta kevadd chīra. 1. (Rahāo)
ਸਭਿ ਸੁਰਤੀ ਮਿਲਿ ਸੁਰਤਿ ਕਮਾਈ ॥	Sabh surti mil surt kamāyi.
ਸਭ ਕੀਮਤਿ ਮਿਲਿ ਕੀਮਤਿ ਪਾਈ ॥	Sabh kīmat mil kīmat pāyi.
ਗਿਆਨੀ ਧਿਆਨੀ ਗੁਰ ਗੁਰਹਾਈ ॥	Giani dhiāni gur gurhāyi.
ਕਹਣੁ ਨ ਜਾਈ ਤੇਰੀ ਤਿਲੁ ਵਡਿਆਈ ॥੨॥	Kahaṇ na jāyi teri til vaddiāyi. 2.

ਸਭਿ ਸਤ ਸਭਿ ਤਪ ਸਭਿ ਚੰਗਿਆਈਆ ॥	Sabh sat sabh tap sabh changiyāyīa(n).
ਸਿਧਾ ਪੁਰਖਾ ਕੀਆ ਵਡਿਆਈਆ ॥	Sidha purkha kīya vaddiāyīa(n).
ਤੁਧੁ ਵਿਣੁ ਸਿਧੀ ਕਿਨੈ ਨ ਪਾਈਆ ॥	Tudh viṇ sidhi kinai na pāyīa(n).
ਕਰਮਿ ਮਿਲੈ ਨਾਹੀ ਠਾਕਿ ਰਹਾਈਆ ॥੩॥	Karam milai nāhi tthāk rahayīa(n). 3.
ਆਖਣ ਵਾਲਾ ਕਿਆ ਵੇਚਾਰਾ ॥	Ākhaṇ vāla kiya vechāra.
ਸਿਫਤੀ ਭਰੇ ਤੇਰੇ ਭੰਡਾਰਾ ॥	Siphti bharay teray bhanddara.
ਜਿਸੁ ਤੂ ਦੇਹਿ ਤਿਸੈ ਕਿਆ ਚਾਰਾ ॥	Jis tu deh tisai kiya chāra.
ਨਾਨਕ ਸਚੁ ਸਵਾਰਣਹਾਰਾ॥੪॥੨॥	Nanak sach savāraṇhāra. 4.2.

Glossary:

ਸਮਾਇ	Samāye	Are rapt
ਗੁਣੀ ਗਹੀਰਾ	Guṇi gahīra	Ocean of virtues
ਚੀਰਾ	Chīra	Extent, Size
ਸੁਰਤੀ	Surti	The adepts in meditation
ਸੁਰਤਿ ਕਮਾਈ	Surt kamāyi	Become immersed
ਕੀਮਤਿ	Kīmat	Value, also appraisers or connoisseurs.
ਗੁਰ ਗੁਰਹਾਈ	Gur gurhāyi	The greatest of teachers
ਸਤ	Sat	Philanthropy
ਸਿਧਾ ਪੁਰਖਾ	Sidha purkha	Masters of the occult mysteries, adepts
ਸਿਧੀ	Sidhi	Perfection
ਕਰਮਿ	Karam	Blessing, Grace of the Lord

In this hymn, the Guru reiterates the theme of the unknowability of the Lord Creator. In the first two lines, he says *suṇ vadda ākhai sabh koye*—people seeking to describe the vastness and mystery of the Lord speak of Him based merely on what they have heard others say. In other words, all putative descriptions of the Lord are based merely on hearsay; none actually knows the reality. He then says *kevadd vadda ddīttha hoye*—only such as have glimpsed the Lord can hope to describe Him, implying that there are hardly any such, because the rare ones who are blessed with that glimpse then become one with Him. The Lord cannot be assessed, measured or described. We have seen the same thought in the Jāp Sahib, where the tenth Nanak says in the opening verse:

ਤਵ ਸਰਬ ਨਾਮੁ ਕਥੈ ਕਵਨੁ ਕਰਮ ਨਾਮ ਬਰਨਤ ਸੁਮਤਿ॥

Tav sarab nām kathhai kavan karam nām barnat sumat.

The Guru is saying who can know your one name, meaning that none knows the full reality of the Lord and no one can say which one name could describe Him. So, we are compelled to describe Him based only on what our limited senses can observe of the actions or powers of the Lord, and of the visible effects of these actions in our limited sphere. Like the blind men describing the elephant, we speak of Him based on what partial knowledge we may have acquired of some aspects of His mighty creation. He cannot be known truly until He chooses to bless us with that eye that can see Him, and the knowledge that will enlighten us. The irony is that when that fortunate event does happen the lucky recipient merges and becomes one with the Lord. Such a one is no longer a mere human like us, with the result that describing the Lord is well nigh an impossible task. This difficulty is enunciated by Guru Nanak in the Japji Sahib, *Pauṛi* 5 when he says, *"jay hau jāṇa akha nāhin kehṇa kathhan na jāyee*", meaning that even if one were to come to know of Him, it would be impossible to put that knowledge into words. The task is like a mute person trying to explain the taste of something delicious. Again in

Pauṛi 37 the Guru concludes with "*Nanak kathhna karṛa sār*", meaning that describing Him is like trying to chew on iron. Describing the Lord is hard indeed.

This is the thought that the Guru touches upon in the fourth line of this hymn, ਕਹਣੈ ਵਾਲੇ ਤੇਰੇ ਰਹੇ ਸਮਾਇ–*kehṇai vālay teray rahay samāye*. Those who seek to speak of Him can do so only after they have been bestowed a glimpse of Him, and at that stage they will become part of Him, be totally immersed. Having gone beyond the human stage they will not be able to speak to us of what they have been graced with. As we have noted above this situation of helplessness to describe the Lord is spoken of elsewhere by the Guru as *gungay ki mitthiāyi* –the mute one seeking to describe the joy of having enjoyed the tastiest sweets. He will babble, the joy will shine on his face, but to us he will not be able to convey the slightest sense of what exactly he has experienced. Before that, in line three, the Guru has described this inability to describe Him with the message, *kīmat pāye na kaheya jāye*–he cannot be evaluated nor described.

The Guru says, in line five, that the Lord is ਗਹਿਰ ਗੰਭੀਰਾ ਗੁਣੀ ਗਹੀਰਾ–*gahar gambhīra guṇi gahīra,* great and deeply profound, and the treasure house of all virtues. None can know, he says in the sixth line, how vast is His ਚੀਰਾ–*chīra,* his extent. His mystery, in other words, is unfathomable. There is a direction for a *rahāo*–a pause, at the end of this line. This is meant to convey that we need to stop and ponder over the line of thought the Guru is stressing. The thought here is that the Lord is impossible to define or measure. Those whom the Lord blesses with a vision of the Reality become then as one with Him, no longer merely human, and therefore, unable to narrate to the rest of us what He is, because mere words can never suffice to explain that which has necessarily to be personally experienced. The mystery thus continues to persist for the uninitiated.

The Guru now, in the seventh line, elaborates further on this inability to describe Him. He says, ਸਭਿ ਸੁਰਤੀ ਮਿਲਿ ਸੁਰਤਿ ਕਮਾਈ–*sabh surti mil surt kamāyi*–all those adepts who strive to develop their insight have sought jointly to exercise their wisdom and intuition to try to asses Him. The word *surt* refers to that part of our mind with which we think. This is therefore, used to describe that category of seekers who strive to train their inner thinking to be focused on the Lord always. The Guru is saying that all such wise ones have worked together to try, through the power of their trained minds, to evaluate Him. Then in the eighth line, the Guru adds, ਸਭ ਕੀਮਤਿ ਮਿਲਿ ਕੀਮਤਿ ਪਾਈ–*sabh kīmat mil kīmat pāyi*, meaning all the evaluators made their assessment. The word *kīmat* means value, price or rate. Here it is used to describe those who have the discriminating power to accurately assess others. What is the outcome of all these efforts? The Guru sums up the lesson as he provides us the answer in the next two lines.

He says in the ninth line that not only these, but also other exalted ones, like the ਗਿਆਨੀ–*giāni,* the learned ones, ਧਿਆਨੀ–*dhiāni*, those who deeply meditate on Him, and *gur gurhāyi*–the Guru of Gurus, meaning the greatest, the highest of teachers, have also tried their best. He then gives us the summation as he says in the 10th line ਕਹਣੁ ਨ ਜਾਈ ਤੇਰੀ ਤਿਲੁ ਵਡਿਆਈ–*kahaṇ na jāyi teri til vaddiāyi*. He is telling us that though all these learned ones may join in, but not even all of them together will be able ever to describe his greatness. The Guru says that any attempt to articulate in words that vast majesty will only be ਤੇਰੀ ਤਿਲੁ ਵਡਿਆਈ–*teri til vaddiāyi*–merely a tiny part, the size of a sesame seed, of the Lord's greatness. In other words whatever we might say to describe

His grandeur, in whatever way the learned ones may seek to picture His great qualities, their efforts can describe His true greatness only to the most minimal extent. The word ਤਿਲ–*til* means the sesame seed, and it is often used as an example of something truly miniscule or petty. So great is He, the Guru is telling us, that human words can have neither the intellect nor the words to depict His true reality.

The Guru now, in lines 11 and 12, speaks to us of other respected categories of beings who meditate on Him. He speaks first of those who have ਸਭਿ ਸਤ–*sabh sat,* meaning great philanthropists, ਸਭਿ ਤਪ–*sabh tap,* meaning those who have performed great austerities while meditating on Him, and ਸਭਿ ਚੰਗਿਆਈਆ–*sabh changiyāyīa(n),* meaning those who have attained all good qualities. In other words, he refers to all those who have attained different types of very desirable virtues. He then adds those who have achieved mystical powers. He says, ਸਿਧਾ ਪੁਰਖਾ ਕੀਆ ਵਡਿਆਈਆ–*sidha purkha kīya vaddiāyīa(n),* referring to the great adepts who through meditating on the Lord attain occult powers.

In line 13 the Guru says ਤੁਧੁ ਵਿਣੁ ਸਿਧੀ ਕਿਨੈ ਨ ਪਾਈਆ–*tudh viṇ sidhi kinai na pāyīa(n).* This means that all these great ones could never have attained these perfect virtues without the blessing of His grace. The term *sidhi* means mystical powers but also means success, fruition, or perfection. Here the Guru is using it in this latter sense. Finally in conclusion the Guru says, in line 14, that success in these activities can be attained only when ਕਰਮਿ ਮਿਲੈ–*karam milai,* the Lord's ਕਰਮਿ–*karam*, His glance of grace, His blessing is bestowed. When this happy event comes about then, he says, ਨਾਹੀ ਠਾਕਿ ਰਹਾਈਆ–*nāhi tthāk rahayīa(n)* meaning none can stand in the way of the lucky recipient getting this blessing.

It might incidentally be useful to note that the last words

in lines 11 to 15, which comprise part 3 of the hymn, though written without the nasal (n) sound, are to be so pronounced when reciting.

In line 15, the Guru says, ਆਖਣ ਵਾਲਾ ਕਿਆ ਵੇਚਾਰਾ–*ākhaṇ vāla kiya vechāra,* meaning that those who speak of the Lord are puny and insignificant; what capacity could he have compared to the subject he is trying to describe? He then says in line 16 that the Lord's ਭੰਡਾਰ–*bhanddār,* His immeasurable stores are full of ਸਿਫਤੀ–*siphti*, virtues and good qualities. This is meant to say that these virtues are not ours to claim as a matter of right, but are the Lord's to bestow when it so pleases Him. In other words, only those attain anything as are lucky enough to be the recipients of His bounty. He underscores this thought in the next line, the 17th, as he says, ਜਿਸੁ ਤੂ ਦੇਹਿ ਤਿਸੈ ਕਿਆ ਚਾਰਾ–*jis tu deh tisai kiya chāra.* This has been deciphered in two ways. Some learned ones understand it to mean that none can stand against the one to whom the Lord has given from His bounty. More appealing, however, is the interpretation adopted by Bhai Vir Singh and some other learned ones that this line means the one to whom the Lord gives these gifts get it as a grace and not through their own ਚਾਰਾ–*chāra,* their own effort. In conclusion, the Guru says, ਨਾਨਕ ਸਚੁ ਸਵਾਰਣਹਾਰਾ–*Nanak sach savāraṇ hāra,* meaning that Nanak says the Lord is the only Truth and by His grace alone can we hope to improve ourselves.

4

IN HIS NAME IS TRUE LIFE

In the next hymn, Guru Nanak speaks to us of the essentiality of immersing ourselves in the Lord's name, which he says is not easy to do but without which we may as well not exist. Even if we do breathe and are nominally alive, we are no better than are the dead. In other words, the life of the spiritually dead man is worthless. This hymn occurs again at page 349, SGGS in the same form. The Guru says:

ਆਸਾ ਮਹਲਾ ੧॥	Āsa Mehla 1.
ਆਖਾ ਜੀਵਾ ਵਿਸਰੈ ਮਰਿ ਜਾਉ ॥	Ākha jiva visrai mar jāo.
ਆਖਣਿ ਅਉਖਾ ਸਾਚਾ ਨਾਉ ॥	Ākhaṇ aukha sācha nāo.
ਸਾਚੇ ਨਾਮ ਕੀ ਲਾਗੈ ਭੂਖ ॥	Sāchay nām ki lāgai bhūkh.
ਉਤੁ ਭੂਖੈ ਖਾਇ ਚਲੀਅਹਿ ਦੂਖ ॥੧॥	Ut(u) bhūkhai khāye chalīai dūkh. 1.
ਸੋ ਕਿਉ ਵਿਸਰੈ ਮੇਰੀ ਮਾਇ ॥	So kiu visrai meri māye.
ਸਾਚਾ ਸਾਹਿਬੁ ਸਾਚੈ ਨਾਇ ॥੧॥ ਰਹਾਉ ॥	Sācha sahib sāchai nāye.1.Rāhao.
ਸਾਚੇ ਨਾਮ ਕੀ ਤਿਲੁ ਵਡਿਆਈ ॥	Sāchay nām ki til vaddiāyi.
ਆਖਿ ਥਕੇ ਕੀਮਤਿ ਨਹੀ ਪਾਈ ॥	Ākh thhakay kimat nahi pāyi.
ਜੇ ਸਭਿ ਮਿਲਿ ਕੈ ਆਖਣ ਪਾਹਿ ॥	Jay sabh mil kai ākhan pāhay.
ਵਡਾ ਨ ਹੋਵੈ ਘਾਟਿ ਨ ਜਾਇ ॥੨॥	Vadda na hovai ghātt na jāye. 2.

ਨਾ ਓਹੁ ਮਰੈ ਨ ਹੋਵੈ ਸੋਗੁ ॥	Na oh marai na hovai sog.
ਦੇਦਾ ਰਹੈ ਨ ਚੂਕੈ ਭੋਗੁ ॥	Deda rahai na chūkai bhog.
ਗੁਣੁ ਏਹੋ ਹੋਰੁ ਨਾਹੀ ਕੋਇ ॥	Guṇ eho hor nāhi koye.
ਨਾ ਕੋ ਹੋਆ ਨਾ ਕੋ ਹੋਇ ॥੩॥	Na ko hoā na ko hoye. 3.
ਜੇਵਡੁ ਆਪਿ ਤੇਵਡ ਤੇਰੀ ਦਾਤਿ ॥	Jevadd āp tevadd teri dāt.
ਜਿਨਿ ਦਿਨੁ ਕਰਿ ਕੈ ਕੀਤੀ ਰਾਤਿ ॥	Jin din kar kai kīti rāt.
ਖਸਮੁ ਵਿਸਾਰਹਿ ਤੇ ਕਮਜਾਤਿ ॥	Khasam visāreh tay kamjāt.
ਨਾਨਕ ਨਾਵੈ ਬਾਝੁ ਸਨਾਤਿ ॥੪॥੩॥	Nanak nāvai bājh sanāt. 4. 3.

Glossary:

ਉਤੁ ਭੂਖੈ	Ut(u) bhūkhai	Because of that hunger
ਖਾਇ ਚਲੀਅਹਿ ਦੂਖ	Khāye chalīai dūkh	Troubles are eaten up or are removed
ਨਾਇ	Nāye	Through His name
ਆਖਿ ਥਕੇ	Ākh thhakay	Exhausted themselves reciting the Name
ਨ ਚੂਕੈ ਭੋਗੁ	Na chūkai bhog	Treasures are inexhaustible, are eternal
ਕਮਜਾਤਿ	Kamjāt	Ignoble one
ਸਨਾਤਿ	Sanāt	Wretched one, outcast

The Guru is here emphasising his oft-repeated message, that we must constantly recite the Lord's name. As we know, Sikhism is known as the *Nām Mārg,* the path of recitation of the Lord's name. A basic tenet of Sikhism is that salvation will be found by living in complete surrender to the Lord and constantly reciting His name. As the Guru tells us in the Japji Sahib *Pauṛi* 32:

ਇਕ ਦੂ ਜੀਭੌ ਲਖ ਹੋਹਿ ਲਖ ਹੋਵਹਿ ਲਖ ਵੀਸ ॥	Ik dū jībhau lakh hoye lakh hoveh lakh vīs.

ਲਖੁ ਲਖੁ ਗੇੜਾ ਆਖੀਅਹਿ ਏਕੁ ਨਾਮੁ ਜਗਦੀਸ ॥	Lakh lakh geṛa ākhiye ek nām jagdīs.
ਏਤੁ ਰਾਹਿ ਪਤਿ ਪਵੜੀਆ ਚੜੀਐ ਹੋਇ ਇਕੀਸ॥	Et rāh pat pavaṛia chaṛīai hoye ikīs.

The Guru is explaining to us the path to the Lord. He says that the staircase to the Lord has to be built through constant recitation of the Name of the Lord. He underlines this by saying that if we had not just one tongue but were that one tongue to become a hundred thousand, nay a further twenty times that, then, with each of these manifold tongues we must repeat the Name of the Lord a hundred thousand times. This, the Guru says will help us build a path to Him, this is the *pavaṛia*–the staircase on which we could hope to climb up to Him.

It is important to pause and ponder on the thought the Guru is conveying to us. He is saying firstly that the path is uphill, it is a climb and hence not to be attained without effort, without some hard work. Secondly, this uphill path, this staircase is built from devotion. This is the staircase to the Lord. However, as the Guru has always told us it is for the Lord to decide when we are to reach Him. It is implicit here that while this is the path we must seek to build, that we must follow, we must not make the mistake of assuming that it has now become our right to reach Him. Since, not by effort alone but by the virtue of His grace only can we reach Him, even those many recitations may not be sufficient; but be sure that it is very much a necessary condition. In other words, our reciting of the name can never be overdone.

Here, in this hymn the Guru puts the same thought in another, even stronger way. He says, *ākha jiva visrai mar jāo*; we are alive only when we remember Him. If we forget then we die, in the spiritual sense. *Visrai* means 'to forget'. If our thoughts are not ever fixed on the Lord then our life is meaningless and, in spiritual terms, we may as well not exist. This birth has been bestowed on us as an invaluable gift and it is our opportunity to seek union with the Lord. We will see later in Rehrās Sahib the same thought strongly underlined when the Guru says:

ਭਈ ਪਰਾਪਤਿ ਮਾਨੁਖ ਦੇਹੁਰੀਆ॥	Bhayee parāpat mānukh dehurīya
ਗੋਬਿੰਦ ਮਿਲਣ ਕੀ ਇਹ ਤੇਰੀ ਬਰੀਆ॥	Gobind milaṇ ki eh teri barīya

The Guru is saying to us that the Lord has bestowed this human form upon you, and that this chance has come our way after many eons so that we can try to reach the Lord. This thought is varyingly but constantly stressed in the SGGS. The concept, borrowed from ancient Indian thought and shared by many belief systems, is that we attain this human form after going through a cycle of many births. During some of the births we really did not have proper opportunity to strive to reach Him. Those were the lower forms of created beings when we lacked an intellect to be able to even think about Him, nor did we have a tongue with which we could recite His name.

Having told us that *ākha jiva visrai mar jā*o–we are truly alive only when we remember Him, the Guru then adds a caveat. He says, ਆਖਣਿ ਅਉਖਾ ਸਾਚਾ ਨਾਉ–*ākhaṇ aukha sācha nāo.* It is tough indeed to meditate on Him. It is of course possible for anyone to sit and parrot the words, but to truly fix your mind on Him to the total exclusion of all else is not easy to achieve. The human mind is forever wandering and fickle. It flits from one worry to the next and lusts for one pleasure after the other. To rise beyond these, to control your emotions and thoughts completely is what is called conquering oneself. The

Guru says, *man jītay jag jīt*–if you control your own mind, you have conquered the entire universe. This is because once you attain such control your mind will immediately focus on Him who created all these huge wonders and who has bestowed the wonderful, invaluable gifts of the human form and a mind upon us, to enable us to meditate on Him and make ourselves worthy of His blessing. A stage has to come when with each breath, we take His name and with each morsel of food, we imbibe Him. That stage of automatic, unspoken prayer is not easy to reach. This is what the Guru speaks of when he says, *Ākhaṇ aukha sācha nāo.*

The Guru then says in lines three and four,

ਸਾਚੇ ਨਾਮ ਕੀ ਲਾਗੈ ਭੂਖ ॥	Sāchay nām ki lāgai bhūkh.
ਉਤੁ ਭੂਖੈ ਖਾਇ ਚਲੀਅਹਿ ਦੂਖ ॥੧॥	Ut(u) bhūkhai khāye chalīai dūkh. 1.

Once the hunger for the Lord's name awakens within us, then it will follow that to satiate that hunger, we will imbibe the Lord's name. Once we have fed on that ambrosia, it will make all the woes that afflict us vanish. The troubles we are talking of here are not merely the worldly afflictions, but pertain more to the diseases that our souls acquire in the spiritually polluted world we live in. The opportunity to attain oneness with the Lord is available to all of us, but the majority among us fritters away that opportunity because we are entangled in the glitter of material pleasures; so enchanting are these to our eyes under the delusion of *Maya*. The soul, thus mislead goes on a spree gorging on these empty baubles. A man who eats only unhealthy food just because it happens to taste good to him will, soon enough, be inflicted with illness and debilitation. Similarly, the soul will be weakened when fed on only material pleasures, and not constantly nourished on the Name of the Lord. Troubles, both spiritual and of this world, are bound to afflict such an unfortunate soul. Therefore, we must hope and pray that the hunger for the Lord will arise within us. When it does arise, we will seek the intake that will satiate that hunger. We will seek the company of those who are *Gurmukh*, who follow the right path. Feeding on this healthy food the soul will bloom in good health; and usually we will find that the body also gains from this approach. We can therefore expect to live peaceful and happy lives nourishing ourselves on the Lord's Name, even while participating fully in the activities that our worldly existence requires of us.

The Guru next says in line five, ਸੋ ਕਿਉ ਵਿਸਰੈ ਮੇਰੀ ਮਾਇ–*So kiu visrai meri māye*, how can we ever afford to forget Him? The Guru is addressing it as a remark to his mother, saying *meri māye,* literally meaning o' my mother. This method of expressing ones thoughts as being addressed to one's mother, meaning a near one is to emphasise that this is his innermost, fondest thought. If we are on the right path, it will indeed be impossible ever to forget Him. Why is that so? He answers that in the next line, the sixth, where he says, ਸਾਚਾ ਸਾਹਿਬੁ ਸਾਚੈ ਨਾਇ॥੧॥ ਰਹਾਉ–*Sācha sahib sāchai nāye.1.Rahāo.* He is saying the Lord is true and true is His Name. He then instructs us to pause and ponder on this thought, the term *rahāo* meaning rest or pause, being an indication that an important point has been made on which we need to pause and reflect. Here the Guru wants to stress that the Lord is immanent in His creation, and He is all-pervading. His name is the underpinning for all creation. Such a one is forever all around us. How, says the Guru, could anyone forget this basic truth? He speaks thus in the full knowledge that there are far too many who do in fact forget Him and thus foolishly squander away this invaluable opportunity, this human birth granted to us so that we can seek to be reunited with Him.

The Guru then returns to the lesson in the previous hymn that the Lord's mystery is beyond human ken. He says in line seven, ਸਾਚੇ ਨਾਮ ਕੀ ਤਿਲੁ ਵਡਿਆਈ–*sāchay nām ki til vaddiāyi.* This literally means, barely an iota of the greatness of that True One. In other words, howsoever much we praise Him, our words can only describe a miniscule part of His true greatness. The next line, the eighth, completes this message when he says, ਆਖਿ ਥਕੇ ਕੀਮਤਿ ਨਹੀ ਪਾਈ–*ākh thhakay kīmat nahi pāyi.* This means that for all their best efforts the learned ones failed to truly evaluate the Lord.

Exactly the same thought was expressed slightly differently in the previous hymn where the Guru told us ਸਭਿ ਸੁਰਤੀ ਮਿਲਿ ਸੁਰਤਿ ਕਮਾਈ–*sabh surti mil surt kamāyi*–all the adepts with capacity to assess Him may join and attempt to assess Him. Not only them but also, the ਗਿਆਨੀ–*giāni* the learned ones and the ਧਿਆਨੀ–*dhiāni* those who deeply meditate on Him, may try. Over and above these, even the *gur gurhāyi*–the Guru of Gurus, meaning the greatest of teachers may make the effort. The Guru says even all of them together will never be able to describe ਤੇਰੀ ਤਿਲੁ ਵਡਿਆਈ–*teri til vaddiāyi*–even a tiny part, the size of a sesame seed, of Thy greatness. There is no way any created being can at all describe or assess Him.

Here, in lines seven and eight, the Guru is saying the ones attempting to describe His vast mystery will tire themselves out in the effort but cannot hope to express even a sesame seed's worth of truth. The Guru then adds in lines nine and ten, *jay sabh mil kai ākhan pāhay, vadda na hovai ghātt na jāye*–that even if everyone, meaning all the learned ones, got together and spoke jointly of His greatness, the Lord will remain His great mysterious self; He will neither grow, nor ever lessen. The point is that the Infinite One is ever the same; there is no question of altering infinity in any way. The praise we sing to Him is not going to affect Him in any way at all. The gain and merit will accrue, interestingly, not to the Lord but to the one who sings. His own self will be purified and he will find it easier to move on the Guru's path.

The Guru, in the next lines speaks again of the great mystery of the Lord. The futile effort to measure Him, describe Him, delineate Him has been commented upon by the Guru as doomed to fail. We can only partially sense and try to understand, even if dimly, some part of that great mystery. Here, in line eleven, the Guru says for the Lord, ਨਾ ਓਹੁ ਮਰੈ ਨ ਹੋਵੈ ਸੋਗੁ–*na oh marai na hovai sog*. He is saying the Lord is beyond Death, therefore, His devotee never has to suffer this sorrow. *Sog* means to mourn, to lament, the usual human reaction that follows when we suffer any loss or death. The Lord's devotee will never have to suffer this trauma. The Guru then adds, in line twelve, ਦੇਦਾ ਰਹੈ ਨ ਚੂਕੈ ਭੋਗੁ–*deda rahai na chūkai bhog*. This means that the Lord's treasures are ever open to us humans. He is ever giving to us; all we have is but His gift. *Bhog* here refers to the treasure house of the Lord from which the material things that the Lord gives us flow forever; this treasure house is never empty.

The Guru then gives another way to describe the Lord and says in line thirteen, ਗੁਣੁ ਏਹੋ ਹੋਰੁ ਨਾਹੀ ਕੋਇ–*guṇ eho hor nāhi koye*. His most notable characteristic, he says, is that there is none to equal Him. This of course is a basic tenet of Sikhism that the creator is unmatched, unequalled and if we just pause to think, this premise is axiomatic because were there some one equal to the Creator then there would be not one but more than one competing Creations. In order to make sense of what visibly exists, it is essential to stipulate that there can be none like the Lord Creator. The Guru then adds that there never was one, and even in the future there would be none such, as he says in line fourteen, ਨਾ ਕੋ ਹੋਆ ਨਾ ਕੋ ਹੋਇ–*na ko hoā na ko hoye.*

The Guru then concludes the hymn by telling us that the Lord is great but equally great are His blessings, as he puts it in line fifteen, ਜੇਵਡੁ ਆਪਿ ਤੇਵਡ ਤੇਰੀ ਦਾਤਿ–*jevadd āp tevadd teri dāt.* He, in line sixteen, then refers to His creation by saying, *jin din kar kai kīti rāt*–He has made the day and the night. This is a poetic way of saying that the laws governing the functioning of the Universe have been set in place by the Lord, and we all exist within the parameters of His rules. He returns to the theme of this hymn, which he had articulated in the opening lines, that forgetting the Lord is death and we are truly alive only as long as we remember Him. He says in line seventeen, ਖਸਮੁ ਵਿਸਾਰਹਿ ਤੇ ਕਮਜਾਤਿ–*khasam visāreh tay kamjāt*– the one who forgets the Lord is among the meanest. In saying so the Guru is also clarifying that high caste or low is not to be measured by the accident of birth. It is by the strength of ones devotion to the Lord that it is to be determined. Driving home the same point, he adds in the last line ਨਾਨਕ ਨਾਵੈ ਬਾਝੁ ਸਨਾਤਿ–*Nanak nāvai bājh sanāt.* He who does not live immersed in the Lord's name is a *sanāt*– very low caste person. The Guru consistently opposed the pernicious caste system that prevailed in his time, and which is unfortunately still alive in our country. However, he has perforce frequently put his message in these terms to drive home a spiritual point; because this was the language his audience spoke routinely and would have more easily understood. He is telling us here that the real low caste one is he who does not remember the Lord, regardless of the accident of his birth.

5

THE FOURTH NANAK

The next hymn, in *Rāg Gūjri,* is by the fourth Nanak, Guru Ram Das. Before examining the lesson contained in it, let us look briefly at the life of the author of this hymn.

Learned ones say he was born in Lahore on *Katak vadi* 2, 1591 *Samvat*, corresponding to 24th September, 1534 AD. His father Hari Das belonged to a family of Sodhi Khatris. His mother's name has been variously mentioned by learned ones as Anupvati, Dayavati or Daya Kaur. Learned ones say that he being the eldest son came to be called *Jettha*. This term derives from *jyeshttha,* meaning eldest or first. He was barely seven years old when he lost his parents. His maternal grandmother then took him to her own village, Basarke. To supplement the family income he took up work as an itinerant saleman. He had, from his youth a great liking for the company of religious men, and one day he came with some devotees to Goindwal to pay homage to the third Nanak, Guru Amar Das *ji*. He was then 12 years old. He was so impressed by the Guru that he chose to stay on in Goindwal and serve the Guru. In the mornings, he would tend to the Guru and then would perform duties in the *langar*–the community kitchen.

Thereafter he would carry on with his salesman's job. His religious fervor, his humility and the visible intensity of his devotion was so impressive that the Guru decided to marry his younger daughter, Bibi Bhani, to him. The marriage took place in 1553 AD. In due course, they had three sons, Prithi Chand, Mahadev and Arjan Dev.

The third Nanak now entrusted Jettha with more and more responsibility. He successfully got a stepped well–*baoli*– constructed in Goindwal Sahib. Guru Amar Das chose him to defend the nascent religion against some false charges that had been made by jealous men before the Mughal emperor. The thrust of the complaints was that the Guru was failing to observe the prescribed caste restrictions and was thus polluting the purity of the religion. Bhai Jettha is said to have very successfully refuted these charges before the court of Emperor Akbar, arguing that according to the Sikh faith birth and caste are of no avail before God. He also initiated the setting up of what is today Amritsar. He purchased land in the villages of Tung, Gumtala and Sultanwind and set up a township in 1574 AD. He named it *Guru ka chak* and got built a *sarovar*, a small lake to the east of it. Later, this township was named Ramdaspur after him and the *sarovar* came to be called Amritsar, meaning pool of nectar. With passage of time, the city itself came to be called Amritsar.

Guru Amar Das duly tested his sons Mohan and Mohri, along with Bhai Jettha and found him the fittest. Eventually Bhai Jettha was ordained on 1st September, 1574 AD as Guru Amar Das's successor and was thereafter to be known as Guru Ram Das. He undertook the further development of the city known today as Amritsar, and of the sacred pool. Pilgrims came in ever-growing numbers to hear the Guru and to help in the excavation work of the tank. He also invited people belonging to different trades so that the city would flourish as a commercial centre apart from its importance as the centre of the Sikh religion.

Guru Ram Das was prolific in composing hymns on the theme of spiritual growth along the path spelt out in the *bāṇi* of Guru Nanak. The Vishvakosh of Dr. Jaggi tells us that there are 640 of his hymns included in the SGGS in the more commonly used forms such as the *Chaupaday, Ashttpadi, Chhant, Paday, Slok* and *Pauṛi*. Most remarkably, his *bāṇi* is to be found in 30 of the 31 *Rāgs* in the Granth Sahib, the most by any Guru; Guru Nanak's hymns are in 20 *Rāgs* and Guru Amar Das's in 18. His growth from an orphan child to being the redeemer of the spiritually orphaned is a remarkable story. He had exhibited excellent orgaisational skills in establishing the infant faith on a sound footing and giving it a base in the shape of the city of Amritsar. His ability as a scholar is evidenced by the fact that he had mastered 30 different *Rāgs* in which he composed his hymns, and the depth of his spiritual immersement is clear from a mere reading of his hymns. His 640 hymns in the SGGS include the hymns that are part of the Rehrās Sahib and the Sohila, the evening prayers prescribed in the *Nitnem*. Apart from the usual forms of stanza, he has additionally composed the *bāṇis* known as *Pahra, Vanjāra, Karhalay, Chhakay-chhant and Ghoṛi*, which are included in the SGGS. He is, importantly, also the author of the *Lāva(n)*, the four sloks of which constitute the pivot around which the Anand, the Sikh marriage ceremony is performed. The couple perambulates around the Sri Guru Granth Sahib four times, once with each slok, sealing the marriage in the same way as the Hindu ceremony of perambulating around the holy fire to the recial of Slokas from the Vedas.

The Guru's message to his Sikhs was that a fulfilling life was not one of merely quiet meditation, but required active participation in life, and in the joys and sorrows of others. This is how one could rid oneself of the prime malady–*haumai*, and ensure one's spiritual uplift. Under his stewardship, Sikhism began to take shape as a vibrant, life affirming belief system where the care of the weak and the helpless became a way of life. Around this time Bhai Gurdas, the son of a cousin of Guru Amar Das also became actively associated with the community. Bhai Gurdas was a mystical poet, a master of classical languages and a learned scholar of comparative religion who would later go on to become the scribe of the first copy of the Sri Guru Granth Sahib, compiled by the fifth Nanak.

He passed from this world on 2 Asu 1638 Samvat, corresponding to 1st September, 1581 AD, passing on the stewardship to his youngest son, Arjan Dev.

We now proceed in the next chapter to try and understand the first of the hymns by the fourth Nanak included in the Rehrās Sahib. It is composed in *Rāg Gūjri* and begins with, ਹਰ ਕੇ ਜਨ ਸਤਿਗੁਰ ਸਤਪੁਰਖਾ॥ *Har kay jan satgur satpurkha.*

6

I SEEK THE BOON OF HIS NAME

In this hymn, the fourth Nanak offers his prayer to the Lord seeking nothing but the gift that he may stay immersed in the Name of the Lord. This hymn, which is on page 10, SGGS, occurs again in the same words on page 492, SGGS. The Guru says:

ਰਾਗੁ ਗੂਜਰੀ ਮਹਲਾ ੪ ॥	Rāg Gūjri Mahla 4.
ਹਰਿ ਕੇ ਜਨ ਸਤਿਗੁਰ ਸਤਪੁਰਖਾ ਬਿਨਉ ਕਰਉ ਗੁਰ ਪਾਸਿ ॥	Har kay jan satgur satpurkha binao karo gur pās.
ਹਮ ਕੀਰੇ ਕਿਰਮ ਸਤਿਗੁਰ ਸਰਣਾਈ ਕਰਿ ਦਇਆ ਨਾਮੁ ਪਰਗਾਸਿ॥੧॥	Hum kīray kiram satgur sarnāyi kar daya nām pargās.1.
ਮੇਰੇ ਮੀਤ ਗੁਰਦੇਵ ਮੋ ਕਉ ਰਾਮ ਨਾਮੁ ਪਰਗਾਸਿ ॥	Meray mīt gurdev mo ko rām nām pargās.
ਗੁਰਮਤਿ ਨਾਮੁ ਮੇਰਾ ਪ੍ਰਾਨ ਸਖਾਈ ਹਰਿ ਕੀਰਤਿ ਹਮਰੀ ਰਹਰਾਸਿ ॥੧॥ਰਹਾਉ॥	Gurmat nām mera parān sakhāyi har kīrat hamri rahrās. 1. Rahāo.
ਹਰਿ ਜਨ ਕੇ ਵਡ ਭਾਗ ਵਡੇਰੇ ਜਿਨ ਹਰਿ ਹਰਿ ਸਰਧਾ ਹਰਿ ਪਿਆਸ ॥	Har jan kay vad bhāg vadderay jin har har sardha har pyās.
ਹਰਿ ਹਰਿ ਨਾਮੁ ਮਿਲੈ ਤ੍ਰਿਪਤਾਸਹਿ ਮਿਲਿ ਸੰਗਤਿ ਗੁਣ ਪਰਗਾਸਿ ॥੨॥	Har har nām milai triptāseh mil sangat guṇ pargās. 2.

ਜਿਨ ਹਰਿ ਹਰਿ ਹਰਿ ਰਸੁ ਨਾਮੁ ਨ ਪਾਇਆ ਤੇ ਭਾਗਹੀਣ ਜਮ ਪਾਸਿ ॥	Jin har har har ras nām na pāiya tay bhāghīṇ jam pās.
ਜੋ ਸਤਿਗੁਰ ਸਰਣਿ ਸੰਗਤਿ ਨਹੀ ਆਏ ਧ੍ਰਿਗੁ ਜੀਵੇ ਧ੍ਰਿਗੁ ਜੀਵਾਸਿ ॥੩॥	Jo satgur saran sangat nahi āye dhrig jīvay dhrig jīvās. 3.
ਜਿਨ ਹਰਿ ਜਨ ਸਤਿਗੁਰ ਸੰਗਤਿ ਪਾਈ ਤਿਨ ਧੁਰਿ ਮਸਤਕਿ ਲਿਖਿਆ ਲਿਖਾਸਿ ॥	Jin har jan satgur sangat pāyi tin dhur mastak likhiya likhās.
ਧਨੁ ਧੰਨੁ ਸਤਸੰਗਤਿ ਜਿਤੁ ਹਰਿ ਰਸੁ ਪਾਇਆ ਮਿਲਿ ਜਨ ਨਾਨਕ ਨਾਮੁ ਪਰਗਾਸਿ ॥੪॥੪॥	Dhan dhan satsangat jit har ras pāiya mil jan Nanak nām pargās.4 . 4 .

Glossary:

ਸਤਪੁਰਖਾ	Satpurkha	The Guru
ਕੀਰੇ	Kīray	Worms, insects, lowly ones
ਕੀਰਤਿ	Kīrat	Praise (of the Lord)
ਰਹਰਾਸਿ	Rehrās	Prayer, can also mean Way of living,
ਤ੍ਰਿਪਤਾਸਹਿ	Triptāseh	Are satiated
ਧ੍ਰਿਗ	Dhrig	Condemnable, Despicable
ਧੁਰਿ	Dhur	Destined
ਲਿਖਾਸਿ	Likhās	Is written

The Guru begins this hymn with a prayer to the teacher, his Guru and says, ਹਰਿ ਕੇ ਜਨ ਸਤਿਗੁਰ ਸਤਪੁਰਖਾ–*Har kay jan satgur satpurkha,* meaning literally 'oh God's own, true Guru, righteous man'. The reference is to his mentor, to whom he accords almost divine status. He then says ਬਿਨਉ ਕਰਉ ਗੁਰ ਪਾਸਿ–*binao karo gur pās*, meaning 'I make this prayer and request to the Guru'. The importance accorded to the Guru, the teacher, the spiritual guide is indeed high in Sikhism.

Individuals would have had their personal Gurus, until early in the eighteenth century when the 10th Nanak ordained that henceforth the Sri Guru Granth Sahib shall be the only Guru for all Sikhs, thus putting an end to the practice of living humans being accorded the status of Guru. In today's terms, therefore, such a prayer is deemed as addressed to the SGGS. The Guru here makes this prayer to his Guru saying *hum kīray kiram*–we are but lowly worms. An absence of vanity and a deeply ingrained sense of humility is a sine qua non of the true devotee. In this tenor the Guru is saying that we are lowly, lacking in purity as well as in power. And, what is the prayer he is making to his Guru? He says, *kar daya nām pargās*–have pity on me and bless me with the enlightenment of the Lord's Name. He then reinforces his prayer by asking his Guru, *meray mīt gurdev mo ko rām nām pargās*. He is saying 'O my friend, my benefactor, divine Guru, grant me the enlightenment that comes with the Lord's name. In other words, he is praying on behalf of all devotees to be blessed with reciting the Lord's Name, from which enlightenment shall follow. This, of course, will happen only when the Lord Creator deems us worthy of His blessing.

The Guru expatiates on the same theme further as he says, ਗੁਰਮਤਿ ਨਾਮੁ ਮੇਰਾ ਪ੍ਰਾਨ ਸਖਾਈ–*gurmat nām mera parān sakhāyi*. He is saying may the Name of the Lord gifted to me by the Guru be the support, the friend, of my soul. *Sakha* is a Sanskrit word, which means a dear and close friend. The Guru's request here is that the companion closest to his heart be none other than the Name of the Lord. With the Lord's Name thus ingrained into the soul, may the constant praise of the Lord become the *rahrās*, the way of life. He says, ਹਰਿ ਕੀਰਤਿ ਹਮਰੀ ਰਹਰਾਸਿ–*har kīrat hamri rahrās*. As we saw, this term *rehrās* has been interpreted in different ways. It can be used for prayer as well as for a way of life. Here the Guru is employing it in the latter sense. The Guru asks us to pause here and ponder on this, the central theme of this hymn. The true devotee seeks nothing more than to be blessed with the ability to recite the Name of the Lord, living in complete concord with His Will and focusing on Him with all his heart. Such a blessing is far greater than any human position of power or any material wealth.

In the second part of this hymn the fourth Nanak says, *har jan kay vadd bhāg vadderay jin har har sardha har pyās.* The Guru is saying that great is the fortune of that man of God in whose heart there is ingrained the thirst for the Lord's Name and whose mind is deeply imbued with the worshipful devotion to the Lord. How then are these devotees to remove their hunger? The Guru says, ਹਰਿ ਹਰਿ ਨਾਮੁ ਮਿਲੈ ਤ੍ਰਿਪਤਾਸਹਿ–*har har nām milai triptāseh*. Such true devotees are satiated only when they feed on the Lord's name. And, how is that food, the Lord's Name to be found? The Guru says, ਮਿਲਿ ਸੰਗਤਿ ਗੁਣ ਪਰਗਾਸਿ–*mil sangat guṇ pargās.* The device prescribed is to consort with those who love the Lord, the *Gurmukhs*, the *sangat*. Company of such persons will engender within us that divine quality. The quality, which is inherent in all of us; that hidden spark of godhead, of our divine origin, which we have forgotten in the glitter of empty baubles that this material world entices us with. Our innate nature will become visible in the light of the Lord's Name recited by His devotees. This hymn thus underlines the prescription that we must shun the company of the *manmukh* the egoistic one who denies his Guru, and seek instead the company of the *Gurmukh*, the one living in accordance with the Lord's will.

The Guru next says that those who have not achieved the joy of the Lord's name are the ਭਾਗਹੀਣ–*bhāghīṇ*, the most unfortunate, and will soon meet their doom and be conquered by death. It is of course the fate of all those who are born to die one day. The flesh is not immortal, regardless of your spiritual merit. Therefore, whenever there is reference in the *Gurbaṇi* to freedom from death, it is meant to convey the state of the soul. The unredeemed soul is bound to suffer the agonies of the cycle of births and death. Here, the Guru's meaning is that those unfortunate ones will not find spiritual redemption.

He then speaks of those who have not attained the joy of taking His Name, when he says, *jin har har har ras nām na pāiya*. *Har ras*–literally means the taste of the Lord, implying that there is a deep sense of delight in the heart of the true devotee. This delight makes him hunger for more and as the devotee feeds on this ambrosial food he is gradually overtaken by a divine bliss. This joy is denied to the one who does not take the Lord's Name, says the Guru. Such *manmukhs* are, he tells us, truly unfortunate and are *bhāghīṇ jam pās*–the unlucky ones who will be as fodder for the messenger of death. In the same vein, the Guru adds that those who do not seek shelter in the way prescribed by the true Guru have wasted their life and can have no hope for their future, which also will be as deplorable. As he says, *jo satgur saran sangat nahi āye dhrig jīvay dhrig jīvās*. The term *dhrig* means damned, despicable, deplorable; *jīvay* means the life they are living and their future life. The term *jīvās* derives from *jīv* meaning life, and *ās* meaning hope. The Guru means that such a life is to be condemned, or in othe words is really wasted. This is in the context of his message that this human birth is a great gift from the Lord and is granted to us so that we may seek to reach Him.

In the last, the fourth part, this hymn speaks of the blessing that awaits those who do attain the stage where they relish the

Lord's name. He says, ਜਿਨ ਹਰਿ ਜਨ ਸਤਿਗੁਰ ਸੰਗਤਿ ਪਾਈ–*jin har jan satgur sangat pāyi,* meaning that those lucky ones who have lived in the company of the true Guru, are blessed with the mark of good fortune on their foreheads. He then says, ਤਿਨ ਧੁਰਿ ਮਸਤਕਿ ਲਿਖਿਆ ਲਿਖਿਆਸ–*tin dhur mastak likhiya likhās*. The blessing of the Lord is marked on them from ਧੁਰਿ–*dhur,* from the very beginning. The implication is that what happens is thus written in our fate, or in other words this good fortune comes as a gift from the Lord. The Guru concludes by saying, ਧਨੁ ਧੰਨੁ ਸਤਸੰਗਤਿ ਜਿਤੁ ਹਰਿ ਰਸੁ ਪਾਇਆ ਮਿਲਿ ਜਨ ਨਾਨਕ ਨਾਮੁ ਪਰਗਾਸਿ–*dhan dhan satsangat jit har ras pāiya mil jan Nanak nām pargās*. This means that blessed are the pious ones, the men of God, who in this fashion form the *satsangat* get together and drink of the nectar of the Lord's name. They will thus be illuminated and will find enlightenment.

The next hymn, also in *Rāg Gūjri*, is by the fifth Nanak, Guru Arjan Dev. Before we discuss it let us take a brief look at his extraordinary life.

7

THE FIFTH NANAK

The fifth Nanak was born on 15th April, 1563. He is widely revered as the very embodiment of godly devotion and selfless sacrifice. He stood steadfast and firm on the principles he believed in and set an example of martyrdom, which is remembered by all even today and which has motivated numerous Sikhs over the ages to show great fortitude and steadfastness against tyranny and injustice even at the cost of their lives. He is often referred to as the foremost among the martyrs.

He was the youngest of the three sons of Guru Ram Das. Prithi Chand, the eldest, was the sharpest in worldly matters, skillfully managing his father's household. The second son, Mahadev had reclusive tendencies and wanted to lead the life of an ascetic. The youngest son, Arjan was much the father's favourite from earliest childhood. The Guru found him to be possessed of a serene nature and deeply imbued with the Name of the Lord. As the story goes, one day, while still an infant he found his way to the throne of his grandfather, the third Nanak, Guru Amar Das. As he sat ensconced comfortably on it, the fond grandfather had smiled and prophesied that the young child would be the support of the Lord's Name. Arjan, though, always kept a low profile and remained deeply involved in service to the *sangat* and ever obedient to his father, the fourth Nanak. It is said that his eldest brother Prithi Chand sensing that the young Arjan was becoming the favourite for the spiritual throne of their father, started scheming to further his own interests. It happened that the young Arjan was sent by their father to Lahore to represent him at a wedding. Taking advantage of this fortuitous development Prithi Chand tried his best to manipulate to make the absence longer. The young Arjan is said to have sent a number of epistles, hinting at his desire for an early return. Some learned ones dispute this story but the fact remains that the beautifully poignant missives said to have been composed at that time, dripping with devotion to the Guru, and equally expressing the plight of a devotee separated from the Lord, now form part of the SGGS, in *Rāg Mājh* at page 96.

It is said that Guru Ram Das soon discovered the true nature of Prithi Chand and deeming him ill suited to provide spiritual leadership to the community, installed Arjan as the fifth Nanak, at a young age of 18. Such was Guru Arjan's magnanimity that he never showed any rancour or resentment to his elder brother. Guru Arjan Dev was married to Mata Ganga on 19th June, 1589 AD. She was the daughter of Bhai Krishan Chand of village Mau, 10 km west of Phillaur in the present day state of Punjab.

The basics of the new religion had, of course, been clearly defined by Guru Nanak, and the next three successors had built considerably on that foundation. Guru Arjan Dev now set upon a mission of putting it on an even more solid footing. He first undertook to complete the *sarovar* at Amritsar and commenced construction of the Harmandir Sahib. Guru Nanak had long ago said 'There is no Mussulman and no Hindu', thus stressing the humanistic approach of the new religion he had founded. In keeping with that spirit, Guru Arjan Dev invited Mian Mir, a Muslim Saint from Lahore to lay the cornerstone of the Harmandir. The open entrances placed on all four sides of the building signified the egalitarian nature of the faith, which equally accepted all the four castes and every religion. The city of Amritsar grew around this holy place.

The fifth Nanak made perhaps the most vital contribution to the development of this new religion when he took up the compilation of the Sri Guru Granth Sahib. This had become essential because with the passage of time many pretenders had appeared claiming to be the true Guru. Their main motivation was their greed to get the material benefits of being treated as a Guru, something that is unfortunately continuing to happen even today. These impostors were distorting and even making their own amendments to the hymns and teachings of the Gurus. Guru Arjan's initiative gave to the community a definitive guide and mentor, and quite appropriately, in due course, came to be installed formally as the Guru for all eternity. In keeping with the egalitarian, casteless and secular nature of the Sikh faith, he included, in addition to his own compositions, the hymns of many well-known mystics of other religions. Thus, we have 116 hymns of Sheikh Farid, and of many other well-known *Bhagats*, not to mention the 11 *Bhatts*–a class of panergysts. Thus, there are 532 hymns of Bhagat Kabir, 61 of Bhagat Nāmdev, 40 of Bhagat Ravi Dās, four hymns of Bhagat Trilochan, three each of Bhagat Dhanna and Beṇi, two each of Bhagat Bhikhaṇ and Jai Dev, and one hymn each of Bhagats Rāmānand, Parmanand, Sadhna, Sain and Pipa. There is also one single line by Bhagat Surdās. Apart from these there is the famous *Vār* of the bards Sata and Balwand, as is the Bāṇi known as *sud* by Baba Sundar, who according to the Mahankosh was a grandson of Baba Mohri and thus a great grandson of Guru Amar Das. This galaxy of great saints and holy men covers not only different periods, but also represents a wide variety of beliefs, sects, and castes from high and low. Sheikh Farid was a Muslim, Kabir *ji* came from a weaver family with uncertain religious affiliation, Dhanna *ji* from a peasant class and Ravi Das *ji* from among the *dalit* classes. Others ranged from what were deemed lowly castes like barber or a dyer, to a Brahmin reckoned as the highest caste.

The common thread in all these is a belief in the one Lord, and a rejection of the ritualistic actions involved in the practice of various faiths and sects. The revelations of the fifth Nanak are of the great spiritual and aesthetic calibre and constitute a substantial part of the Guru Granth Sahib.

In order to ensure proper administration and guidance for the community, which was by now quite well spread, Guru Ram Das had introduced the institution of *Masands* who were to represent the Gurus for the community located at distant places, acting both as agent and as missionary. He also put in place the principle of the *Dasvandh*, the tithe, which requires all individuals to contribute a tenth part of their income for the Guru's *Langar*, the community kitchen, and for other acts of benevolence for the benefit of the poor. This practice is also common among the followers of Christianity, and in a slightly different form among the followers of Islam.

Under his stewardship, the community grew and was well favoured in the imperial circles, as long as Emperor Akbar was the ruler. The Mughal King is said to have visited Goindwal and partaken of the *Langar*; sitting on the floor with the congregation which included people from all castes and communities. It also helped that the Muslim Saint, Mian

Mir who had great affinity with the Guru's domain was well respected by the Emperor Akbar. Therefore, when on one occasion a few impostors including the Guru's elder brother Prithi Chand and his followers, and some jealous Brahmin priests, levelled some false charges against the Guru, the complainants were virtually thrown out of the King's court. They however, did not forget this humiliation and continued their evil machinations. Unfortunately, after the death of Akbar, when prince Saleem ascended the throne as Jahangir, they met with greater success. Jahangir was more under the influence of the Muslim clergy who had been of help to him in the struggle for the throne. To repay their favour he soon discarded Akbar's secular ways and reinstated the *Shariat*. Saleem's son, Prince Khusro, was of a more liberal bent of mind and his grandfather Akbar had favoured him to head the kingdom. This Prince made an abortive attempt at the throne but was defeated and had to run for his life. While passing through Punjab he had halted at the Guru's camp at Tarn Taran and received the help and blessings that the Guru gave to all humanity. This event was to become the cause of much trouble later.

The new faith was fast gaining popularity and both Hindus and Muslims flocked to the Guru's house in equal intensity to pay their homage. This naturally dismayed the Muslim clergy. Another event occurred at that time bringing the crisis to a head. One Chandu Shah, a wealthy Hindu, who was an official at the Emperor's Court at Lahore, had sought to arrange the marriage of his daughter with Guru Arjan Dev's only son, Hargobind, but the Guru had rejected the proposal. He was seething at this rebuff.

These inimical forces now joined and complained about the Guru's activities claiming that he was trying to subvert the primacy of the Muslim faith and of the royal court. The Emperor was persuaded of the truth of these false accusations, as would be clear from the following excerpt from the Tuzuq-e-Jahangiri, his autobiography:

"A Hindu named Arjan lived at Goindwal...simple minded Hindus and ignorant and foolish Muslims have been persuaded to adopt his ways... this business has been flourishing for three generations. For a long time it had been in my mind to put a stop to this affair or to bring him into the fold of Islam..."

Prince Khusro had, in the meanwhile been captured and imprisoned. Jahangir then summoned the Guru to Lahore, and highly prejudiced as he had become he refused to accept the explanation about the shelter given to Khusro. Labelling the Guru as a party to the rebellion, he wanted to punish him with death. Pīr Mian Mir intervened and the Emperor commuted the sentence to a fine of two lakh rupees plus an order to erase a few verses from the Granth Sahib. The Guru naturally refused to do so. It is said that the Sikhs of Lahore wanted to pay off the fine but the Guru flatly refused any attempt to pay an unjust fine.

The Guru was then imprisoned and brutally tortured. In the scorching heat of May-June sun, he was made to sit on burning-hot sand, and his naked body was immersed in boiling hot water. It is said that angered at this cruelty to a saintly person, Pīr Mian Mir approached him and offered not only to again intercede on his behalf but some say that he even offered to punish the rulers by using his occult powers and demolish the whole city of Lahore. The Guru refused this help, holding that all that was happening was by God's will. Finally, on 30th May, 1606, he immersed his tortured body in the River Ravi and passed from this world. He left behind a much stronger body of the faithful and a great tradition of refusing to bow to the unjust and to accept the Lord's will readily and without complaint.

We can now proceed to look at the first of his compositions included in the Rehras Sahib, where he stresses for us to have complete faith in the Lord. It begins with:

ਕਾਹੇ ਰੇ ਮਨ ਚਿਤਵਹਿ ਉਦਮੁ ਜਾ ਆਹਰਿ ਹਰਿ ਜੀਉ ਪਰਿਆ ॥
Kāhay ray man chitveh udam ja āhar har jīo paria.

8

THE LORD SUSTAINS HIS OWN

Let us now try to understand the next hymn, the author of which is the fifth Nanak, the foremost among those who have surrendered completely to the Lord. He tells us that the Lord provides for all, so have faith in Him, do your duty, live the right life and leave to the Lord the results of your actions. Your duty is to act and it is for Him to decide on the outcome. Be assured that those who have faith will never lack for anything. This hymn, which is on page 10, SGGS, occurs again in the same form on page 495, SGGS. The Guru says:

ਰਾਗੁ ਗੂਜਰੀ ਮਹਲਾ ੫ ॥	Rāg Gūjri Mahla 5
ਕਾਹੇ ਰੇ ਮਨ ਚਿਤਵਹਿ ਉਦਮੁ ਜਾ ਆਹਰਿ ਹਰਿ ਜੀਉ ਪਰਿਆ ॥	Kāhay ray man chitveh udam ja āhar har jīo paria.
ਸੈਲ ਪਥਰ ਮਹਿ ਜੰਤ ਉਪਾਏ ਤਾ ਕਾ ਰਿਜਕੁ ਆਗੈ ਕਰਿ ਧਰਿਆ ॥੧॥	Sail pathhar meh jant upāye ta ka rijak āgai kar dharia.1.
ਮੇਰੇ ਮਾਧਉ ਜੀ ਸਤਸੰਗਤਿ ਮਿਲੇ ਸੁ ਤਰਿਆ ॥	Meray mādhao ji satsangat milay so taria.
ਗੁਰ ਪਰਸਾਦਿ ਪਰਮ ਪਦੁ ਪਾਇਆ ਸੂਕੇ ਕਾਸਟ ਹਰਿਆ ॥੧॥ ਰਹਾਉ ॥	Gur parsād param pad pāia sūkay kāsatt haria. 1. Rahāo.
ਜਨਨਿ ਪਿਤਾ ਲੋਕ ਸੁਤ ਬਨਿਤਾ ਕੋਇ	Janan pita lok sut banita koye

ਨ ਕਿਸ ਕੀ ਧਰਿਆ ॥	na kis ki dharia.
ਸਿਰਿ ਸਿਰਿ ਰਿਜਕੁ ਸੰਬਾਹੇ ਠਾਕੁਰੁ ਕਾਹੇ ਮਨ ਭਉ ਕਰਿਆ ॥੨॥	Sir sir rijak sambāhay tthākur kāhay man bhao karia. 2.
ਊਡੇ ਊਡਿ ਆਵੈ ਸੈ ਕੋਸਾ ਤਿਸੁ ਪਾਛੈ ਬਚਰੇ ਛਰਿਆ ॥	Ūdday ūdd āvai sai kosa tis pāchhai bachray chharia.
ਤਿਨ ਕਵਣੁ ਖਲਾਵੈ ਕਵਣੁ ਚੁਗਾਵੈ ਮਨ ਮਹਿ ਸਿਮਰਨੁ ਕਰਿਆ ॥੩॥	Tin kavaṇ khalāvai kavaṇ chugāvai man meh simran karia. 3.
ਸਭਿ ਨਿਧਾਨ ਦਸ ਅਸਟ ਸਿਧਾਨ ਠਾਕੁਰ ਕਰ ਤਲ ਧਰਿਆ ॥	Sabh nidhān dus asatt sidhān tthākur kar tal dharia.
ਜਨ ਨਾਨਕ ਬਲਿ ਬਲਿ ਸਦ ਬਲਿ ਜਾਈਐ ਤੇਰਾ ਅੰਤੁ ਨ ਪਾਰਾਵਰਿਆ ॥੪॥੫॥	Jan Nanak bal bal sad bal jāīai tera unt na pārāvaria. 4.5.

Glossary:

ਚਿਤਵਹਿ	Chitveh	Ponder upon, think about
ਆਹਰਿ	Āhar	Effort, task
ਸੈਲ	Sail	Rock, boulder
ਰਿਜਕੁ	Rijak	Livelihood
ਪਰਮ	Param	Highest
ਕਾਸਟ	Kāsatt	Wood
ਧਰਿਆ	Dharia	Support
ਸੰਬਾਹੇ	Sambāhay	Sends, Reaches to, makes available
ਛਰਿਆ	Chharia.	Has left behind
ਦਸ ਅਸਟ	Dus asatt	Eighteen (here used for the 18 *sidhis*)
ਕਰ ਤਲ	Kar tal	palm of the hand

In the first line, the Guru says *kāhay ray man chitveh udam*–literally meaning why do you worry so much about the outcomes of your efforts. The Guru is here stressing the need to believe that the Lord looks after his creation and it is not necessary to overly obsess about our livelihood.

It is necessary here to understand that this is not a prescription for inaction. The Guru is not saying that we should sit back, do nothing and wait for things to drop into our laps; that without moving a finger the Lord will provide us with all that we need. The Sikh faith never advocates inaction or quietism. It is essentially life affirming and advocates living the life of the active householder, striving, earning an honest living, and then sharing part of it with the less privileged. The fifth Nanak makes this very clear in the following hymn from *Rāg Gūjri Mahla* 5, page 522, SGGS:

ਉਦਮੁ ਕਰੇਦਿਆ ਜੀਉ ਤੂੰ ਕਮਾਵਦਿਆ ਸੁਖੁ ਭੁੰਚੁ॥
Udam krediya jio tu(n) kamāvdiya sukh bhunch(u).

The Guru is saying 'strive while you are alive and by honest earnings live at peace'. The Sikh is required, therefore, to always work hard and earn his bread by the sweat of his brow. What the Guru is telling us here is that while we must strive but we must not be uneccessarily panicky about the outcome of our efforts. There is a huge difference between doing nothing and leaving it to the Lord to provide for us, and doing our task sincerely with full energy and then leaving the result thereof to the Lord. It is the latter course the Guru is recommending here; do your best and leave the results to the Lord, do not worry about it any further.

The Guru is telling us in this hymn not to let our minds dwell overly on how we will live, because the Lord is there to take care of us. Just do your duty with sincerity and leave the rest to the Lord. He says, *sail pathhar meh jant upāye ta ka rijak āgai kar dharia*–there are created beings inside huge rocks and boulders and even inside that seemingly inhospitable environment the Lord provides for their means of living.

Instead of wasting time fretting and needlessly worrying, concentrate on seeking the Lord. As much of your daily needs as the Lord decides are enough for you will come your way, as long as your efforts are sincere. Leave idle worries behind and go spend time in the company of the godly in the congregation, the *satsangat*. Because, says the Guru, *satsangat milay so taria*–he who cultivates the company of those who follow the Guru's path will be saved. The word used is *taria*, literally meaning'swam', or was saved from sinking. Here it is used to indicate salvation, implying that such a one achieves freedom from the cycle of death and rebirth. The term *taria* has reference to the belief that we have to cross an ocean of fire to reach the Lord, and we need a very special vessel for that difficult journey. That vessel is the Lord's name, and we will be able to board this vessel by following the Guru's path and keeping the company of the right minded. The human mind is fickle and easily taken in by the glitter that *Maya* spreads all through this world. The baubles of wealth, power and of sensual pleasures will easily take hold of us if we are not vigilant. To avoid these pitfalls we must shun the company of the *manmukh*–those who are lost in the glitter, and cultivate the company of the *gurmukh*–those who have learned to avoid these pitfalls.

The Guru then gives us a further lesson as he says, *gur parsād param pad pāia.* He is saying that the lofty state of bliss is attained only through the Guru's blessings, his *parsād*. The term *param pad* means the supreme, the highest rank. This alludes to the spiritual stage known as the *turia avastha*, a state of spiritual attainment when the Lord's name resonates within us effortlessly with each breath. The Guru's blessing can help us reach this state and when that blessed event happens even the most arid, the most barren of souls will start living and growing again, or as he puts it *sūkay kāsatt haria*–the dry wood sprouts afresh and lives anew.

The Guru speaks of the need for single-minded faith in the Lord. He says *janan pita lok sut banita koye na kis ki dharia*–mother, father, friends, children or wife, none of these will be your support. Who will then be our support? The Guru restates the lesson of the opening line and says *sir sir rijak sambāhay tthākur kāhay man bhao karia*–to each the Lord reaches his livelihood why should then the mind be full of fear?

The Guru gives now another example to stress the same point. He says *ūdday ūdd āvai sai kosa tis pāchhai bachray chharia*–comes flying hundreds of miles leaving behind the children. The term *chharia* means left behind, but has also been interpreted by some learned ones as 'the deserted one, alone' and they render the line as, the little ones have been deserted. However, the more appealing rendering is that the mother bird has left them behind. There is, of course, no serious difference in the meaning either way. The reference here is probably to the *sarus*- Crane, a variety of white coloured, long legged bird that migrates long distances; it could as much be a reference to any mother bird that has gone foraging for its little ones left behind in the nest. The Guru says this bird has travelled such a long distance and its little ones are alone in the nest, with the mother so far away. Who, asks the Guru, is taking care of their sustenance? The mother bird bears constantly in her heart the thought that her little ones must be fed; and the Lord takes care of even those lonely little birds. This example of the bird leaving her offspring in the nest has also been used by the fourth Nanak in *Rāg Gauṛi Bairāgaṇ, Mahla* 4, page 168 SGGS, where he says:

ਜੈਸੀ ਗਗਨਿ ਫਿਰੰਤੀ ਉਡਤੀ, ਕਪਰੇ ਬਾਗੇ ਵਾਲੀ ॥
ਓਹ ਰਾਖੈ ਚੀਤੁ ਪੀਛੈ ਬਿਚਿ ਬਚਰੇ, ਨਿਤ ਹਿਰਦੈ ਸਾਰਿ ਸਮਾਲੀ ॥
Jaisi gagan phiranti ūddti kapray bāgay vāli
Oh rākhay chit pīcchai bich bachray, nit hirdai sār samāli.

Kapṛay bāgay means the white attired one, referring to the white feathers of the crane. *Gagan phiranti* means travelling in the skies and it refers to the fact that the crane is a migratory bird and often flies long distances.

Lastly, in this hymn the Guru says about the Lord, *sabh nidhān dus asatt sidhān tthākur kar tal dharia*–all the treasures and the eighteen adept powers lie on the palm of the Lord's hand. Having something on the palm of the hand indicates a desire to give. The Guru is saying that He is the large-hearted Eternal Donor who stints not and gives readily without the slightest delay. The gifts that the Lord bestows are openly available and are given in a trice, without stinting. The term *nidhān* means treasures and the Guru is saying that all that exists is a gift from the Lord, the entire creation is His and whatever we may attain in our journey through this life is but a blessing from that Divine treasury.

Hindu mythology, speaks of nine types of *nidhis*–treasures, which are under the control of Lord Kubera. Similarly, there are supposed to be 18 types of occult *sidhis.* The Guru is using the term *Dus asatt sidhān,* meaning ten and eight, or eighteen, *sidhis*. The Guru has given their number in two parts, ten plus eight; because there are supposed to be ten minor ones, and eight major *sidhis*.

The Guru says all these *nidhis* and *sidhis*, these various desired gifts which so many are desperately seeking and for which they perform hard austerities are lying on the open palm of the Lord. This implies two things, firstly that all these are gifts from the Lord; none acquires it just by dint of his own efforts. Secondly, the Guru is saying that these greatly coveted things are as nothing to the Divine one, these lie on His open palm meaning that these are readily given without a second thought. The essence of the message here is that such powers and gifts are automatically available to those who meditate on the *Nām*.

The Guru concludes with *bal bal sad bal jāīai tera unt na pārāvaria*, meaning that he would sacrifice himself to the Lord not once but a hundred times, and that the Lord is immeasurable; His limits are not *pārāvaria*–the ends are not within human ken to decipher.

With this hymn, the five hymns under the heading '*So Dar'* are complete. We now come to the next group, which consists of four hymns under the title '*So Purakh*'.

9

THE UNTAINTED ONE

The first of the four hymns under the title *So Purakh* is by the fourth Nanak. It occurs again at page 348, SGGS, with some minor differences. For example, in line 12 the word *tūtti* becomes *ttūtti* at page 348. Similarly, the word *ji* occurring in lines 12, 13, 14 and 15 becomes *jio* at page 348.These minor variations make no difference to the message of this hymn. The Guru says:

ਰਾਗੁ ਆਸਾ ਮਹਲਾ ੪ ਸੋ ਪੁਰਖੁ	Rāg Āsa Mahla 4 So Purakh
ੴ ਸਤਿਗੁਰ ਪ੍ਰਸਾਦਿ ॥	Ik Onkār Satgur Parsād
ਸੋ ਪੁਰਖੁ ਨਿਰੰਜਨੁ ਹਰਿ ਪੁਰਖੁ ਨਿਰੰਜਨੁ	So purakh niranjan har purakh
ਹਰਿ ਅਗਮਾ ਅਗਮ ਅਪਾਰਾ ॥	niranjan har agma agam apāra.
ਸਭਿ ਧਿਆਵਹਿ ਸਭਿ ਧਿਆਵਹਿ	Sabh dhiāveh sabh dhiāveh
ਤੁਧੁ ਜੀ ਹਰਿ ਸਚੇ ਸਿਰਜਣਹਾਰਾ ॥	tudh ji har sachay sirjaṇhāra.
ਸਭਿ ਜੀਅ ਤੁਮਾਰੇ ਜੀ ਤੂੰ ਜੀਆ	Sabh jiw tumāray ji too(n) jīa
ਕਾ ਦਾਤਾਰਾ ॥	ka dātāra.
ਹਰਿ ਧਿਆਵਹੁ ਸੰਤਹੁ ਜੀ ਸਭਿ	Har dhiāvoh santoh ji sabh
ਦੂਖ ਵਿਸਾਰਣਹਾਰਾ ॥	dūkh visāraṇhāra.
ਹਰਿ ਆਪੇ ਠਾਕੁਰੁ ਹਰਿ ਆਪੇ ਸੇਵਕੁ	Har āpay thākur har āpay sevak
ਜੀ ਕਿਆ ਨਾਨਕ ਜੰਤ ਵਿਚਾਰਾ ॥੧॥	jei kiya Nanak jant vichāra. 1.
ਤੂੰ ਘਟ ਘਟ ਅੰਤਰਿ ਸਰਬ ਨਿਰੰਤਰਿ	Too(n) ghatt ghatt antar sarab

ਜੀ ਹਰਿ ਏਕੋ ਪੁਰਖੁ ਸਮਾਣਾ ॥	nirantar ji har eko purakh samāṇa.
ਇਕਿ ਦਾਤੇ ਇਕਿ ਭੇਖਾਰੀ ਜੀ ਸਭਿ ਤੇਰੇ ਚੋਜ ਵਿਡਾਣਾ ॥	Ik dātay ik bhekhāri ji sabh teray choj viddāṇa
ਤੂੰ ਆਪੇ ਦਾਤਾ ਆਪੇ ਭੁਗਤਾ ਜੀ ਹਉ ਤੁਧੁ ਬਿਨੁ ਅਵਰੁ ਨ ਜਾਣਾ]	Too(n) āpay data āpay bhugta ji hau tudh bin avar na jāṇa.
ਤੂੰ ਪਾਰਬ੍ਰਹਮੁ ਬੇਅੰਤੁ ਬੇਅੰਤੁ ਜੀ ਤੇਰੇ ਕਿਆ ਗੁਣ ਆਖਿ ਵਖਾਣਾ ॥	Too(n) pārbrahm beant beant ji teray kia guṇ ākh vakhāṇa.
ਜੋ ਸੇਵਹਿ ਜੋ ਸੇਵਹਿ ਤੁਧੁ ਜੀ ਜਨੁ ਨਾਨਕੁ ਤਿਨ ਕੁਰਬਾਣਾ ॥੨॥	Jo seveh jo seveh tudh ji jan Nanak tin kurbāṇa.2.
ਹਰਿ ਧਿਆਵਹਿ ਹਰਿ ਧਿਆਵਹਿ ਤੁਧੁ ਜੀ ਸੇ ਜਨ ਜੁਗ ਮਹਿ ਸੁਖਵਾਸੀ॥	Har dhiāveh har dhiāveh tudh ji say jan jug meh sukhvāsi.
ਸੇ ਮੁਕਤੁ ਸੇ ਮੁਕਤੁ ਭਏ ਜਿਨ ਹਰਿ ਧਿਆਇਆ ਜੀ ਤਿਨ ਤੂਟੀ ਜਮ ਕੀ ਫਾਸੀ ॥	Say mukat say mukat bhaye jin har dhiāia ji tin tūtti jam ki phāsi.
ਜਿਨ ਨਿਰਭਉ ਜਿਨ ਹਰਿ ਨਿਰਭਉ ਧਿਆਇਆ ਜੀ ਤਿਨ ਕਾ ਭਉ ਸਭੁ ਗਵਾਸੀ॥	Jin nirbhau jin har nirbhau dhiāia ji tin ka bhau sabh gavāsi.
ਜਿਨ ਸੇਵਿਆ ਜਿਨ ਸੇਵਿਆ ਮੇਰਾ ਹਰਿ ਜੀ ਤੇ ਹਰਿ ਹਰਿ ਰੂਪਿ ਸਮਾਸੀ ॥	Jin sevia jin sevia mera har ji tay har har rūp samāsi.
ਸੇ ਧੰਨੁ ਸੇ ਧੰਨੁ ਜਿਨ ਹਰਿ ਧਿਆਇਆ ਜੀ ਜਨੁ ਨਾਨਕੁ ਤਿਨ ਬਲਿ ਜਾਸੀ ॥੩॥	Say dhan say dhan jin har dhiāia ji jan Nanak tin bal jāsi.3.
ਤੇਰੀ ਭਗਤਿ ਤੇਰੀ ਭਗਤਿ ਭੰਡਾਰ ਜੀ ਭਰੇ ਬਿਅੰਤ ਬੇਅੰਤਾ ॥	Teri bhagat teri bhagat bhanddār ji bharay beant beanta.
ਤੇਰੇ ਭਗਤ ਤੇਰੇ ਭਗਤ ਸਲਾਹਨਿ ਤੁਧੁ ਜੀ ਹਰਿ ਅਨਿਕ ਅਨੇਕ ਅਨੰਤਾ ॥	Teray bhagat teray bhagat salāhan tudh ji har anik anek ananta.
ਤੇਰੀ ਅਨਿਕ ਤੇਰੀ ਅਨਿਕ ਕਰਹਿ ਹਰਿ ਪੂਜਾ ਜੀ ਤਪੁ ਤਾਪਹਿ ਜਪਹਿ ਬੇਅੰਤਾ ॥	Teri anik teri anik kareh har puja ji tap tāpeh japeh beanta.

ਤੇਰੇ ਅਨੇਕ ਤੇਰੇ ਅਨੇਕ ਪੜਹਿ ਬਹੁ	Teray anek teray anek paṛeh
ਸਿਮ੍ਰਿਤਿ ਸਾਸਤ ਜੀ ਕਰਿ ਕਿਰਿਆ	baho simrit sāsat ji kar kiria
ਖਟੁ ਕਰਮ ਕਰੰਤਾ॥	khatt karam karanta.
ਸੇ ਭਗਤ ਸੇ ਭਗਤ ਭਲੇ ਜਨ ਨਾਨਕ	Say bhagat say bhagat bhalay
ਜੀ ਜੋ ਭਾਵਹਿ ਮੇਰੇ ਹਰਿ	jan Nanak ji jo bhāveh meray
ਭਗਵੰਤਾ ॥੪॥	har bhagvanta.4.
ਤੂੰ ਆਦਿ ਪੁਰਖੁ ਅਪਰੰਪਰੁ ਕਰਤਾ ਜੀ	Too(n)ād purakh aprampar
ਤੁਧੁ ਜੇਵਡੁ ਅਵਰੁ ਨ ਕੋਈ ॥	karta ji tudh jevadd avar
	na koi.
ਤੂੰ ਜੁਗੁ ਜੁਗੁ ਏਕੋ ਸਦਾ ਸਦਾ ਤੂੰ ਏਕੋ	Too(n) jug jug eko sada sada
ਜੀ ਤੂੰ ਨਿਹਚਲੁ ਕਰਤਾ ਸੋਈ ॥	too(n) eko ji too(n) nihchal
	karta soi.
ਤੁਧੁ ਆਪੇ ਭਾਵੈ ਸੋਈ ਵਰਤੈ ਜੀ ਤੂੰ	Tudh āpay bhāvai soi vartai ji
ਆਪੇ ਕਰਹਿ ਸੁ ਹੋਈ ॥	too(n)āpay kareh so hoyi.
ਤੁਧੁ ਆਪੇ ਸ੍ਰਿਸਟਿ ਸਭ ਉਪਾਈ ਜੀ	Tudh āpay sristt sabh upāyi ji
ਤੁਧੁ ਆਪੇ ਸਿਰਜਿ ਸਭ ਗੋਈ ॥	tudh āpay siraj sabh goyi.
ਜਨੁ ਨਾਨਕੁ ਗੁਣ ਗਾਵੈ ਕਰਤੇ ਕੇ ਜੀ	Jan Nanak guṇ gāvai kartay
ਜੋ ਸਭਸੈ ਕਾ ਜਾਣੋਈ ॥੫॥੧॥	kay ji jo sabhsai ka jāṇoyi.5.1.

Glossary:

ਨਿਰੰਜਨੁ	Niranjan	Beyond the taint of *Maya*, pure
ਅਗਮਾ	Agma	Beyond reach
ਅਪਾਰਾ	Apāra	Immeasurable
ਵਿਸਾਰਣਹਾਰਾ	Visāraṇhāra	He who dispells
ਘਟ ਘਟ	Ghatt ghatt	In each person
ਸਰਬ ਨਿਰੰਤਰਿ	Sarab nirantar	For ever in all time and space
ਚੋਜ	Choj	Play, doing
ਵਿਡਾਣਾ	Viddāṇa	Wonderful one
ਭੁਗਤਾ	Bhugta	Consumer

ਸੇਵਹਿ	Seveh	Serve, here meaning meditate on
ਅਨੰਤਾ	Ananta.	Endless, eternal, infinite
ਤਪੁ ਤਾਪਹਿ	Tap tāpeh	Perform austerities
ਖਟੁ ਕਰਮ	Khatt karam	Six rites prescribed in Hindu religion
ਸਿਰਜਿ	Siraj	To make, to create
ਗੋਈ	Goyi.	Destroyed
ਜਾਣੋਈ	Jāṇoyi	One who knows

The title of the hymn '*So Purakh*' translates as 'that Entity, or Being'. Here, the Guru is referring to the Lord, as he makes abundantly clear by adding *har purakh*–Lord the Creator. The Guru in this hymn speaks to us about the qualities by which we can sense the Lord and His relationship with his creation. It is an oft-repeated lesson that the Lord is beyond the ken of the ordinary human. How then is He to be described so that the ordinary mortal could try to make some sense of this great mystery? Masters, regardless of religion or region, use roughly the same technique. They try to make things comprehensible by referring to some basic postulates that are essential to an almighty Deity, and then describing His more evident and perceptible characteristics as revealed in the events and things around us that we can see and experience. Here the Guru begins by saying, *so purakh niranjan har purakh niranjan.* Thus, the first thing he highlights is that the Lord is *niranjan*–free from any taint whatsoever. Then he adds, *har agma agam apāra*–the Lord is beyond our reach and is beyond our capacity to measure. Then he says, *sabh dhiāveh*–all creation worships the Lord who is *sachay sirjaṇhāra*–the true one who creates and sustains. With these words, the Guru has told us of some of the qualities by which we can get a glimpse of Him. He says that the Lord is the Creator, is the only Truth, in the sense that he is eternal, and is ever the same while all else is subject to the ravages of time. He further says the Lord is *dātāra*–the one who gives, the source of all that exists. All creation belongs to Him and it is by His beneficence that we are sustained. The Lord is also the *dūkh visāraṇhāra*–the dispeller of all our troubles. The Guru exhorts all godly ones to meditate on that Lord who rids us of all our troubles. The Guru says we poor helpless humans are not capable of anything on our own strength; all we see is the Lord manifest, *har āpay thākur har āpay sevak*–the Lord is the master and is at the same time also the servant. This is a way of saying that the Lord is immanent in all creation and in every being.

In the second part of the hymn, he says the Lord is *ghatt ghatt antar*–within each being. The term *ghatt* means a vessel, but is also frequently used to describe the innermost being, the heart, of all created things. Having highlighted His immanence in these words the Guru now adds the Lord is *sarab nirantar*–within all at all times and places. Then he adds, *har eko purakh samāṇa*–the Lord is uniquely one and He is within all existence. This is again an allusion to the Lord's immanence and to the fact that He is axiomatically the One, like whom there can be none other. The visible differences that we may see around us are an illusion. *Ik dātay ik bhekhāri*–some are donors and others are beggars, seemingly absolute opposites but in reality merely a part of the Lord's play, a manifestation of the variety in which the Lord manifests His presence in this Universe. The Guru says, *sabh teray choj viddāṇa*–all this is just a wonderful frolic put on by the supreme Lord. He makes it clearer in the next line when he says, *āpay dāta āpay bhugta*–Himself the donor and himself the consumer.

The Lord is the only reality; the differences we see are just the various manifestations, which our eyes, limited and deluded by *Maya*, are deceived into seeing Him. He is the *dāta*–provider, the sole source of our sustenance; but in the form of His immanent self is also the *bhugta*–the consumer. The Guru says, *hau tudh bin avar na jāṇa*–I see none except you.

In other words, the Guru is telling us that there is but one Reality, and that is the Lord Himself. That Lord, he says, is *pārbrahm*–transcendent. He is also *beant*–literally meaning endless but used here to say He is the immeasurable one whose limits we cannot fathom. He then says that the Lord's virtues are beyond our capacity to enumerate or recite, expressing his helplessness in describing the myriad qualities and virtues of the Lord by saying, *teray kia guṇ ākh vakhāṇa.* So great are these powers and qualities that we cannot even know where to begin. He concludes this part of the hymn by saying, *jo seveh tudh ji jan Nanak tin kurbāṇa*–Nanak would sacrifice himself to those whose minds are fixed on the Lord. The word *seveh* means 'to serve', but what way could there be to serve a Lord who is Himself the source of all that can be seen? The only possible way is to recite His name fixing one's mind on Him and surrendering to His will. How this *sewa* can be rendered to the Lord has been well put by the third Nanak in *Soratth Mahla* 3, *ghar* 1, page 599, SGGS when he tells us: ਸੇਵਕ ਸੇਵ ਕਰਹਿ ਸਭ ਤੇਰੀ ਜਿਨ ਸਬਦੇ ਸਾਦੁ ਆਇਆ–*sevak sev karay sabh teri jin sabday sād āiya.* This means those who have begun to relish Thy Name serve Thee. The gift of relishing the Lord's Name also comes from Him and thus only those can serve Him whom He blesses with this glance of grace. Those who follow the path of fixing their mind on Him and surrendering to His will are the true servants of the Lord. The position of the true devotee is lofty indeed in Sikhism and the totally immersed devotee is almost like the Lord Himself, deserving of great reverence.

In the third part of this hymn, the Guru speaks further on this very theme, of the high position of those who worship Him. He says, *har dhiāveh tudh ji say jan jug meh sukhvāsi*–those who meditate on the Lord shall have an easy existence in this world. Then he tells us that they shall achieve salvation. He puts it in these words, *mukat bhaye jin har dhiāia*–meditating on the Lord they are saved, or attain salvation. The Guru tells us that they obtain freedom from the cycle of life and death, as he says, *tin tūtti jam ki phāsi*–for them the noose of death is smashed. He stresses this further in the next line as he says, *jin har nirbhau dhiāia ji tin ka bhau sabh gavāsi*–the one whose mind is fixed on the fearless one shall be rid of all fear. *Nirbhau*–the fearless one–is a term used to describe the Lord as would be seen in the *mool mantra* itself. Here, the Guru is using it to drive home the lesson that the one who worships the fearless Lord shall have his own fears fully allayed. He then takes a step further up and says, beyond losing all fear, *jin sevia mera har ji tay har har rūp samāsi*–those who serve, meditate on the Lord shall merge into that divine form. Implied here is the path to God-realisation, which in Sikhism is through *Nām Simran*–recitation of His name. Those who would serve Him must immerse themselves in the recitation of His *Nām*. In the last line of this part, the Guru sums up his praise of the devotee by saying, *say dhan say dhan jin har dhiāia ji*–blessed are those who have meditated on the Lord. Then he concludes with, *Nanak tin bal jāsi*–Nanak would sacrifice himself to such devotees, thus reiterating the thought he had expressed in the last line of the previous part when he said, *Nanak tin kurbāṇa*–Nanak would sacrifice himself to those.

In the fourth part of the hymn, the Guru continues on the theme of worship and of the devotees who worship the One Lord. He first addresses the Lord with, *teri bhagat(i) teri bhagat(i) bhanddār ji bharay beant beanta*–the treasury of devotion to Thee is ever full, unlimited, beyond measure and infinite. This lends itself to more than one interpretation. Firstly, it could mean that because myriad devotees have been worshipping the Lord since the very beginning, the stores of devotion to Him are ever replete. The second view could be that the Lord has filled the created worlds with the store of devotion to Him and countless devotees have fulfilled themselves from these stores of devotion. This seems the more appealing view since it tallies with the thought that even the devotion to Him is a gift. The Guru then refers to these *bhagats* in the next line where he says the words '*bharay beant beanta*', which would then mean that countless *bhagats* have fulfilled themselves.

He then speaks of the devotees who worship the Lord and says, *teray bhagat teray bhagat salāhan tudh ji har anik anek ananta*–thy devotees sing thy praises, and such devotees are myriad and they always singin various and diverse ways the praise of the Lord who is *ananta*–without any end.

The Guru then enumerates some of these various ways of worship practiced in this part of this world. He says, *Teri anik teri anik kareh har puja ji tap tāpeh japeh beanta*–many are those who worship the Lord through *tap tāp*- performing severe austerities, and many are those who worship through *jāp*–recitation of His name. The Guru may also have been referring to those who worship through recitation of mystical chants, *mantras*, as that was the more popular form among his Hindu followers. The message here is that all those who sincerely seek Him are true devotees worthy of respect and reverence, regardless of region, religion, sex or caste.

He then speaks of another category of worshippers, as he says, *teray anek teray anek paṛeh baho simrit sāsat ji*– many are the erudite ones who worship through study of the many *Simritis* and *Shāstras.* These are the the main Hindu religious scriptures enshrining ancient lore and wisdom and deemed especially holy, which provide guidance according to the Hindu system to the seekers of the One Lord. Lastly, at the end of the same line he refers to another set of important Hindu religious practices. He says, *kar kiria khatt karam karanta*–they perform the six prescribed rituals and the other religious actions as prescribed in these scriptures. According to the Mahan Kosh the Manu Smriti describes six requisite duties for a Brahmin; *viz*, studying, teaching, performing *yagya*, helping others perform *yagya*, taking alms and, lastly, giving alms. Another list of six prescribed actions is given in the same *Simriti* as, reading the *Vedas*, performing *tap*(austerities), acquiring *gyān*(knowledge), controlling the senses, *ahimsa*(eschewing violence), and serving the Guru. Other scriptures list various other sets of six actions.

The Guru concludes with, *say bhagat say bhagat bhalay jan Nanak ji jo bhāveh meray har bhagvanta*–Nanak says that sublime are those devotees with whom the Lord God is pleased.

It can be seen that the choice of examples the Guru has quoted here pertain mainly to the more popular forms of worship among his Hindu followers, and speaks only of the Hindu forms of worship and rituals.

This is easily explained if we keep in mind that the Guru's audience would have been mainly Hindu at that time.

Equally, however, this lesson would apply to other forms of worship or ritual laid down in any other belief system.

The thrust of the message is that the Worlds in the Universe are infinite, and in those, there must exist an uncountable variety of beings. Each of these will have their own way of worshipping the One Lord, who is the Lord not only of this small piece of land but of the entire created universe. The Guru is highlighting the truth that the passage to an infinite Lord can be found in an infinite ways. All those who sincerely seek Him are true devotees worthy of respect and reverence.

In fact, from the evidence within the SGGS we know that the Guru's vision was not limited to merely the tract he happened to live in, or even just this world. He saw the infinite worlds that stretch through the endless space-time continuum the Lord has brought into existence. The Guru was not looking at the petty personal or regional differences among those who happened to be among his flock at that time. He tells us in the 22nd *pauṛi* of the Japji Sahib, *pātāla pātāl lakh āgāsa āgās*–the number of the heavens and of the nether worlds is not limited. The term lakh means a hundred thousand but is here intended to denote a very large number. In all these different worlds, there would be life forms of diverse types that are sure to have evolved in widely varying shapes and forms, some not even remotely like our human form. Among all these created beings there are sure to be those who seek the Lord Creator in their own way. The directions that their seeking, their endeavours take are bound to vastly vary. Here in this hymn the Guru hints at this variety. He then mentions some specific forms of worship that existed among the dominant Hindu religion at that time, such as reading the *Simritis* and the *Shāstras*, performimg religious rituals and the six prescribed religious activities. In the last line, he sums up with the caveat that of all these devotees, only those will be successful whom the Lord chooses to accept. This is meant to tell us that of all the myriad devotees paying obeisance in their own ways, through austerities or whatever other method, none can expect to claim as a matter of right the results of their efforts. That is a gift the Lord holds to Himself, to be given at His own sweet will. Therefore, of all the devotees practicing diverse forms of worship, the lucky ones are those, *jo bhāveh meray har bhagvanta* –who please the Lord, says the Guru. These are the ones who will receive the glance of grace from the Lord and be freed from the circle of rebirth.

In the last part of the hymn, the Guru speaks in words of deep devotion about the Lord. He says the Lord is *ād purakh aprampar karta*, meaning He is the Primal Being, beyond the ken of human understanding, and the Creator. As the Guru says in the *mool mantra*, the Lord is the *ād sach*, the Truth from the very beginning. As the Creator, he has, by definition, to be the Primal Being, the one who existed before anything came into being. There is also, similarly, none who could be His equal. In the same vein he adds in the second line that the Lord is *jug jug eko sada sada too(n) eko ji too(n) nihchal karta*–eternally the same through the ages, ever and ever the unique one, the constant one, the Creator. This is a message that has repeatedly been stressed throughout the SGGS, starting with the very first line, the *mool mantra*. The Guru then speaks of the Lord's omnipotence by saying, *tudh āpay bhāvai soi vartai ji, too(n) āpay kareh so hoyi*–what You will, comes to happen; and what You ordain comes to pass. The Guru stresses the Creator function of the Lord in the next line when he says, *tudh āpay sristt sabh upāyi ji tudh āpay siraj sabh goyi*–You have created the universe and having brought it into existence You also destroy it when You so will. The cycle of creation and destruction, of life and death, is here the subject. The Lord, at His sole pleasure creates the universe and then at the appointed time, which only He determines, again destroys it. While it exists, it functions as the arena, the field of action where the souls separated from the Lord are given the invaluable gift of the human form bringing with it an opportunity of trying to regain their original place within Him.

In the last line, the Guru concludes with further words of adoration as he says, *jan Nanak guṇ gāvai kartay kay ji jo sabhsai ka jāṇoyi*–Nanak sings the praises of that omniscient Lord, the Creator.

10

THE TRUE LORD

The next hymn, which is by the fourth Nanak, occurs again on page 365, SGGS in the same form. The Guru says:

ਆਸਾ ਮਹਲਾ ੪ ॥	Āsa Mahla 4
ਤੂੰ ਕਰਤਾ ਸਚਿਆਰੁ ਮੈਡਾ ਸਾਂਈ ॥	Too(n) karta sachiyār maidda sā(n)yi.
ਜੋ ਤਉ ਭਾਵੈ ਸੋਈ ਥੀਸੀ ਜੋ ਤੂੰ ਦੇਹਿ ਸੋਈ ਹਉ ਪਾਈ ॥੧॥ ਰਹਾਉ ॥	Jo tau bhāvai soyi thhisi jo too(n) deh soyi hau pāyi.1. Rahāo.
ਸਭ ਤੇਰੀ ਤੂੰ ਸਭਨੀ ਧਿਆਇਆ ॥	Sabh teri too(n) sabhni dhiāia.
ਜਿਸ ਨੋ ਕ੍ਰਿਪਾ ਕਰਹਿ ਤਿਨਿ ਨਾਮ ਰਤਨੁ ਪਾਇਆ ॥	Jis no kirpa kareh tin nām ratan pāia.
ਗੁਰਮੁਖਿ ਲਾਧਾ ਮਨਮੁਖਿ ਗਵਾਇਆ ॥	Gurmukh lādha manmukh gavāia.
ਤੁਧੁ ਆਪਿ ਵਿਛੋੜਿਆ ਆਪਿ ਮਿਲਾਇਆ ॥੧॥	Tudh āp vichhoṛia āp milāia.1.
ਤੂੰ ਦਰੀਆਉ ਸਭ ਤੁਝ ਹੀ ਮਾਹਿ ॥	Too(n) darīāo sabh tujh hi māh(i).
ਤੁਝ ਬਿਨੁ ਦੂਜਾ ਕੋਈ ਨਾਹਿ ॥	Tujh bin dūja koyi nāheh.
ਜੀਅ ਜੰਤ ਸਭਿ ਤੇਰਾ ਖੇਲੁ ॥	Jiw jant sabh tera khel.

ਵਿਜੋਗਿ ਮਿਲਿ ਵਿਛੁੜਿਆ ਸੰਜੋਗੀ ਮੇਲੁ ॥੨॥	Vijog mil vichhuṛia sanjogi mel.2.
ਜਿਸ ਨੋ ਤੂ ਜਾਣਾਇਹਿ ਸੋਈ ਜਨੁ ਜਾਣੈ ॥	Jis no tu jāṇāyeh soyi jan jāṇai.
ਹਰਿ ਗੁਣ ਸਦ ਹੀ ਆਖਿ ਵਖਾਣੈ ॥	Har guṇ sad hi ākh vakhāṇai.
ਜਿਨਿ ਹਰਿ ਸੇਵਿਆ ਤਿਨਿ ਸੁਖੁ ਪਾਇਆ ॥	Jin har sevia tin sukh pāia.
ਸਹਜੇ ਹੀ ਹਰਿ ਨਾਮਿ ਸਮਾਇਆ ॥੩॥	Sehjay hi har nām samāia.3.
ਤੂ ਆਪੇ ਕਰਤਾ ਤੇਰਾ ਕੀਆ ਸਭੁ ਹੋਇ ॥	Tu āpay karta tera kīa sabh hoye.
ਤੁਧੁ ਬਿਨੁ ਦੂਜਾ ਅਵਰੁ ਨ ਕੋਇ ॥	Tudh bin dūja avar na koye.
ਤੂ ਕਰਿ ਕਰਿ ਵੇਖਹਿ ਜਾਣਹਿ ਸੋਇ ॥	Tu kar kar vekheh jāṇeh soye.
ਜਨ ਨਾਨਕ ਗੁਰਮੁਖਿ ਪਰਗਟੁ ਹੋਇ ॥੪॥੨॥	Jan Nanak gurmukh pargatt hoye.4‖2.

Glossary:

ਮੈਡਾ	Maidda	Mine
ਥੀਸੀ	Thhisi	Will happen
ਦਰੀਆਓ	Darīāo	River, ocean, a vast stream
ਵਿਜੋਗਿ	Vijog	The fate that separates
ਸੰਜੋਗੀ	Sanjogi	The fate that joins or unites
ਜਾਣਾਇਹਿ	Jāṇāyeh(n)	To make understand, to explain
ਵਖਾਣੈ	Vakhāṇai	Speaks
ਸਹਜੇ	Sehjay	Easily

The Guru begins this hymn with, *too(n) karta sachiyār maidda sā(n)yi*, addressing the Lord as the creator, the true reality and saying He is his Lord and master. The description of the Lord as the underlying truth and reality of this created universe is a recurring theme in the Guru's message. The phrase *maidda sā(n)yi* is in *lehndi Punjabi* prevalent in western Punjab, and is an affectionate way of expressing his devotion to the Lord, calling Him 'my master'. The devotee can approach the Lord in various ways as we can see in different belief systems. The Lord in these various belief systems can sometimes be the terrible one whom we must fear and obey; he can be the loving husband with whom we have an intimate relationship and so on. In Sikhism, the basic relationship postulated is of the master and his devoted servant, though at places in the SGGS, He is also depicted as the husband or lover, and some places as father. We are His to command, ever in complete surrender to Him, ever willing to comply with all He ordains and ever content with anything that He may choose to give us. This personal relationship is unique between each soul and the Lord. Here the Guru stresses this aspect, and speaks of his own acceptance of this position, saying the Lord is his master.

He then says, *jo tau bhāvai soyi thhisi jo too(n) deh soyi hau pāyi*–whatever the Lord pleases will come to pass and we will get only what He decides to give us. The formulation that events occur entirely as determined by the Lord occurs repeatedly in the SGGS, and some take it to mean that they need make no efforts at all and must passively wait for events to unfold. Such a negative approach is not in consonance with the Sikh belief system. So, a caveat needs to be entered here, and this formulation is to be clearly understood as not a prescription for passive inaction. It is rather a lesson that underpinning all our efforts must be the constant realisation that the result of these is entirely in the hands of the Lord. The pause marked after this line makes that aspect clearer. It is meant as a direction to stop and ponder on this, the central point of his message. The Guru goes on and says, *sabh teri too(n) sabhni dhiāia*–all creation is the Lord's and all created beings have ever meditated on that one Lord. This priceless jewel, this gift of being able to meditate on His name is however not for everyone. The Guru says, *jis no kirpa kareh tin nām ratan pāia*–only he gets this invaluable gift who has the good fortune to be blessed by the Lord's glance of grace. The truth of this can be seen at a glance in the world around us. The vast majority of us are completely absorbed in pandering to the senses, in worshipping wealth, power and other similar baubles. The ones who do not succumb are indeed blessed. Such lucky ones are few indeed, and the message here is that it has to be our constant endeavour to strive to be among those lucky ones, to be fit for His grace by living the right life and following the path that the Guru has laid down.

The Guru further alludes to this stark reality in the next line. He speaks of the many *manmukhs* who, in *Maya* engendered ignorance, follow their own desires, ignoring the Guru's path. The Guru says, '*gurmukh lādha manmukh gavāia'*. The *manmukh* are the egoistic ones who are not guided by the Guru, while the *gurmukh* are those who follow the path delineated by the Guru. *Lādha* means has gained, has achieved; while *gavāia* means 'has lost'. So, the Guru is saying the *gurmukh* will gain, will achieve God-realisation, and the *manmukh* will be the losers. All this will of course happen only as per the Lord's will. He will determine who is to be sundered and distanced from the Lord and who will have the great joy and blessing of being merged back into Him.

In the second part of the hymn, the Guru says *too(n) darīāo sabh tujh hi māhi*–the Lord is the vast stream, the ocean within which all creation exists. The term *darīāo*, literally means a river. Here, however, it connotes a vast all-encompassing stream into which all smaller streams merge, the vast ocean within which all existence is sustained. The Lord is the *darīāo* outside of which nothing can exist. The Guru says *tujh bin dūja koyi nāheh*–the Lord is the one and only reality, beyond whom nothing exists. Within this vast reality, he has created beings of various types. The Guru says about these created beings, *jiw jant sabh tera khel*–the creation, of all these people and animals, is your play. This has to be understood in the context of why we are put on this world. Great thinkers offer various reasons and rationalisations of why they think the Lord has put us here. In Sikhism, the belief is that no one but the Lord Himself can know the full explanation to this mystery. Therefore, to us all this can be seen at best as the Lord at play. His creation is at His will, its sustenance He ensures at His own will, and its destruction He causes when He desires. The real mystery behind all this play only He knows. It should suffice for us to know that we have been put here in the midst of this mysterious creation for one purpose alone; to use this opportunity to seek reunion with the Lord. So, the mystery of why things happen stays unsolved for us mortals, and all we can see is that the Lord separates and unites people at His own sweet will. These events we humans call *sanjog* and *vijog*.

The Guru expresses this reality here by telling us, *vijog mil vichhuṛia sanjogi mel.* Some learned ones have rendered this phrase to mean that the terms *sanjog* and *vijog* here pertain not to separation from or union with the Lord, but to meeting the *sādh sangat*. They would thus render it as meaning that those who have the *sanjog* to meet up with the saintly, the *sādh sangat*, will attain to God and those who have the *vijog* to distance themselves from the *sādh sangat* will be distanced from the Lord. As will be seen this does not materially alter the sense, except to say that the passage to God-realisation is through the *sādh sangat,* which of course is also very true. The more appealing view, taken by most of the learned ones is however, that the reference is to the union with, or separation from the Lord, both of which are not in our hands and which the Lord himself bestows when He so pleases.

The Guru says in the third part of the hymn, *jis no tu jāṇāyeh(n) soyi jan jāṇai*–only those to whom the Lord grants the blessing will acquire knowledge of the reality. This is to tell us that by our own effort we cannot expect to learn the answer to the ultimate mystery. We may indeed acquire much knowledge of mundane things, or even of the esoteric. Some may even acquire supernatural or occult powers. However, the knowledge that really matters, the knowledge of the Lord, is not ours to acquire; it is the Lord's to bestow. That will happen only when He so decides; hence, says the Guru, *jis no tu jāṇāyeh(n).* The Guru then adds that such a one will *har guṇ sad hi ākh vakhāṇai* –forever then sing the Lord's praises, recite the endless list of the Lord's uncountable virtues. Singing the praises of the Lord, reciting His name such a devotee will forever have peace and with *sehaj* become immersed in the Lord or, as the Guru says, *jin har sevia tin sukh pāia sehjay hi har nām samāia.* Being rapt entirely in recitation of the Lord's name is the same as being immersed in Him. This is the path to salvation.

The term *sehaj* needs to be understood clearly. Its dictionary meaning is 'easy', and so this line would translate as 'with ease he will become immersed in the Lord's name'. The Mahan Kosh, however, gives a dozen different meanings of this term. The Kosh says it can mean, born with, a twin. It can also mean basic nature, habit, as Bhagat Kabir ji says in *Rāg Āsa*, page 481, SGGS, ਅੰਮ੍ਰਿਤੁ ਲੈ ਲੈ ਨੀਮੁ ਸਿੰਚਾਈ॥ ਕਹਤ ਕਬੀਰ ਉਆ

ਕੋ ਸਹਜ ਨ ਜਾਈ॥ –*amrit lai lai neem sinchāyi kahat Kabir uwa ko sehaj na jāyi*–one may nurture the *neem* tree with nectar but it will not lose its basic nature. Thirdly, the Kosh says, *sehaj* can mean thought, ability to discriminate and consider. Fourthly, *sehaj* can mean knowledge, awareness, the sense in which the third Nanak has used it in Anand Sahib, *pauṛi* 18, where he says, *karmi sehaj na upjai vin sehjay sahsa na jāye*–knowledge will not come through the *karm kāndd*–ritual actions, and without knowledge our minds will never be free from doubts. Fifthly, it can mean bliss; the third Nanak says in *Sri Rāg* page 68, SGGS, ਚਉਥੇ ਪਦ ਮਹਿ ਸਹਜੁ ਹੈ ਗੁਰਮੁਖ ਪਲੈ ਪਾਇ–*chauthhay pad meh sehaj hai gurmukh palai pāye*–in the transcendent state of the mind there is bliss which the *gurmukh* gains through the Guru. It can also mean without an effort, as the third Nanak tells us in the Ānand Sahib, *pauṛi* 1, page 917 SGGS, ਸਤਿਗੁਰੁ ਤ ਪਾਇਆ ਸਹਜ ਸੇਤੀ–*satgur ta pāiya sehaj seti*. It can mean 'in the natural course', as we are told in the SGGS, page 1281 in *Vār, Rāg Malhār, Mahla* 3, ਜੋ ਕਿਛੁ ਹੋਇ ਸੁ ਸਹਜੇ ਹੋਇ–*jo kichh hoye so sehjay hoye,* whatever happens will be in the natural course. The same meaning can be inferred also from Bhagat Kabir's *slok* number 59, at page 1367, SGGS, *mukat duāra mokla sehjay āvo jāo*–the door to salvation shall become conveniently wide, and with ease you may go through it. This seems here the more appealing interpretation. The one who sings the praises of the Lord will, with ease, be immersed in Him. In other words, it will become his nature to be ever rapt in devotion to Him.

In the last part of this hymn, the Guru stresses the uniqueness and the creator function of the Lord. He says, *tu āpay karta tera kīa sabh hoye*–You are the underlying cause of all that happens, You are the doer. He then underlines this with, *tudh bin dūja avar na koye*–there is none other than You.

He is telling us that the Lord creates and the entire created universe then continues to exist and act in strict accordance with the inexorable laws that He has set in place for its orderly function. No other power or entity can claim this special position, nor alter one whit of this Reality. He then says, *tu kar kar vekheh jāṇeh soye*–You have created and now You watch it in action, and You are the only one aware of its vast mystery. This is meant to further underline the Lord's unique position as the sole power responsible for the creation of this vast universe, and who alone knows its functioning. The Guru in this line is stressing the Lord's omnipotence and His role as the Creator. Lastly, he says, *jan Nanak gurmukh pargatt hoye*–sayeth Nanak through the Guru the Lord becomes known to His devotees.

This stress on the need for a Guru will be seen throughout the SGGS. Individuals have sometimes interpreted this in a self-seving way, exploitatively setting themselves up as god-men, claiming that the prescription in the SGGS is for a living Guru. While there may be some who genuinely lead their followers on the path to God-realisation, but many so-called god-men flourish by cheating the innocent seeker. For a Sikh the Guru is eternally available in the form of the SGGS as the tenth Nanak ordained early in the 18th century, before he passed away from this world to his eternal abode. There is no place, therefore, for any other Guru in Sikhism.

11

THIS LAKE OF FIRE

The next hymn, in *Rāg Āsa,* is by Guru Nanak, and he speaks to us of the journey of the human soul as we struggle with the travails of existence on this World full of temptations and other spiritual perils. This hymn occurs again at page 357, SGGS, in the same form in the compositions under *Rāg Āsa*. The Guru has delineated here a picture of our spiritual existence in this world where the fire of falsehood burns bright and men are constantly fooled by false attachments to material things and the glitter of *Maya*. He says:

ਆਸਾ ਮਹਲਾ ੧ ॥	Āsa Mahla 1
ਤਿਤੁ ਸਰਵਰੜੈ ਭਈਲੇ ਨਿਵਾਸਾ	Tit sarvaraṛai bhayīlay nivāsa
ਪਾਣੀ ਪਾਵਕੁ ਤਿਨਹਿ ਕੀਆ ॥	pāṇi pāvak tineh kīya.
ਪੰਕਜੁ ਮੋਹ ਪਗੁ ਨਹੀ ਚਾਲੈ ਹਮ ਦੇਖਾ	Pankaj moh pag nāhi chalai
ਤਹ ਡੂਬੀਅਲੇ ॥੧॥	hum dekha tah ddūbīalay.1.
ਮਨ ਏਕੁ ਨ ਚੇਤਸਿ ਮੂੜ ਮਨਾ ॥	Man ek na chetas mūṛ mana.
ਹਰਿ ਬਿਸਰਤ ਤੇਰੇ ਗੁਣ	Har bisrat teray guṇ galiya.1.
ਗਲਿਆ ॥੧॥ ਰਹਾਉ ॥	Rahāo.
ਨਾ ਹਉ ਜਤੀ ਸਤੀ ਨਹੀ ਪੜਿਆ	Nā hao jati sati nahi paṛia
ਮੂਰਖ ਮੁਗਧਾ ਜਨਮੁ ਭਇਆ ॥	mūrakh mugdha janam bhaiya.

ਪ੍ਰਣਵਤਿ ਨਾਨਕ ਤਿਨ ਕੀ ਸਰਣਾ	Paraṇvat Nanak tin ki sarṇa
ਜਿਨ ਤੂ ਨਾਹੀ ਵੀਸਰਿਆ ॥੨॥੩॥	jin tū nāhi vīsria.2.3.

Glossary:

ਸਰਵਰੜੈ	Sarvararạai	In the Lake
ਪਾਵਕੁ	Pāvak	Fire, here used for material desires
ਪੰਕਜ	Pankaj	Mud, sticky morass
ਡੂਬੀਅਲੇ	Ddūbīalay	Sink, become immersed in
ਮੂੜ	Mūṛ	Fool
ਬਿਸਰਤ	Bisrat	To forget
ਗਲਿਆ	Galiya	Eroded
ਮੁਗਧਾ	Mugdha	Thick headed
ਪ੍ਰਣਵਤਿ	Paraṇvat	Humbly, with respect
ਵੀਸਰਿਆ	Vīsria	Forgotten

In the first part of this brief hymn, Guru Nanak says, *tit sarvararạai bhayīlay nivāsa*–I am forced to live in that lake. What lake is that? He provides the answer in the second half of this line as he says, *pāṇi pāvak tineh kīya*–which the Lord has filled with the fire of desires. This world in which we live is an inferno fueled by our unending desires for material things like power, wealth or position. It is through this terrifying lake of fire that the human soul residing in this body has to navigate its way back to oneness with the Lord. Why has the Lord created such a difficult world for us? He has done so to give us the opportunity to reunite with Him, because this is our *Karam Bhūmi*, our field of action. This is where the souls, separated from the Lord through the effects of their own wrong actions and their *haumai*, are sent so that they can use this invaluable human birth to seek redemption and reunion with the Lord. In this arena, the soul will be tested. Here it will be seen whether we are able to overcome the effects of that *pāvak*, that all-consuming fire, the fire of desires, of false attachments and of misdirected ambitions. If we are able to withstand this attack and are able to negotiate the right path through these temptations then we will perhaps become worthy of His grace and maybe our exile, our separation from Him will end; of course only when He so deems fit. The lake of fire is, therefore, a necessary adjunct to the tests our souls have to undergo.

Using a different analogy the Guru now compares our position to a man mired in thick mud. He says, *pankaj moh pag nāhi chālai*–the thick sticky mud, the morass of attachments drags us down and we are unable to move our feet. So, living within this lake of fire we are also shackled by the chains of our false attachments. Our feet will not move forward because we have tied ourselves down with the weight of our own foolish desires. Thus stuck in the mire of our own follies we sink; as the Guru says, *ham dekha tah ddūbīalay*–even as we watch, they are sinking and drowning, meaning that we can see all around us those who are being sucked in yet we learn nothing. It is a tragic truth that fully knowing that the material allurements that surrounds us will only lead to our spiritual downfall we are still ensnared and are unable to save ourselves. It is, as if we know an accident is about to happen to us, but we do not have the sense or the ability to get out of the way and avoid the tragedy.

The Guru then describes this inability or the unwillingness to save ourselves with the remark, *man ek na chetas mūṛ mana*–foolish man why do you not fix your mind on the One. The only path to escape from this terrible trap is to fix the mind on the Lord, recite His name with every breath and live in complete surrender to His will. In this way only is a path to be found out of this lake of fire and the morass of our foolish, meaningless attachments. We can hope to escape the *pankaj moh* and the *pāṇi pāvak* only by this route. If we choose instead to keep moving on our ego-driven path, losing ourselves in the false pleasures of this *Maya*, then the Guru says, *har bisrat teray guṇ galiya*–not remembering the Lord your good qualities will be eroded, you will lose your virtue. The term *galiya* can mean eroded, rotting, or degrading. Here it is used to describe the gradual but sure dissolution of all our merit if we do not turn to the right path and fix our minds on the Lord. If we insist on ignoring the Lord then we will be without any merit and will not ever be able to escape this troubled place. We shall continue to suffer all the sorrows of the seemingly attractive lake made from our attachments to the false baubles that *Maya* has strewn around us. The lake actually contains *pāṇi pāvak,* the fire of our misplaced desires.

In the humble style of the truly achieved soul, the master now says he is unworthy to approach the Lord. As he puts it, *nā hao jati sati nahi paṛia mūrakh mugdha janam bhaiya*–I am neither a *jati*, possessor of occult powers gained through continence and austerities; nor a *sati*, the lover of truth or great philanthropist; nor *paṛia,* wise and knowledgeable. He adds that not only does he lack all these qualities, but also he is *mūrakh mugdha*–foolish and ignorant from *janam*– birth. This is the Guru's way of stressing that you do not approach the Lord on the strength of any mystical, supernatural powers acquired through strict continence and hard austerities, or great observance of truthful philanthropic living, or the acquisition of great knowledge; these cannot entitle us to salvation. The escape from this lake of fire, this morass of attachments is not to be found through such devices. It will come only when the

Lord Himself decides to cast on us His glance of grace. That gift is His to give at His own will, it is not ours to acquire. In any case, compared to the immeasurable ocean of all qualities that is the Lord our puny powers are as nothing. We must, therefore, approach the Lord in a spirit of total humility, as the Guru, with his God-realised soul yet chooses to do here. He says that possessing no qualities, which could entitle him to the Lord's favour, he is *paraṇvat*–humbly requests, begs the Lord. In other words, he is in a state of total surrender, and prays to Him.

And what is his prayer? He begs for the protection and shelter of those who have never forgotten the Lord as he says, *tin ki sarṇa jin tū nāhi vīsria*. This is in tune with the constant refrain in the SGGS to come into the company of the *sādh sangat*–the congregation of the saintly ones. The idea is that the allure of *Maya* is too overpowering. Singly, by ourselves we may continue to succumb. The company of those who have overcome this weakness will help strenghthen our resolve to stay out of the coils of this enchantress. The synergic effect of the *gurmukhs* reinforcing each other's resolve will help us more easily keep control of ourselves and will ease our journey to re-union with the Lord.

12

YOUR CHANCE TO REACH THE LORD

We now come to the last hymn of this part under the set of four *sloks* commencing with *So Purakh*. This is by the fifth Nanak, in *Rāg Āsa,* and he speaks to us of the need to properly utilize this golden opportunity of the human birth that the Lord has granted us. The same hymn occurs again in the same form at page 378, SGGS in the compositions under *Rāg Āsa* . The Guru says:

ਆਸਾ ਮਹਲਾ ੫ ॥	Āsa Mahla 5
ਭਈ ਪਰਾਪਤਿ ਮਾਨੁਖ ਦੇਹੁਰੀਆ ॥	Bhayi parāpat mānukh dehuriya.
ਗੋਬਿੰਦ ਮਿਲਣ ਕੀ ਇਹ ਤੇਰੀ ਬਰੀਆ ॥	Gobind milaṇ ki eh teri bariya.
ਅਵਰਿ ਕਾਜ ਤੇਰੈ ਕਿਤੈ ਨ ਕਾਮ ॥	Avar kāj terai kitai na kām.
ਮਿਲੁ ਸਾਧਸੰਗਤਿ ਭਜੁ ਕੇਵਲ ਨਾਮ ॥੧॥	Mil sādhsangat bhaj keval nām.1.
ਸਰੰਜਾਮਿ ਲਾਗੁ ਭਵਜਲ ਤਰਨ ਕੈ ॥	Saranjām lāg bhavjal taran kai.
ਜਨਮੁ ਬ੍ਰਿਥਾ ਜਾਤ ਰੰਗਿ ਮਾਇਆ ਕੈ॥੧॥ਰਹਾਉ॥	Janam britha jāt rung māia kai.1. Rahāo.
ਜਪੁ ਤਪੁ ਸੰਜਮੁ ਧਰਮੁ ਨ ਕਮਾਇਆ ॥	Jap tap sanjam dharam na kamāia.
ਸੇਵਾ ਸਾਧ ਨ ਜਾਨਿਆ ਹਰਿ ਰਾਇਆ ॥	Seva sādh na jānia har rāia.

ਕਹੁ ਨਾਨਕ ਹਮ ਨੀਚ ਕਰੰਮਾ ॥	Kaho Nanak ham nīch karamma.
ਸਰਣਿ ਪਰੇ ਕੀ ਰਾਖਹੁ ਸਰਮਾ ॥੨॥੪॥	Saraṇ paray ki rākho sarma.2.4.

Glossary:

ਦੇਹੁਰੀਆ	Dehuriya	Body, the human birth
ਸਾਧਸੰਗਤਿ	Sādhsangat	Saintly company
ਸਰੰਜਾਮਿ	Saranjām	Effort
ਭਵਜਲ	Bhavjal	The passage to the other world
ਤਰਨ	Taran	To swim
ਬ੍ਰਿਥਾ ਜਾਤ	Britha jāt	Is wasted
ਸੰਜਮੁ	Sanjam	Control, continence
ਨੀਚ ਕਰੰਮਾ	Nīch karamma	Of lowly actions
ਸਰਮਾ	Sarma	Honour

The Guru says this gift of *mānukh dehuriya*–human form, has been granted to us as a precious opportunity to seek reunion with the Lord. He says *bhayi parāpat mānukh dehuriya*–you have been given this human birth, this body, because *gobind milaṇ ki eh teri bariya*–this is your turn to achieve union with the Lord. The importance of the human form has oft been stressed in the SGGS. It is the Guru's point that of all created shapes this is the only one capable of giving us the wherewithal to try and make ourselves fit to even be considered for His blessing. When we are in other, lesser forms, we cannot speak and our mind does not possess the power or the intellect to discriminate between right and wrong. As Bhagat Kabir says in *Rāg Gūjri* at page 524, SGGS, ਚਾਰਿ ਪਾਵ ਦੁਇ ਸਿੰਗ ਗੁੰਗ ਮੁਖ ਤਬ ਕੈਸੇ ਗੁਨ ਗਈਹੈ–*char pav doye sing gung mukh tab kaisay gun gayihai.* Kabir *ji* is saying when you are born as a dumb four-footed beast with horns, how will you sing His praises? The same thought is expressed slightly differently by the fifth Nanak in the Sukhmani Sahib in *Asttapadi* 4, *pauṛi* 6 when he says, *kaha bisanpad gāvai gung*–how will the dumb one sing of the Lord. The prescription for God-realisation is constant recitation of the Lord's name. There can never be enough of that, as the Guru says in the Japji Sahib, *pauṛi* 32, *ik du jibho lakh hoye lakh hoveh lakh vīs*–if we had one hundred thousand tongues and then twenty times that. With each of these if we were to recite the name of the One Lord hundreds of thousands of times, then that is the path towards union with the Lord. The absence of the ability to speak and a mind to understand what we are speaking makes us incapable of following this essential path. In all forms other than the human, we did not have the capacity, or the opportunity; it has been accorded to us only in this form.

The Guru then provides further confirmation of this prescription and says, *avar kāj terai kitai na kām*–no other effort is of any avail to you. In the same breath, he also specifies the effort or method, which will work when he adds *mil sādhsangat bhaj keval nām*–sit in the company of the saintly, the men of God, the *gurmukhs*, and recite the name of the Lord. Humans often think that they can reach Him through austerities, or through exercise of the intellect, or through good deeds. All these are desirable practices in their own way useful. Controlling the body and the mind will be to an extent helpful; but as a way to God-realisation they will usually not work, for the simple reason that as we acquire these assets the ego also starts to get bloated with the success. We start acquiring pride and thinking of ourselves as special and more deserving than other humans. We may even foolishly start to believe that we have acquired the wherewithal to reach the Lord on our own strength, through our efforts. Pride and ego are the biggest enemies of our efforts on the path to the Lord. When these come, we will slip sharply behind on our journey towards Him. That journey has the best chance of success when it is marked by a sense of humility, of our utter inadequacy before the Lord's great might. That useful attitude will come to us when we start to keep the company of the *sādhsangat*, and along with them join in the recitation of the Lord's name.

The Guru then gives us the central idea of this hymn as he says, *saranjām lāg bhavjal taran kai, janam britha jāt rang māia kai.* This translates as 'get busy in the effort to swim across the dreadful waters else your birth is wasted in the glitter of *Maya*'. The term *saranjām* derives from the Persian *sar* and *anjām*, meaning bringing something to completion. As the Guru tells us, the only task worth attempting is to try to make ourselves worthy of the Lord's glance of grace, so that this separated soul may be allowed to rejoin Him. He now tells us to get busy and make arrangements for bringing the task to a successful culmination. What is the task? The task is to, somehow, safely cross from this mortal world to the eternal world where we may live as one with the Lord. The Guru calls the separating gulf the *bhavjal*, which means the 'water of dread', or dreadful ocean. This is a phrase often used by various belief systems, especially the Eastern ones. Since the event of cessation of our life on this Earth is shrouded in total darkness for us, so it is naturally an object of fear. When our journey here ends, when we take our departure from this *Karma Bhūmi,* we will be embarking on uncharted seas. When an endevour is very hard, and shrouded by uncertainity, the only sensible course is to prepare for it as completely as we can. It behoves us, therefore, to so order our actions while we have the breath to do so, that we are adequately prepared for that journey. This preparation is what the Guru has been instructing us on in this hymn. Join with the *sādhsangat*, he says, and recite His name; other efforts being of no avail. Do this quickly because time is fleeting and we are wasting our precious treasure in *rang māia kai*–chasing after the glitter of that which is false and but an illusion. At the end of this line the Guru says *rahāo*, instructing us to pause and ponder on this important lesson.

In the last hymn, the Guru had concluded with the admission that he had no skills or virtues and prayed to the Lord to put him in the company of the godly ones who ever remember the Lord. He now expresses a similar thought as he says, *jap tap sanjam dharam na kamāia*–I have observed no austerities, nor attempted strict continence, lacking the ability to control my senses I have performed no task which could be spiritually elevating. One can see again, here, the same tremendous modesty from this great and achieved soul. He then adds *seva sādh na jānia har rāia*–I have not served the godly ones and have not acquired any knowledge about the Lord. He concludes this hymn with a direct prayer to the Lord for protection. He says, *kaho Nanak ham nīch karamma*–sayeth Nanak that lowly are our actions. The Guru is surrendering himself totally to the Lord by recounting all his many failings and a total lack of merit. He has, he says, not only failed to practice various devices for approaching the Lord, but even his actions have been lacking in any virtue. With so many shortcomings hindering his path, he yet hopes to reach the Lord. How? He now makes the only possible appeal he can in these circumstances to the Lord and says *saraṇ paray ki rākho sarma*–I am surrendering myself to Your protection, it is now for You to save my honour. In other words, he says on my own merits I deserve nothing at all, but

I surrender myself fully to the Lord, and beg Him to save the one who has thus sought shelter with Him. It is a basic tenet in Sikhism that the Lord's basic nature is to be forgiving and loving. It is the Guru's message that the Lord has created us, we are His children, and even when we are misguided, and stray from the path, we are entitled to His love, because He is a compassionate and kindly parent, so seek shelter with Him, surrendering yourself to His Will.

With this, we conclude the nine hymns comprising the *So Dar* and the *So Purakh*.

We now come to the *Benti Chaupayi*, which the *Rehat Maryāda* prescribes to be recited as part of the Rehrās Sahib. This *Chaupayi* is by the tenth Nanak, Guru Gobind Singh.

13

THE TENTH NANAK

Before we commence to examine the lessons contained in the *Chaupayi*, it would be interesting to take a brief look at the life of the very remarkable author of this composition.

Guru Gobind Singh, the tenth Nanak, the creator of the Khalsa, sojourned briefly on this earth, hardly 42 years. He was born on *Poh sudi* 7, the 23rd day of the month of *Poh* in the year 1723 *Bikrami*, corresponding to 22 December 1666 A.D. He was to leave us on 7 October 1708, but in this short period, he achieved amazing heights as a great scholar, poet, an inspiring leader, and above all a mystical seer ever in touch with the Lord. It was he, who gave to the Sikhs their present day distinctive appearance.

Principal Satbir Singh writes that a Muslim mystic, Pīr Bhikhan Shah, in far away Siyana in Punjab (today in Haryana), sensed the birth of a great soul in the East. He travelled to Patna and tested the infant Guru by placing before him vessels, one containing water and the other milk, representing in his own mind Hinduism and Islam. The young master put his hands on both and then overturned them. The Pīr concluded, rightly, as it turned out, that this master would treat all alike and would show a new path to the Lord.

The Guru returned to Anandpur Sahib when he was about seven years old. There he received his early education, acquiring mastery in languages, such as Punjabi, Braj, Arabic, Sanskrit and Persian; and in martial skills, such as archery, riding and shooting.

He was barely nine years old when Kashmiri Pandits, who were being greatly oppressed by the Mughal Governor, sent a delegation seeking help from Guru Tegh Bahadur. It is said that the Guru decided that a great sacrifice would be needed, and was wondering who could be worthy enough, when the young Gobind Rai said that there could be none more worthy than the Guru himself. The Guru went to Delhi and confronted the Emperor saying that if he wanted the Pandits to convert to Islam he should first deal with the leader. He was imprisoned, and then tortured to press him to accept Islam. His closest followers were brutally put to death before his eyes, but he refused to bend. The Emperor finally had him beheaded.

Learned ones say that the tenth Nanak was installed on *Maghar sudi* 5, eleventh day of *Maghar* 1732, *Bikrami*, corresponding to 11 Nov 1675 AD. He was at that time not quite yet nine years of age. Notwithstanding this, his handling of the concerns of the community was marked by a sure handed skill from the very beginning.

He moved from Anandpur to Nahan in 1684 at the invitation of the Raja of Sirmour, shifting then to nearby Paonta where a Gurdwara stands today.

It is generally accepted that much of the Guru's creative literary work was done during his stay of about four years at Paonta Sahib, and the *Vār Sri Bhagauti ji ki*, also called

Chanddi di Vār, describing a mythical contest between gods and the demons, was most probably his first composition.

The Guru's compositions, even where the subject matter is purely spiritual, employ martial meters and rhythms, designed to infuse the martial spirit among his followers. He glorified the sword as the emblem of manliness and self-respect, to be used for upholding justice, or in self-defense, only as a last resort and never for aggression. The *Zafarnama* says, *Chu kār az hama hilate dar guzasht. Halāl ast burdan ba shamshir dast*–when all other means fail it is righteous and lawful to take the sword in hand. His philosophy does not advocate total non-violence, but does put the shackles of rightfulness on any aggressive response.

The Guru's sacrifice and his military prowess have often been highlighted, but it must be stressed that his spiritual status was also of the highest. His compositions, even where the tone is martial, reveal the divine principle and communicate his personal vision of the Supreme Being. His compositions are replete with the message of love and equality and a strictly ethical and moral code of conduct. He, in line with Nanak's philosophy, preached the worship of the One Supreme Being, deprecating idolatry and superstitious beliefs and ritual observances.

Over time, conflicts arose with the rulers of the various states in the surrounding hill states and battles were fought, the first being a fierce engagement at Bhangāṇi, about 10 km Northeast of Paonta. The Guru won this and numerous other battles against the hill rulers, the imperial forces, and against the both combined, even when his forces were outnumbered.

Gradually, however, the hostility with the Mughals eased after Prince Muazzam was appointed viceroy of a region that included Punjab, and there was a lull in the hostilities against the Sikhs.

The Guru set about reforming the system into which weaknesses had crept in. He began by surgically cleansing the institution of *masands* that had once rendered great service to the community, but with the passage of time had become corrupt. He instructed the *sangats* to bring their offerings directly to Ānandpur, thus establishing a direct relationship with his Sikhs and addressed them as his Khalsa, which is a Persian term used for crown-lands as distinguished from lands under the feudal chiefs.

The institution of the Khalsa was given concrete form on 30 March 1699 in Ānandpur at the annual festival of Baisakhi. It is said that the Guru, naked sword in hand, asked for a Sikh to offer his head to the Guru as a sacrifice. After the initial moment of surprise and disbelief, one Daya Ram, a Khatri of Lahore, came forward. The Guru took him to a tent and returned with his sword dripping blood. In this way, four more Siks offered themselves. They were, Dharam Das, a Jatt from Hastinapur, Mohkam Chand, a washer man from Dwarka, in present day Gujarat, Himmat, a water-carrier from Jagannathpuri in present day Orissa, and Sahib Chand, a barber from Bidar in Karnataka. These five are popularly called the *Panj Piāray*, the five beloved ones.

It will be seen that they came from all the far-flung corners of this vast country, Punjab and Uttar Pradesh in the North, Gujarat in the West, Orissa in the East and Karnataka in the South. They also represented a cross-section of the then prevailing caste structure, with the higher caste Khatri being joined by the so-called lower castes like barber or washer man. This in another way stresses the universal appeal of this new religion, which recognised no differences among humans.

The Guru then performed the ceremony of initiation with the *Khandday di Pahul*. This *pahul* was prepared by stirring sweetened water in an iron vat with the *khandda*, double-edged broadsword, while reciting the prescribed *Bāṇis*. Thousands of Sikhs were initiated to the Khalsa on that occasion, some put the number at 20000, others say 25000.

The initiates were required to affix the surname Singh, meaning lion; and to sport the five symbols of the Khalsa. These are *Kesh*–unshorn hair and beard, *Kangha*, a comb, *Kaṛa*, a steel bracelet, *Kachh*, short breeches, and *Kirpan*, a sword. They were enjoined to be ever ready to help the oppressed, to have faith in one God and to consider all human beings equal, irrespective of caste and creed. In personal conduct, they were required, *inter alia*, to retain unshorn hair and beards, never to use tobacco, not to have sexual relationship outside the marital bond, nor eat the *kuttha*–flesh of animals killed ritually in the Muslim way. Incidentally, it may be of interest that similar injunctions had already existed in the Sikh faith. Principal Satbir Sing says in Purakh Bhagwant, his biography on the tenth Nanak that the seventh Nanak had told a follower named Bhai Nand Lal Puri during a discourse at Galottia Khurd, "Do not use Tobacco, do not cut your hair and do not wear a cap".

The Guru then set a new precedent by taking the initiatory rites from the *Panj Piāray*, now invested with authority as Khalsa, and had his name changed to Gobind Singh. Bhai Gurdas says of this, *wahu wahu Guru Gobind Singh, āpay gur chela*–it is a wondrous sight where Guru Gobind Singh is himself Master as well as disciple.

This Bhai Gurdas is not to be confused with Bhai Gurdas Bhalla the great mystic and poet who authored the well known *Vārs*. In his commentary on the *Vārs* Bhai Vir Singh tells us, as the Mahankosh also confirms, that there have been four Sikhs named Bhai Gurdas, and the one who authored this Slok lived many years after the passing of the tenth Nanak and some of his work is found in the Sarb Loh Granth.

With this unique initiation, the Guru formed a unique bond with his followers, through which he lives on today, in the form of the Sikh Nation, the Khalsa Panth.

Alarmed by these developments the chiefs of the Hill states, rallying under the leadership of the Raja of Bilaspur in whose territory Anandpur was located, sought to expel him. Their expeditions during 1700-1704 having failed, they sought imperial help and reinforced by the imperial army, they laid siege to the city in May 1704.

For seven months, the Sikhs stood firm despite great hardship and scarcity of food. The besiegers thus frustrated then resorted to trickery. They offered the Sikhs safe passage upon sacred oath, but then treacherously set upon them as they were crossing the swollen Sirsa rivulet. Many precious lives, as also most of the manuscripts of the Guru's compositions were lost.

The Guru reached to Chamkaur Sahib, 40 km away. A fierce engagement took place there on 8 *Poh* 1761 *Bikrami.* The corresponding date is reckoned as 7 December 1704 AD, though some learned ones take it as 21 December.

This confusion is because of the difficulty in converting from one era to the other. S. Pal Singh Purewal, the expert who has designed the *Nanakshahi* calendar, says in his analysis that the problem arises because the *Bikrami* calendar is lunisolar. This means that its one part is solar according to which all *Sangrands*, the first day of the month, are decided; and the other part is lunar which determines *tithis.* These are the *sudi,* meaning the part of the lunar month when the moon waxes, and the *vadi*, meaning when the moon is waning. The *gurpurabs* are determined according to these *tithis*. The problem with the solar part is that *Baisakhi* has shifted in relation to seasons. He says that according to *Surya Siddhantic* calculations, *Baisakhi* occurred on the day of the Spring Equinox in 532 CE. Nowadays the Spring Equinox occurs on 20 / 21 March, but *Baisakhi* on 13 / 14 April. In another thousand years, it will start occurring in May. His *Nanakshahi* calendar was an endeavor to resolve this problem.

In the battle of Chamkaur the Guru's older two sons, Baba Ajit Singh and Baba Jujhār Singh were martyred fighting valiantly against overwhelming numbers. When only five Sikhs were left, they bade the Guru to save himself in order to reconsolidate the Khalsa. One of the remaining Sikhs, Sangat Singh who resembled the Guru, sallied forth sporting the Guru's attire and weapons. The Guru meanwhile escaped, accompanied by two of the *Panj Pyaras*, Bhai Daya Singh, Bhai Dharam Singh, and another Sikh named Mān Singh. The enemy forces trailed him to Macchiwaṛa, but two Muslim devotees, Ghani Khan and Nabi Khan, are said to have helped him escape once again, carrying him through the enemy lines in a palanquin proclaiming him their preceptor, the *Uch da Peer*. The Guru refers to some of these events in the *Zafarnama*.

Soon after, another tragedy struck when an old retainer Gangu betrayed the Guru's two younger sons Zorāwar Singh (b.1696) and Fateh Singh (b.1699), and his mother, Mata Gujari to the *faujdār* of Sirhind. The *faujdār* had the children cruelly executed a few days later, despite opposition from some fair-minded nobles–notably the Nawab of Malerkotla. Mata Gujari is said to have died of grief the same day.

The Guru reached the Malwa region of Punjab and camped

in village Dina Kāngaṛ from where he sent the *Zafarnama*, which was a severe indictment of the Emperor and his commanders who had perjured their oath and treacherously attacked him. It emphatically reiterated the sovereignty of morality in the affairs of State as much as in the conduct of human beings and held the means as important as the end.

The Sikhs were to prevail in another hard fought engagement against overwhelming numbers in the marshy wetland of *Khidrāṇa,* near the present day town Muktsar in Punjab. Here, a group of 40 Sikhs who had deserted during the siege of Anandpur redeemed themselves with their valorous show fighting under the leadership of a brave and devoted woman, Mayi Bhago. The Guru pardoned their apostasy and blessed them as the 40 *muktay*–saved ones, or liberated souls.

The Guru camped for nine months at Talwandi Sabo, now called Damdama Sahib. He dictated a fresh rescension of the Sri Guru Granth Sahib, with the celebrated scholar, Bhai Mani Singh as amanuensis. A number of scholars gathered here round Guru Gobind Singh and great literary activity was initiated, leading to the place being known as the Guru ki Kāshi, or seat of learning like Varanasi, which is also known as Kāshi.

The *Zafarnama*, harshly critical though it was, seems to have touched the heart of Emperor Aurangzeb and he initiated steps to conciliate the Guru, directing the provincial officials to arrange for his journey to the Deccan, but the meeting was not to be. The Guru was in Rajasthan, when the Emperor died on 20 February 1707.

In the ensuing struggle for succession, the Guru helped the eldest claimant, Prince Muazzam, whose relations with the Sikhs had been good during the period he was viceroy of the Punjab region. A contingent of Sikhs fought at his side in the successful battle of Jajau, on 8 June 1707. Muazzam ascended the throne as Bahadur Shah. He received the Guru most respectfully at Agra on 23 July 1707. Some scholars say that the Guru accompanied the Emperor on his expedition to the Deccan against his youngest brother, Kam Baksh. The Guru reached Nanded, on the Godavari in August. Here he met a recluse named Madho Das, whom he converted to a Sikh, renaming him Gurbakhsh Singh, though he is better known by his popular name Banda Singh. Guru Gobind Singh gave Banda Singh five arrows from his own quiver and an escort, including five of his chosen Sikhs, and directed him to go to the Punjab and carry on the campaign against the tyranny of the provincial overlords. It is said that Nawab Wazir Khan of Sirhind, feeling threatened by the Emperor's conciliatory treatment of the Guru commissioned two trusted Pathans to assassinate the Guru. They reached Nanded, where one of them stabbed the Guru in the left side below the heart in his chamber as he was resting after Rehrās. The Guru struck him down, while the assassin's fleeing companion was felled by his Sikhs. Bahadur Shah sent expert surgeons, including an Englishman named Cole, to the Guru. It is said that the wound was stitched and appeared soon to have healed but, as the Guru one day applied strength to pull a stiff bow, the wound re-opened. The Guru passed away on 7th October 1708.

Before the end came, the Guru asked for the Sri Guru Granth Sahib and offering five pice and a coconut, he bowed to it. He then commanded the *sangat* to acknowledge the Granth Sahib in his place. The Sikhs *ardās* has since then enjoined upon the Sikh, *Guru Granth ji maniyo pargatt gura(n) ki deh, jo Prabh ko milbai chahay khoj shabad mai lay* – Deem the Guru Granth Sahib the living embodiment of the Gurus and he who seeks to reach God should look for it in the Word. He thus ended the line of personal Gurus and firmly established the concept of seeking God through the *shabad Guru*. The SGGS thus became the ever present Guru for the Sikhs. He told his Sikhs in those last hours that the Guru's spirit will henceforth be in the Granth and the Khalsa. Where the Granth is with the *Panj Piāray*, the five beloved Sikhs representing the Khalsa, there will the Guru be. Let us now look at the *Benti Chaupayi* of the tenth Nanak, which is a part of the Rehrās prescribed in the *Rehat Maryāda.*

14

THE BENTI CHAUPAYI

The *Benti Chaupayi* is a *bāṇi* taken from the Dasam Granth, where it is inscribed at page 1386 to page 1388 of the 1428 page volume brought out by Chatar Singh Jiwan Singh. The *bāṇi* is actually longer but only 25 quatrains of it have been included in the *Nitnem* as per the *Rehat Maryāda.* Many *guttkas* brought out by respected organisations, however, include two additional quatrains occurring immediately after the 25th at the end making the total 27. These two are the one beginning with, *kripa kari hum pur jagmāta*, and the other beginning with, *sri asidhuj jub bhaye dyāla*. These *guttkas* also include an *aṛil* and an additional *chaupayi*. These also include a hymn beginning with *pun rācchas ka kātta sīsa* at the start of the *Benti Chaupayi*. All of these are from the same hymn in the Dasam Granth. Discussion of this longer version and related matters will surely be of interest to the devotee, but here we have to confine ourselves to the *bāṇi* as specified in the *Rehat Maryāda*. However, a discussion of these additional hymns, as also another *chaupayi* that some scholars think should be rightly the part of the *Nitnem* would be the subject of a separate book.

The *Benti Chaupayi* begins with,

ੴ ਵਾਹਿਗੁਰੂ ਜੀ ਕੀ ਫਤਿਹ॥	Ekonkar Waheguru ji ki fateh.
ਪਾ: ੧੦	Pātshāhi 10
ਕਬਿਯੋ ਬਾਚ	Kabiyo bāch
ਬੇਨਤੀ ਚੌਪਈ॥	Benti Chaupayi.

It is almost uniformly the custom when beginning any important task to invoke divine help, so that the work is completed without hindrance. The Guru, therefore, begins this composition with an invocation to the Lord. In Hinduism, the usual invocation is to Lord Ganesha, also called *Vighneshwar*–remover of obstacles. The invocation in Sikhism is always to the Lord God Himself. The SGGS begins with the invocation, which has since been called the *Mool Mantra*, the basic creed that defines the Sikh belief system. In its full form it says, *Ik onkār sat nām karta purakh nirbhau nirvair akāl moorat ajooni saibhang gur prasād.* Giani Harnām Singh Chākar says in his commentary on the Jāp Sahib, that this full form of the invocation has been used 33 times in the SGGS. A shorter form *ik onkār sat nām karta purakh gur prasād* has been used nine times, and an even shorter form *ik onkār sat nām gur prasād* twice. The most commonly employed form, used 522 times in the SGGS, he says, is the briefest, *ik onkār satgur prasād.* The Tenth Nanak had also used this form in the opening *Bāṇi* of the Dasam Granth, the Jāp Sahib. Here for this *chaupayi* he uses a similar but somewhat different form, retaining the *ik onkār* and adding the phrase *Waheguru ji ki fateh*–victory is to the Lord God.

This shorter form of the invocation, *ik onkār,* used here is intended to stress, as throughout the SGGS, the unique oneness of the Lord. He is the *Ik*–the 'One'- the only

Reality, and by implication the creator and the sustainer of all that exists. He is also the *Onkār*, the One who has made this all, brought all creation into existence. The word *Om* has had mystical connotations from the earliest in the Hindu belief system, and has always been used as a synonym for the Lord. It is meant to indicate the 'Word'- the Lord made manifest. The formulation that the Lord creator brought everything into existence with the 'Word' is common to many belief systems. The suffix *kār* appended with *Om* is, however exclusively part of Sikhism. By appending it the Guru meant to signify that the Lord performs the act of shaping, molding or creating. The composite word *Ikonkār* thus speaks to us of a Lord, Unique, above, and beyond all that exists in the material universe, and who is the creator of all that exists.

The Guru then adds the phrase *Wahe Guru ji ki fateh*– Victory to the Lord. This was a form of greeting popularised after the tenth Nanak had created the Khalsa on the *Baisakhi* day of 1699 AD at Anandpur Sahib. This is also the form employed at the beginning of the *Ardās*–the prayer–prescribed in Sikhism. It is meant to indicate that in all our battles, worldly or spiritual, victory comes not through our efforts but by the grace of the Lord. The evils within us, not only the five demons of *kām, krodh, lobh, moh, ahnkār*– lust, anger, greed, false attachments and pride–within our souls, but also our *haumai,* that lead us away from the Lord will be overcome only with His help. Salvation, in other words is to be attained through His glance of grace. Our more mundane successes are also, of course, a gift from Him.

There then follows the inscription, *pātshāhi* 10. This is meant to convey that the hymn is a composition by the tenth Nanak. In the SGGS, the same purpose was served by the inscription *Mahla* followed by the number to indicate which of the ten Nanaks has composed the hymn.

The Guru then says, *kabyo bāch benti.* He is telling us that this composition is being offered by the poet as a *benti*–which means plea or prayer. *Kabyo bāch* derives from *kavi*–poet–and the Sanskrit *uvāch*–meaning 'says'.

It will be seen that, as we had discussed earlier also, the tone of this *bāṇi* is martial even though it is a prayer. This tone is, perhaps in full consonance with the use of the salutation *Waheguru ji ki fateh* by the Guru.

Finally, the Guru says that this prayer to the Lord is in the form of a *chaupayi*, a quatrain consisting of four lines. The Gurus have employed the *chaupayi* form extensively in the SGGS also.

Let us now proceed to discuss the lesson the Guru has imparted to us through this composition. In the first of these 25 quatrains, the Guru begins the prayer with a plea for protection. He says:-

ਹਮਰੀ ਕਰੋ ਹਾਥ ਦੇ ਰੱਛਾ॥	Hamri karo hāthh day rachha
ਪੂਰਨ ਹੋਇ ਚਿੱਤ ਕੀ ਇਛਾ॥	Puran hoye chit ki ichha
ਤਵ ਚਰਨਨ ਮਨ ਰਹੇ ਹਮਾਰਾ॥	Tav charnan mann rahay hamāra
ਅਪਨਾ ਜਾਨ ਕਰੋ ਪ੍ਰਤਿਪਾਰਾ॥ ੧॥	Apna jān karo pratipāra. 1.

Glossary:

ਤਵ ਚਰਨਨ	Tav charnan	Your feet
ਪ੍ਰਤਿਪਾਰਾ	Pratipāra	Nurture

Simply put, in this quatrain the Guru prays to the Lord to keep a protective hand over our heads. May our hearts desires be fulfilled, he says, and may the Lord's feet ever reside in our hearts, or, to put it in another way, may our hearts forever stay fixed on the Lord's feet. May the Lord nurture us as His own.

Seeking protection, help and fulfillment is of course a basic ingredient of most prayers, whether to mortal powers or to the ultimate power, the Lord Himself. We approach all sorts of mundane authorities and ask favours of them for our earthly problems. When we are seeking to approach that highest of all authorities, our creator, our prayers will necessarily take on a higher tenor. We will often seek worldly success too, but we will not be restricted merely to earthly matters, which are after all transient and will cease to exist soon enough. Here, therefore, we need to see this composition as not referring merely to earthly issues, though those too can be important without a doubt. For instance, if we do not have basic security and comfort, our energies will be mainly subsumed in the daily struggle. While some who are strong in their faith in that situation will be able to fix their minds on the Lord even more firmly, many will perhaps find that too difficult. Therefore, the Guru seeks two things here.

Firstly, he asks for *hāthh day rachha*–keep me under your protective hand. The Guru is seeking protection and succour from the vicissitudes that make our daily existence hard, as also from the temptations of this world that imperil our soul. He then adds, *puran hoye chit ki ichha*–may our hearts desires be fulfilled. The very basis of a *benti*–a prayer–is to seek the achievement of what we desire. The desire expressed here is that the protection of the Lord be ever available to us.

Secondly, he seeks an even more important boon, when he says, *tav charnan mann rahay hamāra*–may our mind be forever fixed on the Lord's feet. This is the most valuable boon to seek from the Lord, the blessing that His feet reside forever in our hearts. This is another way of saying that we should remain immersed in Him. The Guru then says, *apna jān karo pratipāra*–nurture us as Your own. The Guru's prayer here is to be treated as belonging to the Lord. In determining our identities, one important consideration is with whom we consort. To be on the side of the high and the noble brings us honour. Therefore, if we can claim to belong to the greatest power then it brings with it the highest honour. It is axiomatic that the Lord is the sole power, and is the highest in this universe. If we belong to Him then there is nothing else, and no other person that we could need.

He continues with the prayer for the Lord's protection in the second quatrain, and says:

ਹਮਰੇ ਦੁਸਟ ਸਭੈ ਤੁਮ ਘਾਵਹੁ॥	Hamray dusatt sabhai tum ghāvo
ਆਪ ਹਾਥ ਦੇ ਮੋਹਿ ਬਚਾਵਹੁ॥	Āp hāth day mohe bachāvoh.
ਸੁਖੀ ਬਸੈ ਮੋਰੋ ਪਰਵਾਰਾ॥	Sukhi basai moro parvāra
ਸੇਵਕ ਸਿੱਖ ਸਭੈ ਕਰਤਾਰਾ॥ ੨॥	Sevak sikh sabhai kartāra. 2.

Glossary:

ਦੁਸਟ	Dusatt	Bad ones, enemies
ਘਾਵਹੁ	Ghāvo	Destroy

Literally rendered, the Guru is praying in this quatrain for the Lord to destroy all his enemies. He prays to the Lord to protect him with His own hands. He prays that his household, servants and Sikhs may remain ever in bliss.

The caveat we had entered in the first quatrain needs especially to be kept in mind here also. The plea for protection here is not to be seen merely in mundane terms as referring to the Guru's personal enemies, friends or family. The term

Dusatt– ਦੁਸਟ–literally means the bad ones, the evil. The Guru's plea, made on behalf of all of us, seeks the Lord's benediction, such that His hand–His protection–is always available to save us from evil.

The theme here has to be understood at two levels. It can be seen firstly, as meaning a normal request as from any human for protection and help to destroy all enemies, all those who oppose him on this earth. However, at a deeper and more relevant level, the plea is to be read as a request for the Lord's help in destroying the evil within. The plea is for destroying evil and not any individuals. The Lord is the creator, the master of all, whether evil or good, whether on the right path or the wrong. The Guru's task is to bring the evil ones to the right path and to lead them back to the Lord from whom we all are separated by the veil of illusion cast by *Maya*. Therefore, the Guru's prayer here is to be seen as meant to rid all of us of our evil.

The Guru then adds here, a further plea that may all his *parvāra*–family–live in peace, and be servants to the Lord, following on a path that is in accordance with His will.

The term ਪਰਵਾਰ–*parvāra*–literally means family. For a *Sat Guru*, the true Guru, it is not to be understood as meaning just the few who may be, by blood or other ties of kinship, linked to him. It has to be seen beyond that, as encompassing the entire humankind. His family of course includes near kin and followers, specifically those who follow on the Lord's path as prescribed by the Guru. However, as we discussed above the prayer is aimed beyond that, at everybody, all human beings, in fact the entire universe.

The Guru continues with his communication with the Lord in the same vein. He says in the third quatrain:

ਮੋ ਰੱਛਾ ਨਿਜ ਕਰ ਦੈ ਕਰਿਯੈ॥	Mo rachha nij kar dai kariyai
ਸਭ ਬੈਰਨ ਕੋ ਆਜ ਸੰਘਰਿਯੈ॥	Sabh bairan ko āj sanghariyai
ਪੂਰਨ ਹੋਇ ਹਮਾਰੀ ਆਸਾ॥	Puran hoye hamāri āsa
ਤੋਰ ਭਜਨ ਕੀ ਰਹੈ ਪਿਆਸਾ॥ ੩॥	Tor bhajan ki rahai pyāsa. 3.

Glossary:

ਨਿਜ ਕਰ	Nij kar	Own hands
ਬੈਰਨ	Bairan	Enemies
ਸੰਘਰਿਯੈ	Sanghariyai	Destroy

Simply rendered, in this quatrain the Guru seeks from the Lord personal protection and immediate destruction of all adversaries. He seeks fulfillment of his heart's desires and that he may ever thirst for the Lord's worship.

The theme continues with a further prayer for personal protection. The Guru asks the Lord to protect him. He says, ਮੋ ਰੱਛਾ–*mo rachha*, my protection, ਨਿਜ ਕਰ ਦੈ ਕਰਿਯੈ–*nij kar dai kariyai*, with Thine own hands bestow. The Guru is seeking the Lord's blessings and seeks to stay under the aegis of the Lord Himself. There is no other power or authority to which we can appeal. It is only the Lord to whom we should supplicate, as the Guru does here.

The Guru then seeks the destruction of all enemies, saying, ਸਭ ਬੈਰਨ ਕੋ ਆਜ ਸੰਘਰਿਯੈ॥–*sabh bairan ko āj sanghariyai*. Now, who are these enemies? As we discussed in the previous quatrain the plea is for destroying evil and not any individuals. The Lord is the creator, the master of all, whether evil or good, whether on the right path or the wrong. The Guru's task is to bring the evil within us, and those who have strayed from the Guru's path, the evil ones, to the right path and to rend the veil of illusion cast by *Maya*.

In the last two lines, the Guru spells out a prayer for the fulfillment of his desires. And, what is that desire? The Guru says, ਪੂਰਨ ਹੋਇ ਹਮਾਰੀ ਆਸਾ–*puran hoye hamāri āsa,* meaning may our desires fructify; and then clarifies what that *āsa*–that hope–is. He answers that question when he says, ਤੋਰ ਭਜਨ ਕੀ ਰਹੈ ਪਿਆਸਾ–*tor bhajan ki rahai pyāsa*, may there ever be in the heart a desire to worship the Lord. The prayer is for such protection against troubles that there remains in our hearts a constant desire to worship the Lord. The rest of the lines about destroying the adversaries etc. are to be seen in the context of this summation. All that he desires is that evil within all of us may be suppressed, and this aim, to forever worship Him, be achieved.

In the fourth quatrain the same theme is continued. He says:

ਤੁਮਹਿ ਛਾਡਿ ਕੋਈ ਅਵਰ ਨ ਧਿਯਾਊਂ॥	Tumhe chhād koyi avar na dhiāu(n)
ਜੋ ਬਰ ਚਹੋਂ ਸੁ ਤੁਮ ਤੇ ਪਾਊਂ॥	Jo barr chāho(n) su tum tay pāu(n)
ਸੇਵਕ ਸਿੱਖ ਹਮਾਰੇ ਤਾਰੀਅਹਿ॥	Sevak sikh hamāray tāriyaih.
ਚੁਨਿ ਚੁਨਿ ਸਤ੍ਰ ਹਮਾਰੇ ਮਾਰੀਅਹਿ॥੪॥	Chun chun satr hamāray māriyaih. 4.

Glossary:

ਧਿਯਾਊਂ	Dhiāu(n)	Meditate upon
ਬਰ	Barr	Blessing, benediction
ਤਾਰੀਅਹਿ	Tāriyaih.	To save, to grant success

Simply rendered the Guru in this quatrain says may one never worship any other than the Lord. May all needs be fulfilled from Him. May He save the Guru's Sikhs and devotees and destroy all foes, the foes being all the evils within us.

Continuing from the last line of the previous quatrain, the Guru stresses in the first two lines that he wishes to worship the Lord alone and to get from Him alone *jo barr chāho(n)*– all that the heart may desire. This is to be seen in the context of the oft-repeated message in *Gurbāṇi* that there ought not to be any duality in the devotion we have for the Lord in our hearts. The Lord is one and uniquely the only real power in this universe. The other powers, gods and godlings that we imagine, such as the various gods and goddesses which are considered part of the Hindu pantheon, are all less than and within the command of the Lord. We must not, therefore, fix our minds ever on a lesser power. We must remember always the Lord alone and fix our mind on Him, for He pervades the entire created worlds and everything moves in accordance with His inexorable will–His *Hukam*. It is also to be seen as a commandment to not deem any earthly power to be worthy of our adoration. We may get some temporary rewards from such powers, but the eternal reward we seek, the liberation from the circle of rebirth is to be obtained only from the Lord.

In construing the last two lines, we will have to keep in view what we had discussed in the previous quatrain. The plea here is for preserving the good and for destroying evil, in its general entirety and not for any exclusive group, or a few individuals. Though at a superficial glance, the Guru's plea to the Lord could be seen as referring only to his followers and devotees, and as being directed against his enemies, but as we discussed in the previous quatrains, the theme here has to be understood at two levels. It is firstly, a normal request as from any human for protection and help to destroy all enemies. At a deeper level, the plea is to be read as a request for the Lord's help in destroying all evil, and more especially the evil within. The Guru's task is to bring the evil ones on the right path and lead them back to the Lord from whom we all are separated by the veil of illusion cast by *Maya*. Therefore, the Guru's prayer here has to be construed accordingly

In the fifth quatrain, the Guru continues with the prayer. He says:

ਆਪ ਹਾਥ ਦੇ ਮੁਝੈ ਉਬਰਿਯੈ॥	Āp hāth day mujhai ubariai.
ਮਰਨ ਕਾਲ ਕਾ ਤ੍ਰਾਸ ਨਿਵਰਿਯੈ॥	Maran kāl ka trās nivariai.
ਹੂ ਜੋ ਸਦਾ ਹਮਾਰੇ ਪੱਛਾ॥	Hū jo sada hamāray pachha.
ਸ੍ਰੀ ਅਸਿਧੁਜ ਜੂ ਕਰਿਯਹੁ ਰੱਛਾ॥ ੫॥	Sri asidhuj joo kariyo rachha. 5.

Glossary:

ਉਬਰਿਯੈ	Ubariai	Raise, uplift
ਤ੍ਰਾਸ	Trās	Dread
ਨਿਵਰਿਯੈ	Nivariai	Save, rescue
ਅਸਿਧੁਜ	Asidhuj	Banner with sword sign

The Guru here reiterates the theme he had laid out in the last two lines of the previous quatrain and repeats his request for the personal intervention by the Lord. He says, *āp hāth day mujhai ubariai*–with Thy own hand grant me succor. He had used the same terminology in the second, where he said, *āp hāth day mohe bachāvoh*–with Thine own hand save me, succor me; and the third quatrain where he said, *mo rachha nij kar dai kariyai*–protect me with Thine own hand. This insistence on the 'Lords own hand' is meant to drive home the point made throughout *Gurbāṇi* that salvation is to be found at no other quarters and there is no power other than the Lord from who help can be sought.

In the second line he says, ‘remove from my mind the fear of death’. Death is feared only because there is uncertainty about what will happen thereafter. If we knew our fate what is there to fear? This earthly sojourn is limited and certain to end in death. It is on the eternity thereafter that we should mainly focus our interest. If we could hope to spend that in oneness with the Lord then it is eternal bliss, something keenly to be awaited and not dreaded. Only the Lord can grant us this culmination. Therefore, the Guru begs the Lord to remove this fear from our minds, or in other words grant us the glance of grace, which will instantaneously bring salvation, and take all fears away.

In the third line, he says, ‘remain forever my support’. In other words, he is praying to the Lord to stand by his side in all times of trouble. The Guru is saying that with a supporter like the Lord what fear could there be of anything at all? Life on this earth will be smooth and when the time comes, salvation will ensue. As the Guru tells us in the Sukhmani Sahib, *Mahla* 5 page 292, SGGS, ਇਹ ਲੋਕ ਸੁਖੀਏ ਪਰਲੋਕ ਸੁਹੇਲੇ॥ ਨਾਨਕ ਹਰਿ ਪ੍ਰਭਿ ਆਪਹਿ ਮੇਲੇ॥–*Eh lok sukhīay pralok suhelay. Nanak har prabh āpeh melay.* This means these lucky blessed ones are happy and comfortable in this life and their life after death is smoothened too. The Lord merges such ones into Himself.

Finally, in the last line the Guru says ‘protect me, oh the one with the sword bannered standard’. It was usual in battle for warriors to sport distinctive signs or emblems, on their personal standards in battle. This was meant to be a distinctive feature so that his own army, as also the enemy, could identify the warrior. Great warriors were renowned everywhere, and the signs marking their standards were equally well known. A great leader could thus be known among the great ones not only by his name but also by the sign on his standard. The

Guru here uses that analogy and seeks to identify the Lord as the great warrior who is *asidhuj*–whose standard carries the sign of the sword. The tenth Nanak, living as he did in tumultuous times entailing continuous struggle and many battles has often used martial terminology in relation to the Lord, and accords the sword a mystical, almost divine status.

In the next, the sixth quatrain, the Guru says:

ਰਾਖਿ ਲੇਹੁ ਮੁਹਿ ਰਾਖਨਹਾਰੇ॥	Rākh leh muh rākhanhāray.
ਸਾਹਿਬ ਸੰਤ ਸਹਾਇ ਪਿਯਾਰੇ॥	Sahib sant sahāye piāray.
ਦੀਨ ਬੰਧੁ ਦੁਸਟਨ ਕੇ ਹੰਤਾ॥	Deen bandh dusttan kay hanta
ਤੁਮ ਹੋ ਪੁਰੀ ਚਤੁਰ ਦਸ ਕੰਤਾ॥ ੬॥	Tum ho puri chatur das kanta. 6.

Glossary:

ਦੀਨ ਬੰਧ	Deen bandh	Friend of the meek
ਪੁਰੀ	Puri	Worlds
ਚਤੁਰਦਸ	Chaturdas	Fourteen
ਕੰਤਾ	Kanta	Lord

Simply rendered, the quatrain addresses the Lord as the saviour, Lord of all, and helper of the saints, the merciful and the destroyer of tyrants. He is the Lord of the fourteen worlds, of the entire created universe.

In this quatrain the Guru's prayer for protection continues. He, in the first two lines, addresses the Lord as the preserver, and begs for His protection; as he says, *rākh leh*–save me. The Lord, he says, who is the master and the beloved, the sustainer of saints. The Lord is of course the sustainer of the entire universe, His benediction being available to every created entity. Here the reference is to the fact that the saints became saints only because the Lord so willed and they remain on the right path because His blessings continue to be upon them. The day that ceases, they can lose the way and stray into the seductive arms of *Maya*. The state of grace is for the Lord to grant, so the Guru says the Lord who is the support of the saints, may grant him, the Guru, similar blessing.

In the third and fourth lines, the Guru says the Lord is the *deen bandh*, the friend of the meek. This is a concept common to almost all religious belief systems. Humility, a lack of aggression, the ability to accept and to forgive, are all universally accepted and advocated characteristics of the truly spiritual person. Since such a life is believed by the savants to be in accordance with the Lord's way, it follows that those who live in this fashion are the friends of the Lord, and equally the Lord is their friend. The second part of the statement is that He is *dusttan kay hanta*–destroyer of the evil. As we discussed in the previous quatrains also, the plea is for destroying evil and not any individuals.

In the last line, he says the Lord is ਤੁਮ ਹੋ ਪੁਰੀ ਚਤੁਰ ਦਸ ਕੰਤਾ–*tumho puri chatur das kanta*, meaning You are the *kanta*–the master of the *puri chatur das*–the fourteen worlds. This concept of there being fourteen worlds is common among different belief systems. In Hindu mythology, there are believed to be seven heavens and seven *pātālas*, netherworlds, making a total of fourteen. The higher worlds are said to be, *bhu*, *bhuvas*, *svar*, *mahas*, *janas*, *tapas and satya.* Of these, the highest is *satya* that is ruled by Lord Brahma, and the lowest is *bhu* that is inhabited by humans. The seven *pātālas* are said to be *atāla*, *vitāla*, *sutāla*, *rasātāla*, *talātāla*, *mahātāla*, *pātāla*.

The Muslim belief system mentions seven skies as mentioned in *Sura* 41.12 of the holy Quran, where it says, 'and He made them seven heavens in two days, and in each heaven made known its office'. There are also said to be seven levels of Hell namely *jahannam, laza, hutamah, sa'ir, saqar, jahim* and *hawiyah.* There is a popular tale of how Guru Nanak was challenged by the Pīr Dastgīr in Baghdad for daring to say, in Japji Sahib, *pauṛi* 22, that there are *pātāla pātāl, lakh āgāsa āgās*–countless heavens and netherworlds, when there were only 14 skies and netherworlds. The *Pīr* wanted the Guru punished for questioning the Muslim belief and it is said the Guru granted him the vision to actually see the infinite worlds, after which he acknowledged the Guru's stature. In simple terms, the Guru is here using this phrase to convey the sense that the Lord's domain comprises the entire created universe. The Guru of course tells us throughout the SGGS that the Lord's creation is infinite.

In the seventh quatrain, the Guru says:

ਕਾਲ ਪਾਇ ਬ੍ਰਹਮਾ ਬਪੁ ਧਰਾ ॥	Kāl pāye Brahma bapp dhara.
ਕਾਲ ਪਾਇ ਸਿਵ ਜੁ ਅਵਤਰਾ॥	Kāl pāye siv joo avtara.
ਕਾਲ ਪਾਇ ਕਰ ਬਿਸਨੁ ਪ੍ਰਕਾਸਾ॥	Kāl pāye kar bisan prakāsa..
ਸਕਲ ਕਾਲ ਕਾ ਕੀਆ ਤਮਾਸਾ॥੭॥	Sakal kāl ka kiya tamāsa. 7.

Glossary:

ਕਾਲ ਪਾਇ	Kāl pāye	At the appointed time
ਬਪ	Bapp	Body
ਅਵਤਰਾ	Avtara.	Came, was created
ਪ੍ਰਕਾਸਾ	Prakāsa	Came to light
ਸਕਲ ਕਾਲ	Sakal kāl	Of entire time
ਤਮਾਸਾ	Tamāsa	Play

Simply rendered, this quatrain says that when the time came, Brahma was born, in due time Shiva was incarnated and so was Vishnu. The entire gamut of time is but a play enacted by the Lord.

The Guru here, while summarising the beginnings of the material universe, in terms familiar to those who would have been aware of Hindu mythology, underlines the unique supremacy of the Lord creator. He says, *kāl pāye Brahma bapp dhara*–the Lord caused Brahma to assume human form at the appropriate time. Brahma is thus not self-created but is a construct of the Lord, brought into existence for a specific purpose and with a specific mandate. The Lord wished for the material world to be created and for that, he caused Brahma to appear. In some belief systems, Brahma is assumed to be *swaibhang*–self-incarnate. Such belief systems then run into the difficulty of explaining the role, and the relative position of Vishnu, the sustainer and of Shiva the destroyer. To overcome this difficulty thinkers have assigned equal status to the three, calling them the *Trimurti*–the trinity. However, within this debate there are many who hold Lord Vishnu to be the creator, from whose navel a divine lotus grew from which Brahma was born. Similarly, some *Purānas* will assign Lord Shiva the primacy. We have within Hinduism sects called *Shaivites* and *Vaishnavites*, believing Shiva or Vishnu to be superior, though this has, fortunately, never led to conflict on this account.

The Guru's formulation clarifies these contradictions. There is but one Lord, and He is above and beyond any other power, including the trinity of Brahma, Vishnu and Shiva (also called Mahesh). It is in this context that this quatrain is to be construed. When that supreme authority so decides He brings Brahma into existence. When the time is right He gives form to Brahma, who, by implication, then proceeds with the creative process according to the laws laid down by the Lord. Brahma is thus not an independent entity, but is an operative power exercising the authority that the Lord creator has bestowed on him. In accordance with the divine laws, he then creates the visible universe.

At the appropriate time, which the Lord alone chooses, the creation of Vishnu and Shiva also similarly takes place. These entities then perform their assigned tasks of sustaining the world for as long as the Lord has so ordained; and then destroy the world at the appointed time. The term of the world and of these powers is pre-assigned. These cosmic time periods are, in the Hindu belief system itself, measured in *Yugas*–ages.

The *Yugas* are reckoned to occur in cycles of four, called *Sat Yuga, Treta Yuga*, *Dwāpar Yuga* and *Kal Yuga*, measuring a total of 4.32 million years in the ratio of 4:3:2:1. The shortest, the *Kal Yuga*, is supposed to last 432000 years. The full cycle is called a *Maha Yuga*. The time scales of creation are measured in terms of the *Maha Yuga.* A thousand such *Maha Yugas* constitute one day of Brahma, the night being of equal length. Brahma is supposed to have a year of 360 such nights and days, and his life span is a 100 years. Thus, we can reach a definite figure for the life span of Brahma, an unimaginably long time in human terms, but finite for all that. Only the Lord's span is infinite. He always is, and He creates the Brahmas through whom this creation is each time brought about, in innumerable cycles of creation and re-creation.

The term ਕਾਲ ਪਾਇ–*kāl pāye*, used in the third line is explained by some learned ones as referring to the Lord as the *Mahākāl*. The term *Kāl* means time or term, and *Mahākāl* would literally mean 'great time'. According to these learned ones, it is used here for the Lord, in the sense of Him being the lord and master of time. The more convincing rendering of *kāl pāye*, however, is 'the right or appointed time'. This implies that the Lord is the authority to decide when these super gods are to take material form to carry out His design of creation, and sustenance thereafter, of the universe thus brought into existence. Time is a construct born from the Lord's will and it is in this sense that the Guru says *sakal kāl ka kiya tamāsa*–meaning that it is a mere play in the hands of the Lord. Throughout all created time, the Lord brings into existence the universe, sustains it for such time as He wills, and when the time comes has it annihilated. The process is eternally repeated, and during that entire exercise, human souls are incarnated and given the opportunity to achieve union with the Lord.

In the eighth quatrain, the Guru says:

ਜਵਨ ਕਾਲ ਜੋਗੀ ਸਿਵ ਕੀਓ॥	Javan kāl jogi siv kiyo.
ਬੇਦ ਰਾਜਿ ਬ੍ਰਹਮਾ ਜੂ ਥੀਓ॥	Beid rāj Brahma joo thhiyo.
ਜਵਨ ਕਾਲ ਸਭ ਲੋਕ ਸਵਾਰਾ॥	Javan kāl sabh lok savāra.
ਨਮਸਕਾਰ ਹੈ ਤਾਹਿ ਹਮਾਰਾ॥ ੮॥	Namaskār hai tāhay hamāra. 8

Glossary:

ਜਵਨ ਕਾਲ	Javan kāl	That Lord
ਬੇਦ ਰਾਜਿ	Beid rāj	Lord of the Vedas
ਲੋਕ ਸਵਾਰਾ	Lok savāra	Created the worlds

This quatrain, simply rendered, says that the Lord of time created the Yogi Shiva. He created Brahma, the Lord and master of the Vedas. The Lord fashioned the entire universe. The Guru says he salutes Him alone.

In the first line, the Guru says that the Lord created the Yogi Shiva, and He also created Brahma the Lord of the Vedas. In the Hindu belief system, the trinity that operates the universe consists of Brahma, Vishnu and Mahesh, who represent the creative, the sustaining and the destructive principles respectively. The Sikh belief system postulates the One Lord who ordained all these activities. Without specifically denying the existence of these super gods, the Guru here emphasises that it is the Lord alone who creates, sustains or destroys. For making this basic truth clear, he says the Lord, the master of time, created the Yogi Shiva. In the Hindu system Shiva is visualised as a recluse who engages in lengthy spells of meditation and maintains an indifferent personal appearance, much in the fashion of the sect known as the *yogi*, or *jogi*, as they are sometimes called in the SGGS. Incidentally, the *yogis* worship Lord Shiva alone as the ultimate divine principle, believing that he alone creates and sustains. The Guru uses the phrase *javan kāl* meaning 'that Lord'. Implicit in the use here of the term *kāl*–is the statement of the absolute mastery the Lord has over time.

In the same vein, he says in the second line that the Lord, as master of time, brought into existence Brahma, master of the Vedas. The allusion here is to the belief that the Vedas emerged out of the mouth of Lord Brahma. In other words, he says, referring to the Hindu belief system that all knowledge flows from this component of the trinity. In this system even his spouse, Saraswati, is visualised as knowledge personified.

In the third line, he says the Lord ordered the entire universe. The allusion is to the belief that before the material universe emerged into its present form, there existed total formlessness, complete random chaos in which only the Lord continued to be and there was nothing else at all, no Brahma, no Vishnu, no Shiva, no visible forms or shapes or beings. All this, the entire material universe, was then ordered into the form we see today. This ordering of chaos into form is what is meant by *sabh lok savāra.*

In the last line, the Guru says that his salutation is to that Lord, implying that there is none else, except Him, who could thus be deserving of adulation.

In the ninth quatrain, the Guru speaks to us further in the same vein. He says:

ਜਵਨ ਕਾਲ ਸਭ ਜਗਤ ਬਨਾਯੋ॥	Javan kāl sabh jagat banāyo.
ਦੇਵ ਦੈਤ ਜੱਛਨ ਉਪਜਾਯੋ॥	Dev dait jachhan upjāyo.
ਆਦਿ ਅੰਤਿ ਏਕੈ ਅਵਤਾਰਾ॥	Ād unt ekai avtāra.
ਸੋਈ ਗੁਰੂ ਸਮਝਿਯਹੁ ਹਮਾਰਾ॥੯॥	Soyi Guru samjhayo hamāra. 9.

Glossary:

ਦੇਵ ਦੈਤ	Dev dait	The gods and the antigods
ਜੱਛਨ	Jachhan	The Yaksha, a class of demigods
ਅਵਤਾਰਾ	Avtāra	Incarnation
ਸਮਝਿਯਹੁ	Samjhayo	Understood, known

Simply rendered, this quatrain says that the Lord, master of time, made the universe, the *devtas* (gods and godlings), *asuras* and *yakshas*. He uniquely is the start and the end. He alone, says the Guru, is my Guru.

In the first line, he repeats the thought stated in the third line of the previous quatrain, that it is the Lord alone who, *sabh jagat banāyo*–made all the worlds. *Javan kāl* here means the Lord. The Guru is saying the Lord is the creator, the sole power that governs the creation and sustaining of the material universe.

In the second line, he says the Lord created the *Dev dait jachhan*. This refers to various types of superhuman beings. The Guru is in this fashion making the statement that the Lord alone is the creator of all beings of all categories. It may, in fact be of interest here, and facilitate the understanding of these passages, to examine the beliefs in Hinduism to which these various references pertain.

The Hindu belief system stipulates these three as the main categories of supra-human creatures. The *Dev* are the gods, representing the principle of good, as opposed to the *Dait* the forces of evil. It is interesting to note that in this belief system both these races are born of the same father, the great sage *Kashyapa* who is one of the *prajāpatis*–progenitors of the created beings. Their mothers, *Aditi* and *Diti*, were the daughters of another *prajāpati* named *Daksha*, who is sometimes called the chief of the *prajāpatis*. *Aditi's* children came to be called the *Devtas*, or *Devas*, whose chief is Indra. *Diti's* children are called *Daitya*, and are supposed to represent the evil, dark forces. Others in the same category are the *Dānavs*, the *Rākshas* and *Asuras*, who are supposed to have had different chiefs from time to time, Rāvana of the Ramayana fame having been one such mighty chief belonging to the race of the *Rākshas*. Another category of divine entities, below the level of gods, is called the *Yaksha*, whose chief is Lord *Kubera*, who happens to be a stepbrother of Rāvana, King of Lanka.

In the last two lines the Guru sums up the lesson by saying that, the Lord is the sole entity existing at the beginning and the end. In other words, the Lord is outside the confines of time, to which all created things are subject. That Lord, says the Guru, is his master. The allusion here is to the concept of *Avtāra*–incarnation. It is believed in Hinduism that in order to curb evil and uphold righteousness Lord Vishnu incarnates from time to time, it being his assigned role to sustain the created worlds. He is worshipped in the form of his various incarnations, of which Rama and Krishna are the best known. The Guru, in keeping with the Sikh belief system's strict monotheistic structure emphasises that there is but one *ād unt ekai avtāra*–the only *Avtāra* from beginning to end. He is telling us that the Lord Himself, as the *Shabad* Guru, the Word incarnate, is eternally present, permeating every atom of the created universe. That Lord, the Creator Himself, is the Master whom the Guru worships.

In the tenth quatrain, the same theme is continued. The Guru says:

ਨਮਸਕਾਰ ਤਿਸ ਹੀ ਕੋ ਹਮਾਰੀ॥	Namaskār tis hee ko hamāri.
ਸਕਲ ਪ੍ਰਜਾ ਜਿਨ ਆਪ ਸਵਾਰੀ॥	Sakal praja jin āp savāri.
ਸਿਵਕਨ ਕੋ ਸਿਵ ਗੁਨ ਸੁਖ ਦੀਓ॥	Sivkan ko siv gunn sukh dīyo.
ਸਤ੍ਰੁਨ ਕੋ ਪਲ ਮੋ ਬਧ ਕੀਓ॥੧੦॥	Satran ko pal mo badhh kīyo. 10.

Glossary:

ਸਕਲ ਪ੍ਰਜਾ	Sakal praja	All created beings
ਸਿਵਕਨ	Sivkan	Servants
ਸਿਵ ਗੁਨ	Siv gunn	Divine qualities
ਸਤ੍ਰੁਨ	Satran	Enemies, opponents

Simply rendered in this quatrain the Guru says he bows only to Him; the Creator of all entities and all created beings who are His subjects, the one who gives divine virtues to His devotees and who in a trice, destroys all enemies.

The essence of the message here is that we must bow only to the one Lord, and not go chasing after sundry powers and beings, all of whom are but the mere creations of the Lord. They have no independent authority beyond what the Lord bestows on each of them, and these powers are given for the performance of specific tasks. We saw in the previous quatrains the Guru spoke of the creation of the super gods like Brahma, Vishnu and Shiva. All other beings, which are believed to be below these powers, are then obviously also His creation, and do not deserve our independent adoration. The Guru is saying do not worship any such entity; worship instead the Lord who creates these entities.

Considering it in this context, we can see that in the first two lines the Guru says, *namaskār tis hee ko hamāri*–our salutation must only be to that Lord who *sakal praja jin āp savāri*–brought all beings, meaning the entire creation, into existence.

In the last two lines he says that not only did that Lord bring them into existence, but He also *sivkan ko siv gunn sukh dīyo*–gave His devotees divine qualities, virtues, and gave them peace and joy. He also *satran ko pal mo badhh kīyo*–destroyed the enemies in a trice. Who, or what, are these enemies? As we have discussed at length in the previous quatrains, these enemies are the evils, the coils of *Maya*, which keep us from moving on the Lord's path. The false glitter and allurements that cause us to go astray, snared in the beguilements and the material trinkets that *Maya* offers in such abundance.

In the eleventh quatrain, the Guru says:

ਘਟ ਘਟ ਕੇ ਅੰਤਰ ਕੀ ਜਾਨਤ॥	Ghatt ghatt kay antar kee jānat.
ਭਲੇ ਬੁਰੇ ਕੀ ਪੀਰ ਪਛਾਨਤ ॥	Bhalay buray kee pīr pachhānat.
ਚੀਟੀ ਤੇ ਕੁੰਚਰ ਅਸਥੂਲਾ॥	Chītti tay kunchar asthūla.
ਸਭ ਪਰ ਕ੍ਰਿਪਾ ਦ੍ਰਿਸਟਿ ਕਰ ਫੂਲਾ॥੧੧॥	Sabh parr kripa dristt kar phūla. 11.

Glossary:

ਘਟ ਘਟ	Ghatt ghatt	Of all things, of each
ਚੀਟੀ	Chītti	Ant
ਕੁੰਚਰ	Kunchar	Elephant
ਅਸਥੂਲਾ	Asthūla	Very large sized
ਫੂਲਾ	Phūla	Blooms, is pleased

Simply rendered, this quatrain says the Lord intimately knows our innermost feelings. He recognises the anguish of all creatures, good or bad. From the tiny ant to the enormous elephant, He protects and cares for all.

Continuing the theme of worshipping none but the one Lord, the Guru touches on some more of the obvious qualities we all ascribe to the Lord, whose vast mystery is of course really beyond any effort at description. He says in the first line that the Lord knows the innermost thought of all created beings. This is, of course, axiomatic. As we have discussed earlier also nothing could possibly be hidden from that omniscient Lord. He permeates all existence, and His presence is to be presumed in each part of it–including within us. Here, though, the stress is not merely on the Lord's omniscience, but the Guru sees Him as an ever-present companion whom we can experience on a continuing basis in every day existence.

In the secondline, he says the Lord recognises the pain and agony in each heart. We will see the same thought enunciated in the first two lines of the next quatrain. Therefore, this concept of the Lord being happy or unhappy needs to be understood, for which it must be seen in the context of the Guru's overall message. The Guru has told us that the Lord is ever with us and is aware of the innermost thoughts of all created things; and so is aware of the pain, the trouble that any created being may feel. This is true not only for the good, the men of God, but also equally for those who do not tread this path and are evil. As Bhai Gurdas says in his *Vārs,* the Lord favours his devotees, but equally he redeems the sinner. For instance, he says in *Vār* 31, *pauṛi* 8:

ਭਗਤਿ ਵਛਲੁ ਭੀ ਆਖੀਐ ਪਤਿਤ ਉਧਾਰਣਿ ਪਤਿਤ ਉਧਰਿਆ॥
Bhagat vachhal bhi ākhiyai patit udhāraṇ patit udhria.

This means that we know Him as not only the uplifter of His devotees but also as the redeemer of the fallen.

All creation is His own, the good or bad, pious or evil. When He sends us to this world, this field of action, He gives us free will. How we use that free will is then up to us. It is for us to make the right choices and try to work our way back to union with Him from whom we were separated temporarily and from whom we will remain distanced until we learn to overcome our *haumai* and realise His existence within us, in fact within all creation. The concept therefore is that He, the loving creator is happy when He sees the child on the right path and is saddened when He sees another child going astray. This also underlines the message that He is not some remote disinterested entity, but is in the closest proximity to each and all of us. This is a theme often stressed in the SGGS also, for instance at page 658, Bhagat Ravidās says, in *Rāg Soratth,*

ਕਹਿ ਰਵਿਦਾਸ ਹਾਥ ਪੈ ਨੇਰੈ ਸਹਿਜੇ ਹੋਇ ਸੁ ਹੋਇ॥
Kah Ravidās hāthh pai nerai sahjay hoye so hoye.

This translates as 'the Lord is closer to us than our own hand and events shall unfold in the normal course as set in place by Him'. The Almighty Lord's omnipresence is stressed here.

The Guru is telling us in the first two lines of this quatrain that the Lord made us and He knows every thought we have, every action we perform and each trouble or joy that we experience. All creation is His own, and He knows our most intimate thoughts regardless of whether we are good or bad. This is not altered by the state of our purity, nor by our might, or our position in worldly affairs.

The Guru says in the third and fourth lines that the Lord grants His love to all equally, to the insignificant *chītti*–ant, as to the *kunchar asthūla*- the mightily impressive elephant. He alone knows who is deserving of His glance of grace, and He grants it at His will and as He deems fit, regardless of how our human eyes may perceive them. Bestowing His blessing to His creation, He is pleased. This is a thought we will find recurring in the *Gurbāṇi.* For instance, in the Japji Sahib in *pauṛi* 37, the Guru says *vekhai vigsay kar vichār*, meaning the Lord is pleased as He watches over His creation, because He loves what He has created. In fact, almost all belief systems hold that the Lord's essence is unadulterated love. Sikhism believes that the Lord constantly showers this love on all. It is a different matter that only a few who have the good fortune of realising this truth, and who can become worthy of accepting it.

The Guru expands the thought further in the twelfth quatrain. He says:

ਸੰਤਨ ਦੁਖ ਪਾਏ ਤੇ ਦੁਖੀ॥	Santan dukh pāye tay dukhi.
ਸੁਖ ਪਾਏ ਸਾਧੁਨ ਕੇ ਸੁਖੀ॥	Sukh pāye sādhan kay sukhi.
ਏਕ ਏਕ ਕੀ ਪੀਰ ਪਛਾਨੈਂ॥	Ek ek kee pīr pachhānai.
ਘਟ ਘਟ ਕੇ ਪਟ ਪਟ ਕੀ ਜਾਨੈਂ॥ ੧੨॥	Ghatt ghatt kay patt patt kee jānai. 12.

Glossary:

ਪੀਰ	Pīr	Pain, agony, troubles
ਘਟ ਘਟ	Ghatt ghatt	Of all things
ਪਟ ਪਟ	Patt patt	Innermost, veiled, hidden

Simply rendered, this quatrain says that when His saints suffer He is pained, and feels happiness when they are happy. He knows the pain of each and every one, and knows the innermost thoughts of all.

The Guru here restates and reiterates the lesson of the previous quatrain. He had said in the previous quatrain that the Lord is aware of our innermost thoughts, and that He knows the pain within each and every created being, whether good or evil. Here, in the first two lines he makes it more specific, and says when the saintly are happy the Lord is pleased. When they are suffering, He is saddened. As we discussed in the previous quatrain He, the loving Creator is happy when He sees the child on the right path and is saddened when He sees another child going astray.

Then, in the third and fourth lines, he reiterates what he had told us in the first two lines of the previous quatrain. He says that the Lord knows the pain in each heart, and He is aware of the innermost secrets of each created being, however hidden we might try to keep these. As we had discussed in the previous quatrain the Lord is the paramount, omniscient creative power, and as such, it is axiomatic that He is aware of all events, all that happens in the created world. There are no inner recesses in which our thoughts could remain hidden from Him. *Ghatt ghatt* means here 'of each entity', while *patt patt* refers to the layers, veils or screen. Thus, the Guru is saying that these innermost thoughts of all created things are transparent to Him, regardless of any effort to screen or veil these.

In the thirteenth quatrain, the Guru speaks of the Lord's creative process, and the process of destruction that cyclically follows it. He says:

ਜਬ ਉਦਕਰਖ ਕਰਾ ਕਰਤਾਰਾ॥	Jab udkarkh kara kartāra.
ਪ੍ਰਜਾ ਧਰਤ ਤਬ ਦੇਹ ਅਪਾਰਾ॥	Praja dhharat tabb deh apāra.
ਜਬ ਆਕਰਖ ਕਰਤ ਹੋ ਕਬਹੂੰ॥	Jabb ākarkh karat ho kabhoo(n).
ਤੁਮ ਮੈ ਮਿਲਤ ਦੇਹ ਧਰ ਸਭਹੂੰ॥੧੩॥	Tum mai milat deh dhhar sabhoo(n).13.

Glossary:

ਉਦਕਰਖ	Udkarkh	Expansive, creative action
ਪ੍ਰਜਾ ਧਰਤ	Praja dhharat	The material beings assume form
ਅਪਾਰਾ	Apāra	Uncountable, numerous
ਆਕਰਖ	Ākarkh	Force of contraction, inward force
ਮਿਲਤ	Milat	Are assimilated
ਦੇਹ ਧਰ	Deh dhhar	Material beings

Simply rendered, this quatrain says that when the Creator projects Himself, His creations assume physical forms. When He decides to take everything back, creation is dissolved and all physical forms merge back into Him.

The arguments on the creation of the universe have raged since ages both in religious and in scientific circles. Various belief systems have evolved their own theories of creation but we need look at what modern Science has postulated. There are two main hypotheses of how the universe came into existence. The first is the 'steady state theory' propounded by Hoyle in 1948 AD, envisaging a continuous creation of matter as the universe expands. The other, older theory, called the 'Big Bang' is today the more accepted. It postulates that there was a moment when all matter was concentrated in one infinitely dense point, which then exploded, and what we are today seeing is a universe continuing to expand as the after effect of that explosion. It says that as the intensely hot and dense point exploded it started to cool, atoms were formed, and ultimately it has over time led to the formation of galaxies and stars, the extent of which has been measured in light-years, with the figures changing as humankind's ability to observe and measure has developed. The Hubble telescope has helped scientists better determine the limits of the known universe such as can be observed by humans.

The formulation put forth in this quatrain describes the creation process as envisaged in most Eastern religions, notably Hinduism. This is also the cosmology that Sikhism adopts. The belief is that the Lord at His will brings into existence the material universe, in which He is then immanent. Why He does it and for how long He sustains it is beyond human knowledge to comprehend. He alone knows, and He alone decides the timing. This manifesting of the material universe happens when *Udkarkh* occurs, or in other words, He extends His creative function, manifests. Matter and energy emanate from Him and things assume form and shape. This universe then exists until the Lord, at His own will determines that it will come to an end. His will then performs the act of *Ākarkh*, or in other words attracts, or forces all these created things to merge back into Him. In other words, the Lord withdraws His immanent presence, though of course He eternally remains in His transcendent form. The process is infinitely repeated, with no end and no beginning known to any created being. This envisages that the super gods, Brahma, Vishnu or Mahesh, envisaged as the creator, sustainer and destroyer respectively, in the Hindu belief system, are also created and destroyed cyclically. In scientific terms, this model would be not far from the Big Bang theory, only going beyond it because though it envisages an instantaneous creation process, it also envisions an equally instantaneous annihilation, only for the process to be repeated ad infinitem.

Thus, in the first two lines the Guru says that when the Lord puts forth His expansive function all beings come into existence. This of course implies that the universe in which these beings are to function also comes simultaneously into existence. In the last two lines, the opposite process is described, and the Guru says when the time comes for the Lord to call everything back into Him then all those who had assumed form merge back into the Lord. The created universe ceases to exist, and there is then nothing but the Lord Himself. This state continues until the Lord decides that it is time again to repeat the process.

In the next quatrain, the 14th, the Guru speaks of our inability to ever comprehend the unknowable Lord. He says:

ਜੇਤੇ ਬਦਨ ਸ੍ਰਿਸਟਿ ਸਭ ਧਾਰੈ॥	Jetay badan sristt sabh dhārai.
ਆਪ ਆਪਨੀ ਬੂਝ ਉਚਾਰੈ॥	Āp āpni būjh uchārai.
ਤੁਮ ਸਭ ਹੀ ਤੇ ਰਹਤ ਨਿਰਾਲਮ॥	Tum sabh hee tay rahat nirālam.
ਜਾਨਤ ਬੇਦ ਭੇਦ ਅਰ ਆਲਮ॥ ੧੪॥	Jānat beid bheid ar ālam. 14.

Glossary:

ਬਦਨ	Badan	Bodies, created things
ਸ੍ਰਿਸਟਿ	Sristt	Creation, the world
ਬੂਝ	Būjh	Understanding
ਨਿਰਾਲਮ	Nirālam.	Apart, unique
ਬੇਦ	Beid	Scriptures, knowledge
ਆਲਮ	Ālam	Learned ones

Simply rendered this quatrain says that the numerous created forms and bodies speak of Him according to their own understanding. The Lord remains detached from them all. The wise ones, and the religious books, know this deep mystery, that He is unknowable.

It is an oft-stated position in the Sikh belief system that the Lord is beyond human ability to comprehend. Only someone who has merged with the Lord can know His extent. However, such a one will find words utterly insufficient to describe the experience. At many places in the SGGS, the Guru has described the predicament of such a person as, ਗੂੰਗੇ ਕੀ ਮਿਠਿਆਈ–*Gūngay ki mitthiāyi*, like a mute person seeking to describe the great pleasure of having tasted the most delicious sweets. He is elated, but has no words available to tell others of what he is experiencing. Another analogy used is of the rivulet reaching the mighty ocean. The waters of the two are then so completely intermingled that it is no longer possible to tell. Any true depiction is therefore inherently impossible, even though we have many claiming to know the Lord. To an extent this is so, because we are limited entities and can speak of the infinite Lord only to the extent our severely limited capabilities enable us to experience Him. In the first two lines, the Guru describes this phenomenon, of how all created beings speak of the Lord in the light of their own limited understanding of the vast mystery. *Jetay badan sristt sabh dhāray, āp āpni būjh uchārai*, he says. This means that the Lord's created beings in this universe all try to depict Him as their understanding may lead them to believe. The understanding is necessarily very limited, but yet all strive to speak of Him. The basic lesson here is that all these depictions can never really define Him, for He is truly unknowable.

In the last two lines, the Guru stresses another basic tenet of Sikhism, that the Lord is unique. There is no peer for the Creator. This is again axiomatic. If the Lord had a peer then He would not be the supreme master. He is *Nirālam*, without a peer, unique and apart from all creation. This is a mystery, says the Guru, which *jānat beid bheid ar ālam*, is known to the scripture and to the learned sages. In other words, the wise and learned ones know that His true form is beyond human ken to know Him in His entirety.

In the next quatrain, the 15th, the Guru expounds further on this theme. He says:

ਨਿਰੰਕਾਰ ਨ੍ਰਿਬਿਕਾਰ ਨਿਰਲੰਭ॥	Nirankār nirbikār nirlambh.
ਆਦਿ ਅਨੀਲ ਅਨਾਦਿ ਅਸੰਭ॥	Ād anīl anād asambh.
ਤਾ ਕਾ ਮੂੜ੍ਹ ਉਚਾਰਤ ਭੇਦਾ॥	Ta ka mūrh uchārat bheida.
ਜਾ ਕਾ ਭੇਵ ਨ ਪਾਵਤ ਬੇਦਾ॥ ੧੫॥	Ja ka bheiv na pāvat beida. 15.

Glossary:

ਨਿਰੰਕਾਰ	Nirankār	Having no specific form
ਨ੍ਰਿਬਿਕਾਰ	Nirbikār	Untainted, immaculate
ਨਿਰਲੰਭ	Nirlambh	Needing no support
ਅਨੀਲ	Anīl	Having no specific colour
ਅਨਾਦਿ	Anād	Having no beginning

ਅਸੰਭ	Asambh	Not subject to birth
ਮੂੜ	Mūrh	Fool, ignorant one
ਭੇਵ	Bheiv	Secret

Simply rendered, this quatrain says the Lord is formless, immaculate and is in need of no support. He is from the beginning, untainted, pure, unblemished, eternal and self-manifest. Only fools can claim to discuss His bounds, which are not known even to the Vedas.

In the first line the Guru describes the Lord, to the extent description is possible within the limits imposed by language and by human understanding. The terms used are restatements of the language and of concepts used extensively in the *Gurbāṇi*. Thus, the Lord is described here as *Nirankār*– having no form. The Lord, in His immanence can be also said to have all possible forms, for He permeates each entity. In reality, though, that only means that he has no one fixed form by which He could be described. He is *Nirbikār*, having no taint, or in other words immaculate. As the sole power in this universe, He cannot have any stain attaching to Him. Whatever He does is right and true. He is also *Nirlambh*, in need of no support. He is the support of all that exists, so what support could He possibly need?

In the second line, the Guru recites some more characteristics we humans ascribe to the Lord. He is *Anīl, Anād, Asambh*, meaning He has no specific colour, no beginning nor end, and is not subject to birth or death. *Anīl* literally means without colour, but is used here to stress that the Lord cannot be described by way of any specific characteristic. He has no specific form, or colour, or distinguishing marks. He is also self-manifest, not created or born. Since the cycle of births and deaths is what characterises the human condition, the distinction here is made to highlight His unique separateness.

In the third and fourth lines, the Guru then reverts to the point he made in the previous quatrain, where he said, *jetay badan sristt sabh dhāray*, *āp āpni būjh uchārai*. Here he says *ta ka mūrh uchārat bheida*. He is saying that it is the *mūrh*–foolish, ignorant ones, who have the temerity to boast that they know His *bheid*–secret, His reality. These are secrets, which even the scriptures have frankly admitted their inability to fathom. All religious belief systems throw up their hands when it comes to defining the shape, form or powers of the Lord. He is unknowable, unfathomable and beyond human capacity to describe. It is only a fool, then, who would dare to claim any true knowledge of the Lord. As the Guru said in *pauṛi* 26 of the Japji Sahib:

ਜੇ ਕੋ ਆਖੈ ਬੋਲ ਵਿਗਾੜ ਤਾ ਲਿਖੀਐ ਸਿਰ ਗਾਵਾਰਾ ਗਾਵਾਰੁ॥
Jay ko ākhay bol vigāṛ ta likhiyai sir gāvāra gāvār[u].

This means that if someone claims to be able to describe or to speak of the true reality of the Lord, then his name will top the list of the foolish. In other words, such a one must be styled as really an utter fool.

The lesson continues in the 16th quatrain, where the Guru says:

ਤਾ ਕੌ ਕਰ ਪਾਹਨ ਅਨੁਮਾਨਤ॥	Ta kau kar pāhan anumānat
ਮਹਾ ਮੂੜ੍ਹ ਕਛੂ ਭੇਦ ਨ ਜਾਨਤ॥	Maha mūrh kachh bheid na jānat.
ਮਹਾਦੇਵ ਕੌ ਕਹਤ ਸਦਾ ਸਿਵ॥	Mahādev kau kahat sada siv.
ਨਿਰੰਕਾਰ ਕਾ ਚੀਨਤ ਨਹਿ ਭਿਵ॥੧੬॥	Nirankār ka chīnat neh bhiv. 16.

Glossary:

ਪਾਹਨ	Pāhan	Stone idol
ਮਹਾ ਮੂੜ	Maha mūrh	Great fool
ਮਹਾਦੇਵ	Mahādev	Shiva
ਸਦਾ ਸਿਵ	Sada siv	The Lord
ਭਿਵ	Bhiv	Secret

Simply rendered, this quatrain says that deeming Him a stone, the fools do not comprehend the mystery. They call the Eternal Lord by the name of *Sada Siv*, and do not know the secret of the Formless Lord.

The Guru alludes to the belief systems where idols are worshipped. This was especially true of many sects within Hinduism. These sects deem the stone idol to be the Lord Himself and worship it. The Guru says in the first two lines that this is a foolish notion and that the *maha mūrh*–great fool, who is entangled in such superficial ritualistic idolatry and is not on the right path, will never be able to reach true understanding. Sikhism does not encourage idol worship at all, a view common to many other great belief systems also such as Islam, and many prominent sections of the Hindu and Christian belief systems. The stress in Sikhism is to fix one's mind on the one Lord, love His creation, and to follow a path in this life that requires great self-control and righteous living. This requires us to follow the path prescribed by the Guru, the essence of which is to unquestioningly accept His *Hukam*, His Will.

In the next two lines, the Guru stresses this further and refers to a sect of Hinduism, the *Shaivites*, who believe that Lord Shiva, who is also called Mahadev, is the creator. The Guru says that the formless Lord is different from and beyond any one of the super gods. Of these super gods, neither Brahma, nor Vishnu nor indeed Shiva can be the Lord, because they all are themselves the creation of that one Lord and will with the passage of their allotted time cease to exist. Only the Lord is eternal. Those who forget this reality and start worshipping any of the other powers have strayed from the path to God-realisation and can never hope to learn the real secret.

In the next quatrain, the 17th, the Guru elaborates and stresses again the thought he put forth in the first two lines of the 14th quatrain. He says:

ਆਪੁ ਆਪਨੀ ਬੁਧ ਹੈ ਜੇਤੀ॥	Āp āpni budhh hai jeti.
ਬਰਨਤ ਭਿੰਨ ਭਿੰਨ ਤੁਹਿ ਤੇਤੀ॥	Barnat bhinn bhinn tuhe teti.
ਤੁਮਰਾ ਲਖਾ ਨ ਜਾਇ ਪਸਾਰਾ॥	Tumra lakha na jāye pasāra.
ਕਿਹ ਬਿਧਿ ਸਜਾ ਪ੍ਰਥਮ ਸੰਸਾਰਾ॥੧੭॥	Keh bidhh saja prathham sansāra. 17.

Glossary:

ਬੁਧ	Budhh	Understanding, intellect
ਬਰਨਤ	Barnat	Describes, states
ਪਸਾਰਾ	Pasāra	Extent, expanse

Simply rendered, this quatrain says that everyone describes the Lord according to his own understanding. The limits of creation cannot be known, nor how in the beginning the Universe was created.

This is a reiteration of the thought put forth in the first two lines of the 14th quatrain, where the Guru had said, *jetay badan sristt sabh dhāray, āp āpni būjh uchārai.* This means that all created beings speak of the Lord in the light of their own limited understanding of the vast mystery. Here in the first two lines he restates this more emphatically. He says, *Āp āpni budhh hai jeti. Barnat bhin bhin tuhay teti.* This means that the ability to describe the unknowable mystery of the Lord is constrained by the level of our understanding. That is why we have so many differing interpretations of this mystery; of what this world is about, why we are here and where we will go at the end of this sojourn. The Lord is one, yet we see Him spoken of by learned ones in such a bewildering variety of ways. This is, says the Guru, because each interpretation is limited by and coloured by the level of our own experience, our intellect, and our capacity to understand. The true devotee of course knows what the reality is, but only after he has become one with Him. For the rest of us, however, the description is tinged inevitably by our own prejudices, beliefs, our own understanding. The irony is that the true devotee, who truly knows is unable to find words to describe Him, while the rest of us who in fact do not know, are only too keen to spout what we believe to be the truth.

The Guru explains in the last two lines the thrust of this message. He says that in reality none can estimate the extent of the Lord, nor say by what device the Lord first created this universe. Only the Lord knows the process of creation. So, says the Guru, *keh bidhh saja prathham sansāra*–how the Lord initially brought this creation into existence is impossible to explain. Why creation took place, how vast is the size and extent of that creation is an issue that has mystified, and fascinated thinking men since the ages. Scientists seek to unravel this mystery by devising finer and more powerful instruments, while mystics depend on their intuitive powers to decipher this mystery. Neither can ultimately succeed because the Lord is not to be known or measured in any human terms. The only way to reach Him is to achieve God-realisation, to become one with Him. This is to be achieved by following the path of righteous living and total surrender to His will, and it will happen when He in His benevolence decides to cast on us His glance of grace.

In the next quatrain, the 18th, the Guru says:

ਏਕੈ ਰੂਪ ਅਨੂਪ ਸਰੂਪਾ॥	Ekai rūp anūp sarūpa.
ਰੰਕ ਭਯੋ ਰਾਵ ਕਹੀ ਭੂਪਾ॥	Runk bhayo rāv kahi bhūpa.
ਅੰਡਜ ਜੇਰਜ ਸੇਤਜ ਕੀਨੀ॥	Anddaj jeraj setaj kīnee.
ਉਤਭੁਜ ਖਾਨਿ ਬਹੁਰ ਰਚਿ ਦੀਨੀ॥ ੧੮॥	Utbhuj khān bahur rach dīnee. 18.

Glossary:

ਰੂਪ	Rūp	Form, shape
ਰੰਕ	Runk	Pauper
ਰਾਵ	Rāv	Noble, wealthy one
ਭੂਪਾ	Bhūpa	Lord, ruler
ਅੰਡਜ	Anddaj	From the egg
ਜੇਰਜ	Jeraj	From the placenta
ਸੇਤਜ	Setaj	From sweat
ਉਤਭੁਜ	Utbhuj	From the ground, vegetation
ਖਾਨਿ	Khān	Source of origin

Simply rendered, this quatrain says the Lord is one, manifest in varied forms. Somewhere He is a poor man, at another a Lord, a rich ruler. The Lord creates beings from various sources, such as from the egg, the womb, the sweat, and from the earth.

Having in the previous quatrains spoken of the complete incapacity of created beings to comprehend the creator, or the method and extent of His creation, the Guru now speaks to us of how that One Lord is manifest in such variegated forms on this world. In the first two lines, he says the Lord is *ekai rūp*–uniquely one, but is *anūp sarūpa*–peerless and manifest in very differing forms and shapes. He is *runk bhayo rāv kahi bhūpa*–at one place appears in the form of a *runk*–pauper, and the same Lord is manifest at another place as the *rāv*–affluent great one and at another place he is the *bhūpa*–the ruler, a king.

The Guru says in the third and fourth lines that the Lord has worked his mystery in different ways while bringing this vast variety of created beings into existence. Thus, he says, some are born from the egg, such as the birds, the fish and many reptiles. Still others are born through the placental route, among this category being almost all mammals that gestate inside the mother's womb before emerging into the world. Some are born seemingly from the sweat. In this group are counted the parasites, such as lice, the birthing process and growth of which is facilitated by the sweat on living bodies, where eggs are laid, incubated and where the young then grow and multiply. Lastly are the *utbhuj*–categories of living things that grow from the earth, the vegetation and the flora. In these various ways, all created beings have been brought into existence on this earth.

In the next quatrain, the 19th, the same theme continues. The Guru says:

ਕਹੂੰ ਫੂਲ ਰਾਜਾ ਹੈ ਬੈਠਾ॥	Kahu[n] phūl raja hai baittha.
ਕਹੂੰ ਸਿਮਟਿ ਭਿਯੋ ਸੰਕਰ ਇਕੈਠਾ॥	Kahū[n] simitt bhiyo sankar ikaittha.
ਸਗਰੀ ਸ੍ਰਿਸਟਿ ਦਿਖਾਇ ਅਚੰਭਵ॥	Sagri sristt dikhāye achambhav
ਆਦਿ ਜੁਗਾਦਿ ਸਰੂਪ ਸੁਯੰਭਵ॥ ੧੯॥	Ād jugād sarup suyambhav. 19.

Glossary:

ਬੈਠਾ	Baittha.	Sitting
ਸਿਮਟਿ	Simitt	Contracted, shrunken
ਅਚੰਭਵ	Achambhav	Wonder, miracle
ਸੁਯੰਭਵ	Suyambhav	Self-created

Simply rendered, this quatrain says that at some places the Lord blooms, enthroned as a king while at other places He is shrunken in the form of Shiva. He shows His miraculous deeds to all His creation of the universe. He is the Primal Power, sui generis and eternal, being there since the beginning, and existing forever and ever, through the ages.

The first line has been rendered in two ways by the learned ones. Some render it more literally, as referring to the worldly kings and paupers, or ascetics. For instance, Reema Ānand and Khushwant Singh render these as, "At some places you are like a flower-bedecked king sitting on his throne. At others you are like a hermit shrunken to the bone." Slightly differently, Prof. Talib puts it as, "In one spot is He expanded as universal monarch, in another is He contracted sole." Iqbal Singh puts it as, "Sometimes Thou sitest as a monarch on the lotus flower, sometimes as Shiva, Thou gatherest up the creation". Yet another scholar sees it quite differently as saying, "In this world there live rich kings and poor *yogis*. This looks strange. Only He, the self-illuminated Master, knows the answer to this riddle." It is obvious that some have rendered *phūl* in the sense of to bloom, to expand or grow. This of course is a quite valid interpretation of the word. However, Bhai Talwāṛa, Bhai Vir Singh, and to quite an extent Iqbal Singh, render it as referring to the creation myth according to which Brahma the creator was born of the lotus flower growing from the navel of the Lord Vishnu, who is here deemed as the one Lord. According to this view, the rendering of these two lines would be that at one place the Lord manifests as Brahma enthroned on the lotus flower, performing the expansive creative role. At another place, the same Lord is manifest also as Shiva performing the destructive function; by dissolving everything and merging it all back into His own eternal self. The latter rendering, explaining as it does the two functions of creation and destruction is in line with the lesson contained in the previous quatrains, of the Lord being unknowable, omniscient and immanent in all creation. This, therefore, seems the more convincing view.

In the last two lines, the Guru sums up the message as he says that the Lord shows us the magnificent wonder of all this variegated creation, while He eternally is omnipresent in each atom of it, immanent, pervading all that exists. He is the Primal Being, existing outside of time and space, and in fact the very basis, the very cause of this universe and of time. He is uncreated, not born, self-created, self-illuminating, and is at the beginning of all existence and through the ages of the created universe.

In the next quatrain, the 20th, the Guru, now makes a very personal prayer to this Lord about who He has been telling us in the previous quatrains. He says:

ਅਬ ਰੱਛਾ ਮੇਰੀ ਤੁਮ ਕਰੋ॥	Ab rachha meri tum karo
ਸਿੱਖ ਉਬਾਰਿ ਅਸਿੱਖ ਸੰਘਰੋ॥	Sikh ubār asikh sanghro.
ਦੁਸਟ ਜਿਤੇ ਉਠਵਤ ਉਤਪਾਤਾ॥	Dusatt jitay utthvat utpāta.
ਸਕਲ ਮਲੇਛ ਕਰੋ ਰਣ ਘਾਤਾ॥ ੨੦॥	Sakal malechh karo ruṇ ghāta. 20.

Glossary:

ਉਬਾਰਿ	Ubār	Uplift, raise
ਸੰਘਰੋ	Sanghro	Destroy, slay
ਉਠਵਤ	Utthvat	Rise
ਉਤਪਾਤਾ	Utpāta	Mischief
ਮਲੇਛ	Malechh	Fithy ones, outcasts
ਰਣ ਘਾਤਾ	Ruṇ ghāta	Destroy in battle

Simply rendered, in this quatrain the Guru prays to the Lord to keep him under His protection, uplift his followers to flourish (in faith, intellect and wisdom) and destroy the enemies (negative thinking). Destroy the filthy evil that dares arise (in the mind).

We need briefly to revert to the discussion we had on quatrains 3 and 4. As we had discussed there the theme here has to be understood at two levels. It can be seen firstly as a request, such as any of us would make for protection and help against those who oppose us. However, at a deeper and more relevant level, the plea is to be read as a request for the Lord's help in destroying the evil within. The plea here again is for destroying the evil within, and not any individuals. The Lord is the creator, the master of all, whether evil or good, whether on the right path or the wrong. The Guru's task is to bring the evil ones to the right path and to lead them back to the Lord from whom we all are separated by the veil of illusion cast by *Maya*.

So, the Guru's prayer here in the first two lines is to be seen as a plea to the Lord to rid us of the evil within. What is the Guru seeking in the 2nd line when he says *Sikh ubār asikh sanghro*? He is not seeking merely the destruction and killing of a few who may be opposing him in life or on the battlefield. The reference here is not to the follower of a particular religion or belief system, but to a way of life. The Sikh he is referring to is the one who is treading the right path, and is striving to attain to God-realisation. The *asikh* is the opposite thereof, one who is immersed in worldly and sensual delights, and who has forgotten that this human birth is an extremely precious gift from the Lord. It is believed in Hinduism that this gift is granted to us after going through a cycle of 8.4 million births in different forms of existence. It is only when the human stage is reached do we get the chance to reach the Lord. As the Guru says in *Āsa Mahla* 5, and as we recite daily in the Rehrās Sahib, *Gobind milan ki eh teri bariya*–this is your opportunity, your chance to realise the Lord. The world of *Maya* is however, so alluring and offers so many glittering diversions that most of us lose our way, and blinded by the false glitter start chasing the mirage of sensuous satisfaction. It is protection against this danger that the Guru seeks to invoke. He prays that the *asikh* way within us may be destroyed by the grace of God.

In the last two lines, this is further stressed. The Guru says in line three, *dusatt jitay utthwat utpāta. Dusatt* means evil, bad or sinful, *utthwat* means raise their heads, and *utpāta* means trouble or mischief. This line therefore refers to the evils that raise their head within us, though at the superficial level these two lines can also be interpreted as referring to the opponents of the Guru, and meaning, "destroy the evil ones who dare raise their heads".

In the next quatrain, the 21st, the Guru continues with this theme. He says:

ਜੇ ਅਸਿਧੁਜ ਤਵ ਸਰਨੀ ਪਰੇ॥	Jay asdhuj tav sarni paray
ਤਿਨ ਕੇ ਦੁਸਟ ਦੁਖਿਤ ਹ੍ਵੈ ਮਰੇ॥	Tin kay dusatt dukhit hwai maray

ਪੁਰਖ ਜਵਨ ਪਗ ਪਰੇ ਤਿਹਾਰੇ॥	Purakh javan pagg paray tihāray
ਤਿਨ ਕੇ ਤੁਮ ਸੰਕਟ ਸਭ ਟਾਰੇ॥ ੨੧॥	Tinn kay tum sankatt sabhh ttāray. 21.

Glossary:

ਅਸਿਧੁਜ	Asdhuj	Banner with sword sign
ਦੁਖਿਤ	Dukhit	Trouble, pain, agony
ਸੰਕਟ	Sankatt	Danger, peril

Simply rendered this quatrain says that whosoever seeks the protection of the Lord, whose banner bears the sign of the sword, his enemies suffer pain and are destroyed. The Lord removes all the afflictions and maladies of those who fall at His feet.

The tenth Nanak has here, as at many places in his compositions, used martial terminology. In olden times armies went to battle with each battle lord riding a chariot or elephant displayed prominently on which was his war banner. These banners carried distinguishing signs and marks, so that both armies would know where he was in the melee of conflicting armies. This was a dare to the enemy and was at the same time a help to his own compatriots. Famous warriors had well known signs, and were even sometimes called by the signs on their banners, in addition to their own names. The Guru uses that analogy here and speaks of the Lord as *asdhuj*–the Lord with the sword-banner. He says in the first two lines that those who come under the aegis of that Lord, are rid of all evils, all troubles. The biggest troublemakers, the biggest enemies that we can have are the evil passions within us. These are destroyed only by total surrender to the will of the Lord.

It is a basic tenet of the Sikh belief system that the only path to the Lord is by total surrender to His will. While doing so one has to live the righteous life, fixing the mind on Him, reciting His name constantly and seeing His presence in every created entity. When the mind is thus trained, we will have surrendered our will to Him. That is the stage when our lives will become free of all trouble. The Guru speaks of this phenomenon in these lines. Not only are all troubles and difficulties removed, but also no dangers no perils will ever cross their paths, if any arise the Lord will divert these away.

In the next quatrain, the 22nd, the Guru says:

ਜੋ ਕਲਿ ਕੋ ਇਕ ਬਾਰ ਧਿਐ ਹੈ॥	Jo kal ko ik bār dhiyai hai.
ਤਾ ਕੇ ਕਾਲ ਨਿਕਟਿ ਨਹਿ ਐ ਹੈ॥	Ta kay kāl nikitt neh ai hai.
ਰੱਛਾ ਹੋਇ ਤਾਹਿ ਸਭ ਕਾਲਾ॥	Rachha hoye tāhe sabh kāla.
ਦੁਸਟ ਅਰਿਸਟ ਟਰੇਂ ਤਤਕਾਲਾ॥੨੨॥	Dusatt aristt ttaray(n) tatkāla. 22.

Glossary:

ਕਲਿ	Kal	The Lord
ਕਾਲ	Kāl	Death
ਦੁਸਟ	Dusatt	Evil ones
ਅਰਿਸਟ	Aristt	Trouble, problems
ਟਰੇਂ	Ttaray(n)	Are averted
ਤਤਕਾਲਾ	Tatkāla	Instantaneously

Simply rendered, this quatrain says that Death cannot come near those who once learn how to meditate on the Supreme Lord. They remain protected at all times. All their enemies and sorrows are removed instantaneously.

The term *kal* has been here used for the Lord. This term can be rendered in various ways. Thus, it can mean a machine or a device. It also means peace or tranquility. It can also be seen as a short form of *akkal*–meaning solitude, loneliness. Bhai Vir Singh sees it as meaning peace, calm or beauty, which he says is used here for the Lord. The Mahan Kosh has the more convincing rendering, and says that it is used here as a short form of *Akāl*–the deathless one, which is the most common appellation used for the Lord. In any case, in all these interpretations it is uniformly accepted that the term is used here to denote the Lord. The Guru is saying that, *jo kal ko ik bār dhiyai hai*–those who once meditate on the Lord are saved from the clutches of *Kāl*, which literally means time but is used commonly to refer to death. The phrase *ik bar* literally means 'once', but is not to be construed as meaning that one fleeting act of meditation is all we need. No, the prescription in Sikhism is to be immersed in Him at all times; with each breath must we take His name. As the Guru said in *Rāg Gauṛi Mahla* 5, page 286 SGGS

ਬਾਰੰ ਬਾਰ ਬਾਰ ਪ੍ਰਭ ਜਪੀਐ॥ ਪੀ ਅਮ੍ਰਿਤ ਇਹ ਮੰਨ ਤੰਨ ਧ੍ਰਪੀਐ॥
Bār[n] bār bār prabh japiyai.
Pee Amrit eh mann tann dhrapiyai.

This means that we must recite His name again and again, and filled with this nectar may we sate our mind. Again, he says at the same page in the SGGS:

ਆਠ ਪਹਿਰ ਪ੍ਰਭ ਬਸਹਿ ਹਜੂਰੇ॥ ਕਹੁ ਨਾਨਕ ਸੇਈ ਜਨ ਪੂਰੇ॥
Ātth pahar prabh baseh hajūray.
Kahu Nanak seyi jann pūray.

This means that the ones who focus on the Lord at all hours, and who take His name with each breath are the fulfilled ones. Yes, there indeed is one event that occurs instantaneously, and that is the liberation of the soul. That does happen in a trice when the Lord's glance of grace is accorded to us, which can happen any time when He so wills, but it is our duty to be ever prepared for which we must live the path the Guru has prescribed.

The Guru then says, *ta kay kāl nikitt neh ai hai*–death will never come near those. This is not to be seen as meaning that the person thus meditating becomes physically immortal. The crux of the message is that if someone has rightly worshipped the Lord, his soul will, in time, but only when the Lord so decides, merge with Him, and will thus be taken out of the cycle of birth and death. That moment is not in our hands; it is for the Lord to determine, but the passage to that happy event lies through worshipping Him. Therefore, even if the body must fall prey to death, as all flesh inevitably has to, the person, the soul, will have been taken out of the purview of *Yama*, the Lord of Death. It is in this sense that the Guru says, *ta kay kāl nikitt neh ai hai*–death cannot come near such a one.

In the third line, the Guru says that *rachha hoye tāhe sabh kāla*–the Lord's protection is ever available though all ages. The Lord Himself ever guards such a one. Lastly, the Guru says *dusatt aristt ttaray(n) tatkāla*–The enemies and the troubles of such devotees are averted in a trice. They do not then have to fight these battles alone; the Lord stands as their protector, instantaneously voiding any difficult moment for them. In other words, the Lord grants such devotees the courage and strength to overcome any difficulty.

In the next quatrain, the 23rd, the Guru speaks further about such devotees, and says:

ਕ੍ਰਿਪਾ ਦ੍ਰਿਸਟਿ ਤੁਮ ਜਾਹਿ ਨਿਹਰਿ ਹੋ॥	Kripa dristt tum jāhe nihar ho.
ਤਾ ਕੇ ਤਾਪ ਤਨਕ ਮੋ ਹਰਿ ਹੋ॥	Ta kay tāp tanak mo har ho.
ਰਿੱਧਿ ਸਿੱਧਿ ਘਰ ਮੋ ਸਭ ਹੋਈ॥	Ridh sidh ghar mo sabh hoyi.
ਦੁਸਟ ਛਾਹ ਛ੍ਵੈ ਸਕੈ ਨ ਕੋਈ॥ ੨੩॥	Dusatt chhāh chhwai sakai na koyi. 23.

Glossary:

ਕ੍ਰਿਪਾ ਦ੍ਰਿਸਟਿ	Kripa dristt	Benevolent glance
ਨਿਹਰਿ	Nihar	Watch, see
ਤਨਕ	Tanak	In a trice, a moment
ਰਿੱਧਿ ਸਿੱਧਿ	Ridh sidh	Adept practices and powers
ਦੁਸਟ ਛਾਹ	Dusatt chhāh	Shadow of trouble or evil

Simply rendered, this quatrain says that when the Lord bestows His benevolent glance on someone all their sins and all their troubles are removed in a trice. They are blessed with spiritual powers and earthly treasures. No evil-doer can touch even the shadow of such a one.

The Guru here continues to tell us about what happens to the one who has followed the path to God-realisation in the correct way and has surrendered his own will to the Lord. He says in the first two lines that, *kripa dristt tum jāhe nihar ho*–when the Lord bestows His glance of grace on someone then, *ta kay tāp tanak mo har ho*–all troubles vanish for that person. It is an oft-repeated message that the Lord is not to be achieved by our own efforts and our will. It is our duty, though, to try to achieve the proper state of mind and live in total surrender to His will. These are necessary conditions but are by no means any guarantee that we will reach Him. That happy circumstance will come about only when He so wills, and when will that happen, only He knows. When the Lord does cast his *kripa dristt*–His glance of grace–the troubles of the devotee *–tā kay tāp*–will be over in *tanak*–a trice, a moment.

The term *Tāp* has many meanings such as 'fever', 'heat', 'trouble or tensions' or 'worries'. In the scriptures, however, there is frequent reference to three types of *Tāp* that afflict created beings. The Mahan Kosh lists these as, firstly the *ādhyātmik*–referring to bodily illness, and troubles and evils in the mind such as anger or lust. The second is *ādhibhautik* –meaning troubles caused to us by other beings; and third is *ādhidaivik*–which are caused by natural agency, such as heat, storms etc. In the SGGS these are referred to as *Ādh, Biyādh* and *Upādh*. For instance at page 297, Rāg Gauṛi, the Guru says in the SGGS:

ਆਧਿ ਬਿਆਧਿ ਉਪਾਧਿ ਰਸ ਕਬਹੁ ਨ ਤੂਟੈ ਤਾਪ॥

Ādh, Biyādh and Upādh ras kabhu na tūttai tāp.

The Shabdarth defines *ādh* as troubles pertaining to the mind, such as worries etc.; *biyādh* as referring to the troubles of the body such as fever, ulcers etc., while *upādh* means troubles caused by illusions etc. In short, the term *tāp* refers to the various types of troubles, physical, mental, psychological, internal or external which afflict us. Here, the Guru is telling us that for those who are under the effect of these three maladies the troubles will not be removed.

In the last two lines, the Guru says *ridh sidh ghar mo sabh hoyi*–meaning that such a devotee will have *ridhi* and *sidhi* in his home. The term *sidhi* translates as 'supernatural powers'. It derives from *sidh*–meaning controlled or adept. It was the practice for the *yogis* and some other sects to follow rituals of arcane nature and practice severe austerities to attain to *ridhis* and *sidhis*–become an adept, with supernatural powers that could bring power and wealth. One who successfully reaches his goal in this endeavor is called a *sidh*.

The Guru's path does not advocate the pursuit of such austerities, or even to have in mind a goal such as achieving miraculous powers. In the Sikh belief system, the only requirement is to surrender to the Lord, fixing one's mind on Him alone and following the path the Guru prescribes. The attainment of any such esoteric powers may incidentally come to such a devotee, but it is not his target–it is a mere byproduct of his having reached God-realisation and in reality; these do not matter to him at all. The Guru touches on this aspect in *pauṛi* 29 of the Japji Sahib, which is one of the four dealing with the *yogi* sect. He says, *āp nāth, nāthi sabh ja ki, ridh sidh avra sād*–meaning the Lord Himself is the true *Nāth*, the master of all creation, and the pursuit of *ridhis* and *sidhis* is nothing but a distraction. The term used, *avra sād*, means a different taste, and here it means that instead of the joy of God-realisation such adepts are on the path of worldly pleasures; in other words have strayed from the right path. Here the Guru is saying that those blessed by the Lord's glance of grace will automatically attain to the temporal and spiritual powers that are so sought after by the adepts.

In the next quatrain, the 24th, the Guru says:

ਏਕ ਬਾਰ ਜਿਨ ਤੁਮੈ ਸੰਭਾਰਾ॥	Ek bār jin tumai sambhāra.
ਕਾਲ ਫਾਸ ਤੇ ਤਾਹਿ ਉਬਾਰਾ॥	Kāl phās tay tāhe ubāra.
ਜਿਨ ਨਰ ਨਾਮ ਤਿਹਾਰੋ ਕਹਾ॥	Jin nar nām tihāro kaha.
ਦਾਰਿਦ ਦੁਸਟ ਦੋਖ ਤੇ ਰਹਾ॥ ੨੪॥	Dārid dusatt dokh tay raha. 24.

Glossary:

ਸੰਭਾਰਾ	Sambhāra	Contemplate
ਕਾਲ ਫਾਸ	Kāl phās	Noose of death
ਉਬਾਰਾ	Ubāra	Uplifted
ਦਾਰਿਦ	Dārid	Poverty, misery
ਦੁਸਟ	Dusatt	Evil,
ਦੋਖ	Dokh	Troubles, pain

Simply rendered, this quatrain says that those who have once learnt how to always remember the Lord are saved forever from even the noose of death. Whosoever meditates on the Lord's name suffers not penury and is spared from evil, and from suffering and adversity.

In the first two lines, the Guru says that those who surrender to the Lord need no longer be in fear of death. The term *sambhāra* comes from *sambhāl*, meaning 'taking care of' or 'handing over for safety or protection'. It also has the dictionary meaning of to prop, to nourish, to support or sustain. The term *sambhāra* can also, however, be used as derived from *sambhāran*, which according to the Mahan Kosh also means to remember or to contemplate. It has in this sense been used in the SGGS when the ninth Nanak says in *Rāg Jaitsari Mahla* 9, page 703, SGGS, ਪਾਵਨ ਨਾਮੁ ਜਗਤ ਮੈ ਹਰਿ ਕੋ ਕਬਹੂ ਨਾਹਿ ਸੰਭਾਰਾ–*pāvan nām jagat may har ko kabhoo nāhe sambhāra.* He is saying to us that you have never contemplated the holy name of the Lord. This is the sense in which we have to construe the phrase here. The Guru says that when a person meditates on the Lord, his fear of death vanishes. Contemplating the Lord means fixing one's mind on Him; when this is successfully done, and if the Lord grants His glance of grace, the devotee becomes one with the Lord.

After that, there is no death and no rebirth. One is taken out of that cycle and will have achieved salvation. Obviously, there is then no question of being afraid of death.

In the last two lines, the Guru reiterates and emphasises the message by saying that the devotee who takes the name of the Lord is saved not only from the fear of death, but also from *dārid dusatt dokh*–is also saved from poverty, evil and pain. In other words, the troubles, material, personal, or spiritual, of such a devotee are removed. The short point is that meditating on the one Lord in the manner prescribed by the Guru will bring freedom from want, from troubles, from evils, and will remove the fear of death, from which all humans otherwise suffer.

The last quatrain, the 25th, completes the prescribed portion of this composition. The Guru says:

ਖੜਗ ਕੇਤ ਮੈ ਸਰਣਿ ਤਿਹਾਰੀ॥	Khaṛag keit mai saran tihāri.
ਆਪ ਹਾਥ ਦੈ ਲੇਹੁ ਉਬਾਰੀ॥	Āp hāth dai leh(u) ubāri.
ਸਰਬ ਠੌਰ ਮੋ ਹੋਹੁ ਸਹਾਈ॥	Sarab tthaur mo hoh sahāyi
ਦੁਸਟ ਦੋਖ ਤੇ ਲੇਹੁ ਬਚਾਈ॥ ੨੫॥	Dusatt dokh tay leh(u) bachāyi. 25.

Glossary:

ਖੜਗ ਕੇਤ	Khaṛag keit	Sword banner
ਉਬਾਰੀ	Ubāri.	Save, uplift
ਠੌਰ	Tthaur	Place, situation

Simply rendered this quatrain says, O Lord of the sword banner, I seek your protection. With Your hands guard and protect me. At all times, and in all situations be my support. Save me from wants, evils and pain.

The term *kharag keit* has the same meaning as the term *asdhuj* employed by the Guru earlier, in the 21st quatrain. *Keit* and *dhwaj* both mean flag, or banner. The term *khaṛag* describes a particular type of sword, double-edged and broad bladed. The Guru addresses the Lord again here as the one with the sword banner and seeks His protection, saying he has come to Him for asylum, for succour. He beseeches the Lord to, *āp hāth dai leh ubāri*–please lend him a helping hand and save him, uplift him.

In the last two lines, he prays to the Lord to *sarab tthaur mo hoh sahāyi*–be his support at all places and in all situations. He then seeks the Lord's protection from evil and from all troubles as he says *dusatt dokh tay leh bachāyi*. As we had discussed in the previous quatrain *dusatt dokh* refers to all sorts of troubles and pains that man is heir to, material, personal, or spiritual. It will be seen that there is recognition here that without the Lord's glance of grace we cannot hope to escape the myriad troubles we face enmeshed as we are in the coils of illusion created by our ignorance, by our inability to look beyond the glitter of *Maya* and see the one and only Reality.

With this the prayer begun in the first quatrain with *hamri karo hāthh day rachha* is brought full circle with *āp hāth dai leh ubāri*, both meaning 'lend your helping hand to protect us'. The Lord's intervention is sought for ridding us of our earthly troubles, but above all for removing from within us all evils and ridding us of our spiritual weaknesses.

The *Rehat Maryāda* prescribes that after the 25 stanzas of the *chaupayi*, there will also be read the *Sawwaiya* and the *Dohra* mentioned there. The *Sawwaiya*, also by the tenth Nanak, consists of four lines and is as follows:

ਸ੍ਵੈਯਾ ॥ SAWWAIYA

ਪਾਂਇ ਗਹੇ ਜਬ ਤੇ ਤੁਮਰੇ ਤਬ ਤੇ	Pā(n)ye gaheh jab tay tumray
ਕੋਊ ਆਂਖ ਤਰੇ ਨਹੀਂ ਆਨਯੋ ॥	tab tay koū ānkh taray nahi ānyo
ਰਾਮ ਰਹੀਮ ਪੁਰਾਨ ਕੁਰਾਨ ਅਨੇਕ	Ram Rahīm Puran Quran anek
ਕਹੈਂ ਮਤ ਏਕ ਨ ਮਾਨਯੋ ॥	kahai(n) mut ek na mānyo
ਸਿੰਮ੍ਰਿਤਿ ਸਾਸਤ੍ਰ ਬੇਦ ਸਭੈ ਬਹੁ ਭੇਦ	Simrit sastra beid sabhay bahu
ਕਹੈਂ ਹਮ ਏਕ ਨ ਜਾਨਯੋ ॥	bhed kahai(n) ham ek na jānyo
ਸ੍ਰੀ ਅਸਿਪਾਨ ਕ੍ਰਿਪਾ ਤੁਮਰੀ ਕਰਿ ਮੈ	Sri aspān kripa tumri kar mai na
ਨ ਕਹਯੋ ਸਭ ਤੋਹਿ ਬਖਾਨਯੋ ॥	kahyo sabh tohe bakhānyo

Glossary:

ਪਾਂਇ	Pā(n)ye	Feet, shelter, refuge
ਸਿੰਮ੍ਰਿਤਿ ਸਾਸਤ੍ਰ	Simrit sāstra	Hindu scriptures
ਆਂਖ ਤਰੇ	Ānkh taray	To have under the eye, to pay attention
ਅਸਿਪਾਨ	Aspān	Wielder of the sword

The Guru says, *pā(n)ye gaheh jab tay tumray tab tay koū ānkh taray nahi ānyo* - 'after I took refuge at Thy feet, I have never looked for protection from any other'. This is a restatement of the basic tenet of the Sikh faith; we must single-mindedly focus on the one Lord. Sikhism is a strictly monotheistic belief system. There is but one God and all other powers that we can think of are merely His creations, functioning as per His command. Having sought refuge with that Lord there should then be no question of relying on any other power, because those powers are bound to be inferior and lesser. Fix your mind on the Supreme Lord, is the message here. *Koyi ānkh taray* translates literally as 'none under my eye'. It is an idiomatic way of saying that the attention remains constantly fixed on the One, does not wander at all; so, the Guru says I do not even look at another.

The Guru then says, *Ram Rahīm Puran Quran anek kahai(n) mat ek na mānyo*. This literally translates as'*Rama* and *Rahīm*, the *Puranas* and the *Quran*, tell us much about their own belief systems, but I do not depend on or follow those teachings'. The term *Rama*, which is the name of one of the incarnations of Lord Vishnu in Hinduism, is frequently used to denote God, and is used here in that sense. The term *Puranas* refers to the eighteen epics, which also contain a great deal of religious instruction and are treated as part of the holy books of the Hindu faith. The term *Rahīm* is used to denote God in Islam and is thus referred to in the *Quran, or Qura'an*, the Holy Book of Muslims. The phrase is therefore meant here to refer to the belief systems of the Hindus and the Muslims, the main belief systems most prevalent then. The Guru is stressing that a new belief system has come into being now and he follows not the old systems, but is focused on this new faith, this new path.

In the same tenor, the Guru speaks further, and this time more specifically of the Hindu belief system, the followers of which were by far the more numerous among the Guru's followers. He says, *Simrit Sastra beid sabhay bahu bhed kahai(n) ham ek na jānyo.* This translates as 'the *Simritis* and the *Sastras*, and the *Vedas*, speak of many esoteric teachings but I credit not a single one'. The *Sastras,* numbering six, are the holy books of the Hindus and considered the repositories of all religious and other connected knowledge. The *Simritis*, reckoned to be 27 in number, are treatises on religious and other mystical matters. The *Vedas*, four in number are supposed to be the last word in religious education. The Guru says all these holy books speak of many secret and esoteric things. They reveal to us knowledge of many a diverse philosophy and a great many things of the world.

The Guru is telling us that rather than expending time and energy on these matters, it is better to focus one's mind on the Lord. Not that these holy and learned ones are useless, but these cannot be our ultimate guide. More important than all these esoteric practices and knowledge is the constant recitation of the name of the Lord. The message is that living an honest and productive life, in complete surrender to Him, is the path we need to follow.

Lastly, the Guru addresses the Lord directly and says, *Sri Aspān kripa tumri kar mai na kahyo sabh tohe bakhānyo.* This translates as 'Oh the Sword-Bearer, it is not by my effort but by your blessing that I am able to say these words in praise of Thee'. The Guru's use of martial imagery, while imparting a spiritual message, is again very visible here. He addresses the Lord as *Aspān*–Wielder of the Sword, and acknowledges the Lord as the source of this message. In other words, the Guru is telling us that our abilities are but gifts from the Lord and whatever worthwhile we are able to do or say is only by His grace.

We finally have the *dohra*, a couplet, with which this part of the Rehrās Sahib is completed. This composition is also by Guru Gobind Singh *ji* and it says:

ਦੋਹਰਾ ॥	DOHRA
ਸਗਲ ਦੁਆਰ ਕਉ ਛਾਡਿ ਕੈ ਗਹਿਓ ਤੁਹਾਰੋ ਦੁਆਰ ॥	Sagal duār kau chhādd kai gahiyo tuhāro duār.
ਬਾਂਹਿ ਗਹੇ ਕੀ ਲਾਜ ਅਸ ਗੋਬਿੰਦ ਦਾਸ ਤੁਹਾਰ ॥	Bā(n)h gahay ki lāj us Gobind dās tuhār.

Glossary:

ਦੁਆਰ	Duār	Door, here refuge
ਬਾਂਹਿ	Bā(n)h	Hand, arm
ਗਹੇ	Gahay	Taken up, held

This couplet literally translates as, 'Ignoring all others, I have taken refuge at Your door. Hold my hand; give me Your protection because I am Your servant'.

The concept of total surrender to the Lord is stressed once again in a different way. The Guru says he has looked at various belief systems but has abandoned all those. The only path he follows now is the path of recitation of the Lord's name; it is only at the Lord's door that he seeks succour. The Guru says since he has handed himself over to the Lord may He hold his hand and keep him safe under His protection. The term ਬਾਂਹਿ ਗਹੇ–*bā(n)h gahay* derives from *bā(n)h*, meaning arm, and *gahay* meaning held or accepted. The Guru is saying that he has handed over his own self to the Lord and placed himself unconditionally in surrender at the Lord's door, at His mercy. Now, therefore, it is for the Lord to do as he wishes with him. The Guru's prayer, however is for the Lord to protect his honour, to uphold the sanctity of the relationship of servant and master that the Guru has voluntarily accepted, after testing many other doors and having found them wanting.

With this, the Chaupayi as prescribed in the *Rehat Maryāda* is complete. There are, however many respected organisations, which believe that some more hymns from the same composition in the Dasam Granth should form part of the Chaupayi, and thus a longer version of this *bāṇi* ought to have been included in the *Nitnem*. Many *guttkas* will be found incorporating the longer version in the *Nitnem*. These issues do deserve a more detailed discussion but this is not the subject of our present study. We must not forget that the *Rehat Maryāda* has been drawn up by very learned men; it has been given the seal of approval by the duly constituted body representing the Sikhs. It, therefore, deserves to be respected and observed. It is, however, an undeniable fact that highly respected bodies of Sikhs prescribe longer versions of the *Nitnem*, which many devotees recite as part of their daily prayers. There can be no objection to this also because there is no bar in the *Rehat Maryāda* from reciting as many additional *bāṇis* as a devotee may choose.

Apart from those who advocate a longer version of the *Chaupayi*, there are also some learned ones who hold that an altogether different *Chaupayi* from the Dasam Granth, beginning with:

pranvo ād ekankāra, jal thal mahial kio pasāra.
ād purakh abgat ab(i)nasi, lok chatrr das jot prakāsi.

should have been accorded higher priority and been included in the *Nitnem* rather than the Chaupayi officially prescribed in the *Rehat Maryāda.*

These issues are of interest to many and deserve detailed discussion. It would, therefore be the subject matter of a separate book, the Lord willing. Here, however, we are confining ourselves to a discussion of only the *bāṇis* included as per the *Rehat Maryāda* in the *Nitnem*.

15

THE THIRD NANAK

We now come to the concluding hymns of the Rehrās Sahib. This part begins with six *pauṛis* from the *Anand Sahib,* which is a composition by the third Nanak. Before we commence to try to understand these six *pauṛis*, it would be useful to take a look at the life of the author of this composition. The third Nanak, Guru Amar Das came to be the spiritual guide of the nascent Sikh community at an unusually late age. He was 73 years old when, in 1552 AD, his mentor, Guru Angad Dev invested him with the Guru's status.

He was born at village Basarke Gillan in Amritsar district on *Vaisakh Sudi* 14th, *Samvat* 1536, corresponding to 5th May, 1479. His father was Tej Bhan Bhalla, and mother's name according to *Guru Granth Vishwakosh* of Dr. Rattan Singh Jaggi, was Lakho. He was married in 1502 AD, on 11 *Māgh Samvat* 1559. His wife's name was Ramo, says the Vishwakosh. They had four children, two sons; Mohan and Mohri and two daughters; Bibi Dani and Bibi Bhani, the latter was to marry Bhai Jettha, who was to become the fourth Nanak, Guru Ramdas. His parents were orthodox *Vaishnavites*, and Amar Das was known for his spiritual bent of mind and he would go on pilgrimages to Hardwar.

It is said that he happened to hear some hymns of Guru Nanak from Bibi Amro, the daughter of Guru Angad, who was married to the nephew of Guru Amar Das. He was so taken by the Guru's message that he went to see Guru Angad Sahib at Khadur Sahib; he decided to stay on there, and serve the Guru. He was then in his sixties and nearly 25 years elder to Guru Angad. He served the Guru with great and single-minded devotion, rising early to fetch water from the Beas River for Guru's bath, and then go gather wood for the *Langar*–the community kitchen.

His unstinting devotion for over a decade won the Guru's acceptance and he was installed as the third Nanak. Guru Angad's sons had shown great resentment at the growing affection the Guru was showing to Amar Das and therefore, the Guru advised him to set up a new town on the banks of Beas. He moved, after his installation, to this new town of Goindwal. The Guru's sons continued their inimical intentions and for some time he decided to withdraw from the affairs of the community. However, he was soon sought out by the elders of the community, led by Baba Buddha and brought back to active participation. The Guru's sons also realised their error and came round.

Guru Amar Das contributed greatly to propagating the Sikh faith. He organised the community into 22 well-marked geographical areas and established centres, called *Manjis*, for each under the charge of a devout Sikh. He himself visited and also sent Sikh missionaries to different parts of India to spread Sikhism. He strengthened the tradition of *Guru ka Langar*–the community kitchen, and made it compulsory for the visitor to the Guru saying, *'Pehle Pangat Phir Sangat'*, meaning that if you want to meet the Guru go sit with the devotees for *Langar*. It is said that even the emperor Akbar when he came to see the

Guru, had to first join in the community meal before he could have an interview with Guru Sahib. It is said that the Emperor, impressed with this egalitarian practice wanted to give a grant for the *Langar*, but the Guru politely declined, and persuaded Akbar to instead, waive off the pilgrim's tax on non-Muslims.

He preached against Sati and advocated widow-remarriage. He asked the women to discard *Purdah*–the veil. He greatly strengthened the new faith by instituting a new set of ceremonies for birth, marriage and death, thus giving the infant faith a distinctive identity. He constructed a stepped well, called *Baoli*, at Goindwal Sahib. This had eighty-four steps and it became the first Sikh pilgrimage centre.

He got compiled into book form the hymns of his predecessors, Guru Nanak and Guru Angad. These books later became a good source when the SGGS was to be compiled. He also composed numerous hymns, the number of which is 885 according to Dr. Jaggi. This includes the Anand Sahib, and hymns in other formats such as the *Ashttpadi*, the *Sohilay*, the *Chhant* and so on. The *Alahnīa(n*) which are recited as part of the death ceremonies are also his composition.

Guru Amardas Sahib found his son-in law, Ramdas to be the most deserving successor, ahead of his own sons. He thus continued the tradition that Guruship was not a birthright, but would go by spiritual merit. He passed away at the age of 95, on *Bhadon Sudi* 14th, *Samvat* 1631, corresponding to September 1, 1574 AD.

16

THE SONG OF BLISS

We now come to this sublime *bāṇi* of the third Nanak, the Anand Sahib, of which the first five and the 40th *pauṛi* are part of the *Nitnem* prescribed in the *Rehat Maryāda*.

The *Shabdarth* of the SGPC tells us that the Anand Sahib was recited by the Guru on the birth of his grandson Ānand, son of Mohri, in 1554 AD. It was of course an occasion of great joy for the family and it is customary at such times to sing and dance and make merry. The hymn was, however meant to convey a much higher lesson. When great souls speak, whatever the context, their words will carry for us a precious message, as the third Nanak himself tells us in *Rāg Suhi Mahla* 3, page 755, SGGS, where he says, ਮਹਾ ਪੁਰਖਾ ਕਾ ਬੋਲਣਾ ਹੋਵੈ ਕਿਤੈ ਪਰਥਾਏ॥ ਓਇ ਅੰਮ੍ਰਿਤ ਭਰੇ ਭਰਪੂਰ ਹਹਿ ਓਨਾ ਤਿਲੁ ਨ ਤਮਾਇ॥– *Maha purkha ka bolna hovai kitai parthhāye. Oye amrit bharay bharpūr heh ona til na tamāye.* The Guru uses the occasion to impart to us a message, which while reflecting in its own way his worldly joy, speaks of a spiritual joy.

He is saying that a much greater *Anand,* bliss, comes from singing the praises of the one Lord. The Guru began this hymn with, *Anand bhaya meri māye*–O my mother I am in bliss. The cause for this elation, he says, is *sat Guru mai pāia* –I have found the true Guru. It follows that when we find the Guru, which for the Sikh today is the SGGS, we can embark on the journey to the Lord. Celebrate this vital first step therefore. Here, in the first five *pauṛis* and the final, the fortieth, *pauṛi* the Guru expatiates on the joys of meeting the Guru, and through him the Lord Himself. It is customary to read these six together on all the important occasions in the life of a Sikh. Thus, these are recited at the conclusion of the nonstop recitation of the SGGS, called the *Akhandd Patth,* in fact at all important ceremonies including the wedding rituals known as *Anand Karaj*.

This set of six *pauṛis* describes progressively the stages of the mind as it learns to be with the Lord. The first *pauṛi* speaks of the joy of the first meeting. The second is a reminder to the mind to not slip up and to steadfastly keep up the relationship. The third *pauṛi* is a prayer to the Lord to grant that this interaction successfully continue, the fourth is an exhortation to the godly ones to remain immersed in the singing of praises of the Lord and in the fifth he says this gift will come from the Lord only to the truly fortunate. In the fortieth *pauṛi,* he concludes this aspect of his message by speaking of the fulfillment of all ones wishes and the attainment of the ultimate knowledge. In the remaining *pauṛis* of the Anand Sahib from the sixth to the 39th, he tells us the process we must follow as we try to move on this path.

The Guru begins this composition with the title and, as is usual in all the Guru's compositions, with an invocation to the Lord. He says:

ਰਾਮਕਲੀ ਮਹਲਾ ੩ ਅਨੰਦੁ	Rāmkali Mahla 3Anand
ੴ ਸਤਿਗੁਰ ਪ੍ਰਸਾਦਿ ॥	Ek onkār satgur prasād

This is one of the shorter forms of the invocation to the Lord, used in the SGGS and the full form of which is the *Mool Mantra* as found at the start of the Japji Sahib at page 1 of the SGGS. The Guru is invoking the Lord's help in successful completion of this composition and he says the Lord is one, he is the only Truth and He is to be reached, or realised, through the Grace of the True Guru. The digit 1-one-is a part of this formulation throughout the SGGS. It is meant to indicate the unique oneness of the Lord; there can be none like Him. *Om* is the celestial sound indicating the immanent aspect of the transcendent Lord, as incarnate in His creation. Here it is used as a combination word *onkār*, deriving from *Om*, as we have discussed, and *kār* meaning the Creator.

We come now to the first *pauṛi* where the Guru says:

ਅਨੰਦੁ ਭਇਆ ਮੇਰੀ ਮਾਏ ਸਤਿਗੁਰੂ ਮੈ ਪਾਇਆ॥	Anand bhaya meri māye satguru mai pāia.
ਸਤਿਗੁਰੁ ਤ ਪਾਇਆ ਸਹਜ ਸੇਤੀ ਮਨਿ ਵਜੀਆ ਵਾਧਾਈਆ ॥	Satgur ta pāia sehaj seti mann vajīya vādhhāīya
ਰਾਗ ਰਤਨ ਪਰਵਾਰ ਪਰੀਆ ਸਬਦ ਗਾਵਣ ਆਈਆ ॥	Rāg ratan parvār parīya sabad gāvaṇ āīya.
ਸਬਦੋ ਤ ਗਾਵਹੁ ਹਰੀ ਕੇਰਾ ਮਨਿ ਜਿਨੀ ਵਸਾਇਆ ॥	Sabdo ta gāvoh hari kera mann jini vasāia.
ਕਹੈ ਨਾਨਕੁ ਅਨੰਦੁ ਹੋਆ ਸਤਿਗੁਰੂ ਮੈ ਪਾਇਆ॥੧॥	Kahay Nanak Anand hoa satguru mai pāia.1.

Glossary:

ਅਨੰਦੁ	Anand	Bliss
ਮਾਏ	Māye	My mother
ਸਹਜ ਸੇਤੀ	Sehaj seti	With spiritual knowledge, alsorendered as 'easil 'easily'

ਰਾਗ ਰਤਨ	Rāg ratan	Precious *rāgs*, musical measures personified
ਪਰਵਾਰ ਪਰੀਆ	Parvār pariya	The *rāginis*, variants of these *rāgs*
ਮਨਿ	Mann	The mind, also heart

The first line translates literally as, 'oh mother mine I am in bliss because I have met the True Guru'. The path to the Lord in Sikhism is said to exist through the true Guru. For the Sikh today this true Guru is the SGGS. The Guru is the one who gives us the right direction, the right guidance so that we learn to recite the name of the Lord within our hearts and start becoming worthier of His grace. Therefore, when we find that Satguru, the true Guru, it is indeed a matter of joy and an occasion to celebrate. The learned ones have construed the term *māye* variously. Bhai Vir Singh, Khushwant Singh and Bhai Harnam Singh view it as 'mother'. Prof Sahib Singh takes it in the sense of companion or the congregation itself. Bhai Talwara takes it to mean sister or close female friend. When we are in the midst of extreme pain or joy it is natural that our thoughts turn to our mothers. It seems the more appealing view that the Guru is using this tender folk idiom to denote his great pleasure and joy.

The Guru then adds in the second line that along with his true mentor, his Guru, he has, also attained *sehaj*. As we had discussed earlier this term has many meanings. Here also many learned ones, for instance Prof. Sahib Singh and Bhai Talwāṛa take the term in the sense of the mystical calmness and steadiness, that spiritual equilibrium which we achieve as we move up the ladder to the Lord. On the other hand, Bhai Vir Singh, Khushwant Singh and the Mahan Kosh, take it in the sense of 'ease'. They render this line as meaning that I have easily found the Guru and therefore my mind resounds with congratulations. The former view assumes that as we find the Guru the *sehaj* also simultaneously comes. The latter view speaks only of the lucky happenstance that has enabled us to find the Guru. It is only after we have walked sufficiently along that tough path the Guru prescribes that we could hope to reach that much coveted stage of *sehaj*. The first view is also valid in its own way, but in the light of this discussion, the latter rendering seems here the more appealing. The term *vadhhāīya*, pronounced with a nasal 'n' sound at the end, literally means 'may it prosper and grow'. It is a commonly used term for congratulating someone who has obtained something highly valuable or desirable. Here the Guru is telling us that his finding the true Guru is deserving of such congratulations, and he says these are ringing out in his heart. It is just another way of saying he is in utter bliss.

The Guru then further resorts to metaphors for joy. He says, *rāg ratan parvār parīya sabad gāvaṇ āiya*(last word to be pronounced with the nasal 'n'). This literally means 'the jewels of musical measures and their sub-measures have come to sing the *shabad*, the Guru's word'. The *rāg* is the musical measure in the Indian system. Not only does it govern all musical composition but also it is ascribed a semi divine status, each as that *rāg* personified. The sub-measures and other slight variations are called the *parvār*, meaning family, and *parīya*, which literally means fairies but is used here to denote the sub-measures of the *rāgs*. The Guru is telling us that the bliss in his heart is getting reflected in an upsurge of the word of God, the *shabad*, in his heart and it feels as if these are being sung in the various musical measures and sub-measures. It is as if all these measures have come as music personified to him and are singing the Lord's message within him.

Then he says to us 'sing the word of God, all those who have Him in the mind'. The presumption here is that at the occasion of great joy in finding a true Guru many have come to share in the joy of their Guru. The Guru is asking them to also join in the singing of the *shabad* of the Lord.

The Guru concludes with 'sayeth Nanak, I am in bliss; I have found my True Guru'. This is just a summing up of the thought with which he had started this hymn. The joy within him is bubbling over. Having had the great good luck to find the true Guru he speaks out his delight again.

In the second *pauṛi,* the Guru says:

ਏ ਮਨ ਮੇਰਿਆ ਤੂ ਸਦਾ ਰਹੁ ਹਰਿ ਨਾਲੇ ॥	Ay mann meriya tu sada rahu har nālay.
ਹਰਿ ਨਾਲਿ ਰਹੁ ਤੂ ਮੰਨ ਮੇਰੇ ਦੂਖ ਸਭਿ ਵਿਸਾਰਣਾ ॥	Har nāl rahu tu mann meray dūkh sabh visārṇa.
ਅੰਗੀਕਾਰੁ ਓਹੁ ਕਰੇ ਤੇਰਾ ਕਾਰਜ ਸਭਿ ਸਵਾਰਣਾ ॥	Angīkār oh karay tera kāraj sabh sawārṇa.
ਸਭਨਾ ਗਲਾ ਸਮਰਥੁ ਸੁਆਮੀ ਸੋ ਕਿਉ ਮਨਹੁ ਵਿਸਾਰੇ ॥	Sabhna gala samrath swāmi so kio manhu visāray.
ਕਹੈ ਨਾਨਕੁ ਮੰਨ ਮੇਰੇ ਸਦਾ ਰਹੁ ਹਰਿ ਨਾਲੇ ॥੨॥	Kahay Nanak mann meray sada rahu har nālay.2.

Glossary:

ਵਿਸਾਰਣਾ	Visārṇa	To forget
ਅੰਗੀਕਾਰੁ	Angikār	To accept
ਸਭਨਾ ਗਲਾ ਸਮਰਥੁ	Sabhna gala samrath	All powerful, omnipotent

The Guru says in the first line *ay mann meriya tu sada rahu har nālay* –O my mind, stay ever with the Lord. In the Anand

Sahib, the Guru has adopted an easy, folksy style of presenting his profound message. As one reads this composition aloud, the soothing lilt carries one into a trance like state where the Lord seems somehow nearer. The Guru sort of uses a musing tone and speaks to himself, in the process asking all of us to follow the same path. He says stay focused on the Lord always. See Him in all that exists, feel his presence in the surroundings, in the air we breathe, in the beauty of nature that we see around us. Keep Him ever in the mind.

He then says, *Har nāl rahu tu mann meray dūkh sabh visārṇa*–O my mind, stay with the Lord for He removes all worries. The message in the first line is slightly elaborated here by the Guru as he adds that the Lord removes all worries. Worries and troubles come from our foolish belief that we can rely on human agency for redressal. The day we realise that all that happens is in the hands of the one Lord, and all human powers are puny and ineffectual in comparison, the state of surrender to Him will start to settle in. Soon all these worldly sorrows will begin to lose their dread for us, they will be forgotten.

The Guru then adds, *angīkār oh karay tera kāraj sabh sawārṇa.* This translates as 'when He accepts you as His own then all your affairs will become straightened out'. In other words, those who surrender to the Lord and become His dear ones will find their worldly problems also resolved without too much effort. As the Guru says in *Soratth Mahla* 3, page 638, SGGS, *achint kamm karay Prabh tin kay jin har ka nām piāra*–the Lord will resolve the issues for His true devotees without their asking. If you love Him, He removes your worldly problems without your even knowing it.

This point is further underscored in the next line where the Guru says, *sabhna gala samrath swāmi so kio manhu visāray.*

This translates as, 'the Lord is omnipotent why do you forget Him'. The lesson in this hymn focuses on the need to stay with the Lord, meaning to surrender entirely to His will and to cast one's actions, one's entire life in accordance with His way, as explained to us by the Guru. Therefore, the Guru stresses the point by telling us that the Lord to whom we are to surrender is all-powerful, can thus meet all our needs, and can look after us in this life and beyond. Do not, therefore, ever forget Him, says the Guru; recite His name with each breath.

In the last line, the Guru says, *kahay Nanak mann meray sada rahu har nālay.* This translates as 'sayeth Nanak, O my mind, stay ever with the Lord: recite His Name'. This repetition in the concluding line is a reiteration of the underlying message of this hymn, which had opened with the line, *ay mann meriya tu sada rahu har nālay.* The Guru is making sure we understand the message which is 'do not ever forget Him; recite His name with each breath'.

In the third *pauṛi* of the Anand Sahib, the Guru says:

ਸਾਚੇ ਸਾਹਿਬਾ ਕਿਆ ਨਾਹੀ ਘਰਿ ਤੇਰੈ ॥	Sāchay sahiba kia nāhi ghar terai
ਘਰਿ ਤ ਤੇਰੈ ਸਭੁ ਕਿਛੁ ਹੈ ਜਿਸੁ ਦੇਹਿ ਸੁ ਪਾਵਏ ॥	Ghar ta terai sabh kichh hai jis deh so pāvay.
ਸਦਾ ਸਿਫਤਿ ਸਲਾਹ ਤੇਰੀ ਨਾਮੁ ਮਨਿ ਵਸਾਵਏ ॥	Sada sipht salāh teri nām mann vasāvay
ਨਾਮੁ ਜਿਨ ਕੈ ਮਨਿ ਵਸਿਆ ਵਾਜੇ ਸਬਦ ਘਨੇਰੇ ॥	Nām jin kai mann vasiya vājay sabad ghaneray
ਕਹੈ ਨਾਨਕੁ ਸਚੇ ਸਾਹਿਬ ਕਿਆ ਨਾਹੀ ਘਰਿ ਤੇਰੈ ॥੩॥	Kahai Nanak sachay sāhib kiya nāhi ghar terai.3.

Glossary:

ਘਰਿ ਤੇਰੈ	Ghar terai	In thy abode
ਪਾਵਏ	Pāvay	Obtains, attains
ਸਿਫਤਿ ਸਲਾਹ	Sipht salāh	Praises, encomiums
ਘਨੇਰੇ	Ghaneray	Numerous, intense

The Guru here points again to the Lord's omnipotence in the first line of this *pauṛi* as he rhetorically poses the question, *sāchay sahiba kia nāhi ghar terai.* This literally translates as 'O true Master, what is not in your house'. This is a colloquial way of saying that all powers, all created things are within the Lord's hand. His is the power to give life and to take it, nay, beyond that to make or unmake the very universe in which we exist. The theme propounded in the previous *pauṛis* is being emphasised again. The Lord is omnipotent, and therefore it is in our own interest that we ever remain under His protection, acknowledging no other master.

The Guru makes the message clear and puts the issue beyond any doubt, as he himself answers the query he had posed in the first line, and further expands the argument. He says, *ghar ta terai sabh kichh hai jis deh so pāvay.* This can be translated as 'everything is to be found in Thine abode and he receives on whom You choose to bestow'. To the question he had raised in the first line, *kia nāhi ghar terai,* he now provides the answer and says, *ghar ta terai sabh kichh hai.* The omnipotence of the Lord having been averred the Guru now makes it clear that the blessings of the Lord exist unbounded but are not ours to take as a matter of right. These come only to those who are blessed with His glance of grace. The hidden message is that we must make ourselves worthy of His beneficence. For reaching that coveted state, we have to live the life of the *Gurmukh*, following scrupulously the path prescribed by the Guru, in other words staying ever with the Lord.

In the third line, the Guru carries his lesson a step further as he says, *sada sipht salāh teri nām mann vasāvay*–ever sing Thy praise and keep Thy Name in our minds and hearts. It is possible to construe this line as meaning that by singing the praises of the Lord constantly, His Name will begin to reside in our hearts. The more appealing rendering, however, is the one followed by most learned ones; that among the innumerable gifts the Lord bestows is the biggest one, the gift of singing His praises and of engraving His Name on our minds. This gift can lead us to salvation and is hence the most precious.

In the next line, the Guru tells us what happens when the Name of the Lord resides constantly in our hearts. He says, *nām jin kai mann vasiya vājay sabad ghaneray*–the mind in which His Name resides, resounds joyously to the strains of the divine music. The term *ghaneray* means numerous, or intense. The term *shabad* literally means word, but is usually employed in Sikhism for the hymns of the saints and the Gurus. The singing of these brings peace and bliss to the mind of the seeker. The lucky event of the Lord's name residing in our hearts will be followed by a joy as if the word of the Lord were resonating intensely within us. To the true devotee that is bliss beyond anything this world can bring.

The Guru then concludes as usual in this composition, repeating the crux of the message he had stated in the first line of the hymn. He says, *kahai Nanak sachay sāhib kiya nāhi ghar terai.* The Guru says, 'sayeth Nanak, O true Lord there is nothing lacking in thy house'. The omnipotent Lord is the Lord creator of all that exists and thus all things, all powers by definition have to be residing with Him.

In the fourth *pauṛi* of the Anand Ṣahib, the Guru now narrates his own state of mind. He says:

ਸਾਚਾ ਨਾਮੁ ਮੇਰਾ ਆਧਾਰੋ ॥	Sācha nām mera ādhāro
ਸਾਚੁ ਨਾਮੁ ਅਧਾਰੁ ਮੇਰਾ ਜਿਨਿ	Sāch nām adhār mera jin
ਭੁਖਾ ਸਭਿ ਗਵਾਈਆ ॥	bhukha sabh gavāīya
ਕਰਿ ਸਾਂਤਿ ਸੁਖ ਮਨਿ ਆਇ ਵਸਿਆ	Kar sānt sukh mann āye vasia
ਜਿਨਿ ਇਛਾ ਸਭਿ ਪੁਜਾਈਆ ॥	jin ichha sabh pujāīya
ਸਦਾ ਕੁਰਬਾਣੁ ਕੀਤਾ ਗੁਰੂ ਵਿਟਹੁ	Sada kurbaṇ kita Guru vittoh
ਜਿਸ ਦੀਆ ਏਹਿ ਵਡਿਆਈਆ ॥	jis diya eh vaddiāīya
ਕਹੈ ਨਾਨਕੁ ਸੁਣਹੁ ਸੰਤਹੁ ਸਬਦਿ	Kahai Nanak suṇho santo
ਧਰਹੁ ਪਿਆਰੋ ॥	sabad dharoh piāro
ਸਾਚਾ ਨਾਮੁ ਮੇਰਾ ਆਧਾਰੋ ॥੪॥	Sācha nām mera ādhāro. 4.

Glossary:

ਆਧਾਰੋ	Ādhāro	Base, support
ਭੁਖਾ	Bhukha	Hunger, greed
ਪੁਜਾਈਆ	Pujāīya	Have fulfilled
ਧਰਹੁ	Dharo	To repose in

(Note: the words, Bhukha, Gavāīya, Pujāīya, ichha, vittoh, diya and vaddiāīya are all to be pronounced with a nasal 'n' sound)

The Guru begins this hymn with, *sācha nām mera ādhāro*– the true Name of the Lord is my only support. The term *ādhāro* literally means base or support, but can also mean the food that sustains life. In either sense, the message remains the same but the rendering as support or base is the more appealing. After having stressed to us the vital importance of forever being with the Lord, the omnipotent one from whom we can hope to receive all possible gifts including the ultimate gift of freedom from the cycle of death and rebirth, he says that for himself the true Name has become the sole support. This means he seeks succour from no other power or authority, he recognises no ruler or master except the one Lord Himself. In other words, he has put into total practice the lesson he has been narrating for us in the previous three *pauṛis*, and lives now with the Lord. The Name of the Lord has become the basis of his very existence.

In keeping with his style, the Guru now gently takes the narration a step further and says, *sāch nām adhār mera jin bhukha sabh gavāiya*–the true Name is my support, it has removed all hunger from within me. This is the delicious irony of this path. The Lord possesses all powers and can, if he so chooses, give us anything that we may crave. However, once His name resides with us, the craving suddenly vanishes. Now we have the possibility of obtaining all the material things we may have been yearning for, but when this stage is reached the hunger also vanishes. We may have started the journey in the expectation of rewards of the things of this world but the successful completion of the journey will remove any such weakness. The Name of the Lord removes the dross of greed and avarice from within us and leaves us happy and fulfilled. This is what the Guru is narrating; he has no hunger, no craving left within him. He has achieved true satiation and satisfaction.

The Guru restates the above position as he says, *kar sānt sukh mann āye vasia jin ichha sabh pujāiya*–I am at peace and joy now resides in my heart and mind, all my desires have been fulfilled. It is of course a well-documented fact that when the name resides in the heart, it ousts all negative thoughts and feelings from within us. The true men of God (as against the bogus godmen who so sorely afflict the Indian polity and society) are known to live quiet lives of peace and serenity and radiate an aura that soothes even the casual bystander. We are in bliss indeed, when the Lord grants us the great gift of residing in our hearts.

In the fourth line, the Guru says, *sada kurbaṇ kita Guru vittoh jis diya eh vaddiāīya*–I am forever a sacrifice to the Guru who has such greatness. The greatness of the Guru lies in his mentoring us on the path to God-realisation. It is the path he outlines, his constant guidance as we wend our way down this blessed path, slipping often and then recovering again as the Guru's message shines like a beacon keeping our feet steady. For the Sikh, this Guru is the SGGS and from it are we to seek daily guidance to see we are not deviating from the path. Here the hymn having told us that peace now resides in the heart he gives credit for it to the Guru and expresses his ineffable love by saying he would gladly be a sacrifice at any time to such a Guru.

In the next, and the concluding, line the Guru says, *kahai Nanak suṇho santo sabad dharoh piāro*–sayeth Nanak, O saints, fix your devotion firmly in the *shabad.* This term has been used here to indicate the name of the true Lord. He is stressing on us that the path requires us to fix our minds on the Lord. He addresses the seeker and prescribes *sabad dharoh piāro.* To attain the goal begin by developing in the heart love for His Name. The terms name, *bāṇi* or *shabad* are often used interchangeably to denote the divine. Love for the Name, or for the *bāṇi*, or *shabad*, is the first step on that path which can lead to the Lord. To make the message clear beyond any doubt the Guru then repeats the first line and says the true Name is his support.

In the fifth *pauṛi,* the Guru says:

ਵਾਜੇ ਪੰਚ ਸਬਦ ਤਿਤੁ ਘਰਿ ਸਭਾਗੈ ॥	Vājay panch sabad tit ghar sabhāgai
ਘਰਿ ਸਭਾਗੈ ਸਬਦ ਵਾਜੇ ਕਲਾ ਜਿਤੁ ਘਰਿ ਧਾਰੀਆ ॥	Ghar sabhāgai sabad vājay kala jit ghar dhārīya
ਪੰਚ ਦੂਤ ਤੁਧੁ ਵਸਿ ਕੀਤੇ ਕਾਲੁ ਕੰਟਕੁ ਮਾਰਿਆ ॥	Panj dūt tudh vas kītay kāl kanttak māria
ਧੁਰਿ ਕਰਮਿ ਪਾਇਆ ਤੁਧੁ ਜਿਨ ਕਉ ਸਿ ਨਾਮਿ ਹਰਿ ਕੈ ਲਾਗੇ॥	Dhur karam pāia tudh jin kao se nām har kai lāgay.
ਕਹੈ ਨਾਨਕੁ ਤਹ ਸੁਖੁ ਹੋਆ ਤਿਤੁ ਘਰਿ ਅਨਹਦ ਵਾਜੇ ॥੫॥	Kahai Nanak teh sukh hoa tit ghar anhad vājay.5.

Glossary:

ਪੰਚ ਸਬਦ	Panch sabad	Melody of five kinds of instruments
ਸਭਾਗੈ	Sabhāgai	Fortunate ones
ਕਲਾ	Kala	Power
ਧਾਰੀਆ	Dhārīya	Sustained
ਪੰਚ ਦੂਤ	Panj dūt	Five evils
ਕਾਲੁ ਕੰਟਕੁ	Kāl kanttak	Fear of death
ਧੁਰਿ ਕਰਮਿ	Dhur karam	Destiny, blessing from the beginning
ਪਾਇਆ	Pāia	Granted

The Guru in this *pauṛi* speaks to us of the bliss that envelops the lucky ones in whose heart the Lord begins to dwell, the ones who are on the right path to God-realisation. In the first line of this hymn, he says, *vājay panch sabad tit ghar sabhāgay*–in that fortunate house the five types of music resounds. The term *panch sabad* derives from the five types of musical instruments commonly recognised in the Indian system of music. The first type is known as the *tār*, meaning strings and these include instruments such as the guitar or the *sitār*. The second category is the *chumm*, meaning leather based, and these include the *tabla,* drums. The third is *dhāt*, meaning metal based instruments such as the cymbals, the *ghungru* or the *chheṇa*. Fourth type is called the *ghaṛay*, meaning pots and referring to Indian instruments such as *jal tarang*. Lastly, we have the *phūk wālay*, meaning instruments working on the blown air, such as the flute or the *shehnāyi*. The sense of the term *panch sabad* here has, however, to be taken as meaning divine music. The playing of the five types of music is meant to indicate the best possible and most melodious tunes. The devotee on the right path, who lives with the Lord in his heart, will feel as if this magnificent music, these blissful tunes are playing within him. The heavenly music drowning out all petty distractions is the reward that the true seeker attains. This is the stage when the mystical tenth door, the *dasam duār*, opens and one gets a glimpse of the Lord. Such an abode is fortunate indeed, which is what the Guru is here telling us when he says, *tit ghar sabhāgai*.

In the second line, he says, *ghar sabhāgay sabad vājay kala jit ghar dhārīya*–fortunate is the house where divine music resounds, where the Lord has bestowed of His might. In the gentle soothing style he adopts in this composition, the Guru adds to his lesson by reiterating the point he made in the first line and then adding *kala jit ghar dhārīya.* The Guru is stressing here that if a person has attained this happy state and the *panj sabad* are resounding within him then be aware that it is a gift from the Lord. The Guru says that it is the *kala*–might or power, infused within that *ghar*–abode or house–which brings this happy result. The reference is obviously to the Lord's might, for only He can bring about this greatly coveted outcome for the lucky recipient. The term *dhāriya* literally means has sustained, taken on, assumed but is to be understood here as meaning injected or infused into something or someone.

In the third line, he says, *panj dūt tudh vas kītay kāl kanttak māria*–You have subdued the five demons and destroyed the pain and dread of death. The term *panj dūt* is commonly used to indicate the five major evils afflicting humans. These are the main obstruction, which we have to overcome before we can move upwards spiritually. These are *kām, krodh, lobh, moh and ahankār*, meaning respectively desire, anger, greed, attachment and ego. The Guru is saying that the Lord has helped overcome these five. The term *dūt* literally means messenger or ambassador but is also used to indicate the agents of *Yama*, the God of Death in the Hindu belief system. The five evils are as dreadful for us as the agents of death. These are overcome for the true devotee, says the Guru. The term *kāl kanttak* literally means the thorn of time or of death. This fear is likened here to a thorn constantly hurting us and making us suffer helplessly. This painful thorn has been removed by the grace of the Lord for these lucky ones, says the Guru.

The Guru then says, *dhur karam pāia tudh jin kao se nām harkay lāgay*–those whom you bless with such good fortune get attached to the recitation of Your Name. After having exhorted us through the previous four *pauṛis* to fix the mind on the Lord and telling us the joy and bliss that ensues, the Guru now puts in a slight caveat. He says only those will be able to fix their minds on the Lord in whose lot the Lord has thus ordained. This refers to the belief that we carry with us the baggage of our past actions. The free will granted by Him to the human enables us to make choices while we wend our way through this life on this earth. Right choices will lead us closer to Him and wrong choices distance us. Unfortunately, too many of us will stray because the false glitter and allure of the material things of the world, and the ephemeral joys of the flesh are more attractive than the seemingly hard path that leads to the Lord. The Lord will assign us the good fortune when He decides we have earned it; that decision being entirely His. Those blessed ones in whose lot the Lord has *dhur karam pāia*, bestowed the glance of His grace will *nām har kai lāgay*, feel the urge to attach themselves to the Name of the Lord. In other words, only these lucky ones will follow the right path, while the rest wander after false attractions.

In the concluding line, the Guru, in keeping with the style he has adopted in this composition, reiterates the point he made in the first line where he had told us, *vājay panch sabad tit ghar sabhāgai*. Here he says, *kahai Nanak teh sukh hoa tit ghar anhad vājay*–sayeth Nanak, peace comes to that house, that mind and the *anhad* resounds. The term *anhad nād*, is used to describe that unstruck melody that echoes through the universe from the very beginning. This divine music is the Lord's signature and it is heard only by those in tune with the Lord's way. The Guru here says that it resounds in that heart, within that *ghar,* which literally means house but refers here to the mind of the true devotee. In that mind, there is the divine symphony playing joyfully and as a result there is *sukh*, peace and calm and serenity and above all freedom from all troubles of the body or the soul.

We now come to the fortieth *pauṛi* of the Anand Sahib, which is prescribed to be read after the first five, as part of the Rehrās Sahib. Here, the Guru sums up the message set out in this composition. He speaks of the joys of fulfillment as he says:

ਅਨਦੁ ਸੁਣਹੁ ਵਡਭਾਗੀਹੋ ਸਗਲ	Anand suṇho vaddbhāgīyo
ਮਨੋਰਥ ਪੂਰੇ ॥	sagal manorath pūray
ਪਾਰਬ੍ਰਹਮੁ ਪ੍ਰਭੁ ਪਾਇਆ ਉਤਰੇ ਸਗਲ	Pārbrahm prabh pāia utray
ਵਿਸੂਰੇ ॥	sagal visūray
ਦੂਖ ਰੋਗ ਸੰਤਾਪ ਉਤਰੇ ਸੁਣੀ	Dūkh rog santāp utray suṇi
ਸਚੀ ਬਾਣੀ ॥	sachi bāṇi
ਸੰਤ ਸਾਜਨ ਭਏ ਸਰਸੇ ਪੂਰੇ ਗੁਰ	Sant sājan bhaye sarsay pūray
ਤੇ ਜਾਣੀ ॥	gur tay jāṇi
ਸੁਣਤੇ ਪੁਨੀਤ ਕਹਤੇ ਪਵਿਤੁ ਸਤਿਗੁਰੁ	Suṇtay punīt kahtay pavit
ਰਹਿਆ ਭਰਪੂਰੇ ॥	satgur rahia bharpūray
ਬਿਨਵੰਤਿ ਨਾਨਕੁ ਗੁਰ ਚਰਣ ਲਾਗੇ	Binwant Nanak gur charaṇ
ਵਾਜੇ ਅਨਹਦ ਤੂਰੇ॥੪੦॥	lāgay vājay anhad tūray.40.

Glossary:

ਮਨੋਰਥ	Manorath	Purposes, aims, ambitions, wishes
ਵਿਸੂਰੇ	Visūray	Frustations, worries
ਸੰਤਾਪ	Santāp	Woes, afflictions
ਸਰਸੇ	Sarsay	Gladdened, made happy
ਪੁਨੀਤ	Punīt	Pure, chaste
ਬਿਨਵੰਤਿ	Binwant	Humbly request
ਤੂਰੇ	Tūray	Bugles, here meant for melodies

The Guru begins this hymn with, *Anand suṇho vaddbhāgīyo sagal manorath pūray,* which literally translates as 'O fortunate ones, listen to *Anand* all your hopes will reach fulfillment'. Those who have followed the lesson set out in the opening stanzas and have, therefore, stayed steadfastly on the path prescribed by the Guru will have their wishes fulfilled, says the Guru. He speaks of these faithful ones as *vaddbhāgīyo*, because they are indeed the fortunate ones. All their *manorath* will be achieved. This term derives from *mann* and *arth*, meaning the mind and aims or ambitions. Whatever you have in mind will be attained following on this path. The men of God will seek union with Him, while many will seek baser, less important things of this world. Even for these there will be fulfillment; it is a different matter though that they will soon realise that baubles can please only for a brief while, the joy they may bring is fleeting. The true lasting joy will come only when the hunger for these toys is overcome and we see the Lord in everything. At that time, we will have achieved the state of being ever with the Lord, which the Guru had described as *sada rahu har nālay.* Having come to this fortunate stage there will be *Anand*, bliss, resounding within us and all our aims will be achieved.

In the second line, the Guru explains why the bliss is now within us. He says, *pārbrahm prabh pāia utray sagal visūray*–the transcendent Lord has been realised and all discord has ended, all frustrations overcome. In life, we are constantly in the midst of strife and troubles. The term *visūray* refers to these afflictions and the Guru says we will be rid of all these; *utray* literally translates as 'will be offloaded, or removed'. All these are off our backs when we have realised the *Pārbrahm prabh*–the Lord who is beyond measure, who is transcendent.

In the third line, the Guru tells us what happens when we listen to the true word. He says, *dūkh rog santāp utray suni sachi bāṇi*–pain, illness, mental-suffering have been cured by listening to the true scripture. The entire lesson in this hymn is to exhort us to recite the name of the Lord and follow the path as delineated by the true Guru. When we obey this dictum our *dūkh rog santāp* will be removed, will vanish. In the previous line, he had said, *utray sagal visūray*. Now in a very similar vein he says, the *dūkh rog santāp* will be removed. These terms literally mean sorrows, illnesses and troubles of the mind respectively. *Rog* is used for illnesses of the body, physical ailments. *Dūkh* is a broader term meant to convey all other types of problems, mainly the ones that are due to causes beyond us, which occur due to outside agency. The term *santāp* is used for troubles within the mind, any issues at all that cause mental agony, from whatever cause. All these various issues will get resolved says the Guru here.

In the fourth line, he speaks of the men of God, the saintly ones, and says *sant sājan bhaye sarsay pūray gur tay jāṇi*–the saintly ones are in bliss having obtained from the perfect Guru the divine knowledge. The vital role of the Guru is stressed here, as is the need to strictly follow the path he delineates for us. If we do that then we become like the saints, the *gurmukhs*, the beloved of the Lord; and our minds will transcend all earthly worries and be ever in divine bliss, experiencing the playing of the celestial music in our hearts. *Sarsay* derives from *sa* and *rus* meaning having joy, or being in bloom. The term here indicates great and growing joy. Having heard the true Guru and obtained from him the true knowledge, the godly ones are now in utter bliss.

In the fifth line, the Guru tells us that those who utter His name and those who hear it from the heart are both purified. He says, *suṇtay punit kahtay pavit Satgur rahiya bharpūray*–those who listen to or recite the *Gurbāṇi* are purified and made holy, and they are imbued totally with the awareness of the true Guru, the Lord Himself. He had begun the message in this hymn with the exhortation to listen to this hymn of bliss and he is now confirming to us that if we listen, and not just superficially but truly imbibe it, then we are bound to be purified. Even those who recite it are made holy, their life is sanctified. The true Guru, in this case, the Lord Himself will wholly reside in the hearts, and they will achieve the coveted realisation that the Lord pervades all that exists. Our lives will then become meaningful for we will be on the path to salvation, which, of course, the Lord will grant only when he so chooses.

The Guru now concludes this lesson with, *binwant Nanak gur charaṇ lāgay vājay anhad tūray*–Nanak humbly sayeth, celestial music will resound within those who are attached to the Guru's feet. Once again, the Guru's vital role in our spiritual journey is stressed here. The Guru here, in the true style of the achieved soul, shows utter humility and puts us profound message in the form of a humble request. It will be seen throughout the SGGS that the Gurus have never ever tried to be aggressive or boastful, notwithstanding their almost divine spiritual status. All their teaching is couched in gentle suggestions and polite requests. The teacher who is proud of his spiritual elevation or of his erudition is never the true guide. The first sign of the right master is the total absence of vanity or pride. This is to be found amply within the SGGS, which for the Sikh is the true Guru, ever present, ever available to guide us through this perilous maze of false worldly attractions. Seek guidance from this Guru, surrender yourself at this Guru's feet and the divine music will resound within you. The term *anhad tūray* refers to the celestial music that has from the day of creation echoed through the universe, as the signature of the Lord creator. *Anhad* means without limit, or immeasurable, beyond human capacity to comprehend. *Tūray* is used for any wind instrument, meaning instrumenst played with the mouth, such as the bugle, the horn or the trumpet. Humans on this earth usually play these on joyful occasions. The Guru says such a great joy will blossom in the heart and mind of the one who surrenders at the Guru's feet, in other words, faithfully follows the path the Guru prescribes.

With this, the six prescribed hymns from the Anand Sahib are complete.

17

THE JEWELS ON THE PLATE

We now come to the concluding part of the Rehrās Sahib. This part begins with the hymn, by the fifth Nanak, known as the *Mundāvaṇi*, which is placed at page 1429, SGGS. This word translates both as the seal and as the riddle as we will discuss later. The Guru says:

ਮੁੰਦਾਵਣੀ ਮਹਲਾ ੫	*Mundāvaṇi Mahla 5*	
ਮੁੰਦਾਵਣੀ	*Mundāvaṇi*	Seal, or Riddle.

The fifth Nanak, while compiling the SGGS has used this hymn called the *Mundāvaṇi* as the concluding hymn. This term means a seal indicating authority or finality, but it can also mean, in the *Potthohāri* dialect, a riddle. This would be clear from the following composition by the third Nanak, in *Rāg Soratth,* page 645, SGGS:

ਥਾਲੈ ਵਿਚਿ ਤੈ ਵਸਤੂ ਪਈਓ ਹਰਿ	Thhālai vich tai vastu paīyo
ਭੋਜਨੁ ਅੰਮ੍ਰਿਤੁ ਸਾਰੁ॥	har bhojan amrit sār
ਜਿਤੁ ਖਾਧੈ ਮਨੁ ਤ੍ਰਿਪਤੀਐ ਪਾਈਐ	Jit khādai mann triptīai paīai
ਮੋਖ ਦੁਆਰੁ॥	mokh duār
ਇਹੁ ਭੋਜਨੁ ਅਲਭੁ ਹੈ ਸੰਤਹੁ ਲਭੈ	Eh bhojan alabh hai santoh
ਗੁਰ ਵੀਚਾਰਿ॥	labhai gur vīchār

ਇਹ ਮੁੰਦਾਵਣੀ ਕਿਉ ਵਿਚਹੁ ਕਢੀਐ	Eh mudāvaṇi kio vichoh
ਸਦਾ ਰਖੀਐ ਉਰਿ ਧਾਰਿ॥	kaddhīai rakhīai ur dhār
ਏਹ ਮੁਦਾਵਣੀ ਸਤਿਗੁਰੂ ਪਾਈ ਗੁਰਸਿਖਾ	eh mudāvaṇi Satguru pāyi
ਲਧੀ ਭਾਲਿ॥	gursikha ladhi bhāl
ਨਾਨਕ ਜਿਸੁ ਬੁਝਾਏ ਸੁ ਬੁਝਸੀ ਹਰਿ	Nanak jis bujhāye su bujhsi har
ਪਾਇਆ ਗੁਰਮੁਖਿ ਘਾਲਿ॥	pāia gurmukh ghāl.

The term *Mundāvaṇi* is here clearly used in the sense of riddle or a poser. The Guru says in this hymn that there are three things served in the platter partaking of which we will achieve satiation in our mind and soul and reach the door to salvation. He then adds that this feast is *alabh*–unmatched–and is to be enjoyed only through meditating on the Lord. He then says we should never let this reality escape from us, rather we should imbibe it deeply in our minds. The true Guru has posed us the riddle and only the *Gursikh* will discover its meaning. Then he concludes with the oft-repeated caveat that it is not merely by our effort that we will find the answer. He says, *Nanak jis bujhāye su bujhsi*, O Nanak only he will unravel the mystery and discover the answer to whom the Lord grants this privilege. He then also presents the path as he says *har pāia gurmukh ghāl*–the Lord will be reached by hard work, following the Guru's path.

As we can see this hymn by the third Nanak presents a thought very similar in content and presentation to the *Mundāvaṇi* used here by the fifth Nanak. It will help us in trying to understand the Guru's message and it makes clear that the term has elsewhere also been used in the SGGS in the clear sense of 'riddle'. The learned ones have interpreted it in both senses. We can take it as meaning that the Guru is putting the final seal of authentication on the SGGS with this riddle, which also contains a profound message.

As we can see, though the word means the authenticating seal of closure but it is, in fact, not the final hymn in the SGGS. After this hymn there are more hymns by the fifth Nanak and then the *Rāg māla* which is the final *bāṇi* in the SGGS. This lists some *rāgas*, Indian musical measures, even though these are not an index of the *rāgas* used in the SGGS and, further, it mentions some *rāgas* not used at all in the SGGS. It is today an inseparable part of the SGGS, as the *Rehat Maryāda* of the Sikhs approved by the SGPC confirms in Article XI, which says:

a. *"The reading of the whole Guru Granth Sahib (intermittent or non-stop) may be concluded with the reading of Mundawani or the Rag Mala according to the convention traditionally observed at the concerned place. (Since there is a difference of opinion within the Panth on this issue, nobody should dare to write or print a copy of the Guru Granth Sahib excluding the Rag Mala). Thereafter, after reciting the Ānand Sahib, the Ardas of the conclusion of the reading should be offered and the sacred pudding (Karhah Prashad) distributed".*

Scholars have since long been arguing whether the *Rāg māla* should be treated as *Gurbāṇi*. Many learned ones think it should, while others just as eminent are of the view that it should not. The purpose of our discussion here, however, is not to argue the relative merits of those arguments and suffice it to say that the SGPC has put the closure to this issue with the above direction contained in the *Rehat Maryāda*. Our concern here is the *Mundāvaṇi*.

The Guru says:

ਥਾਲ ਵਿਚਿ ਤਿੰਨਿ ਵਸਤੂ ਪਈਓ ਸਤੁ ਸੰਤੋਖੁ ਵੀਚਾਰੋ ॥	Thhāl vich tin vastu paīyo sat santokh vīchāro

ਅੰਮ੍ਰਿਤ ਨਾਮੁ ਠਾਕੁਰ ਕਾ ਪਇਓ ਜਿਸ ਕਾ ਸਭਸੁ ਅਧਾਰੋ ॥	Amrit nām tthākur ka paiyo jis ka sabhas adhāro
ਜੇ ਕੋ ਖਾਵੈ ਜੇ ਕੋ ਭੁੰਚੈ ਤਿਸ ਕਾ ਹੋਇ ਉਧਾਰੋ ॥	Jay ko khāvai jay ko bhunchai tis ka hoye udhāro
ਏਹ ਵਸਤੁ ਤਜੀ ਨਹ ਜਾਈ ਨਿਤ ਨਿਤ ਰਖੁ ਉਰਿ ਧਾਰੋ ॥	Eh vasat taji nah jāyi nit nit rakh ur dhāro
ਤਮ ਸੰਸਾਰੁ ਚਰਨ ਲਗਿ ਤਰੀਐ ਸਭੁ ਨਾਨਕ ਬ੍ਰਹਮ ਪਸਾਰੋ ॥੧॥	Tamm sansār charan lag tarīai sabh Nanak brahm pasāro

Glossary:

ਥਾਲ	Thhāl	A metallic serving plate, a salver
ਭੁੰਚੈ	Bhunchai	Consumes, eats
ਉਰਿ ਧਾਰੋ	Ur dhāro	Hold in the heart
ਪਸਾਰੋ	Pasāro	Expanse, spread

The Guru says in the first line of this hymn, *thhāl vich tin vastu paīyo sat santokh vīchāro*–in the plate are three things: truth, contentment, and contemplation. What is the platter the Guru refers to here? Most learned ones render it as metaphorically referring to the SGGS, the scripture. Prof. Sahib Singh, however, construes it to mean that the platter is the heart and mind of the human where these three gifts will reside when he immerses himself in the Name. The more appealing view is the former. The Guru is now summing up and says that in the holy book that you have just read these three invaluable assets are to be found. Bhai Vir Singh renders this line to mean that in the platter there are *sat santokh*–truth and contentment, on which we should ponder. He takes the word *vīchāro* as an exhortation from the Guru to think and ponder about these. The third gift, he says, is the *amrit nām* mentioned in the next line where the Guru says, *amrit nām tthākur ka paiyo*. Thus, according to Bhai Sahib the nectar of the Lord's name is the third offering along with truth and contentment. Most learned ones however take the view that *vīcharo*–meditation–is the third gift, and this seems the more appealing rendering, though both views make eminent sense.

Then in the next line, the Guru says, *amrit nām tthākur ka paiyo jis ka sabhas adhāro*–there is the nectar, the name of the Lord, which sustains all. He thus lists a fourth, and most valuable, article also to be found on this platter. He says there is also the Name of the Lord, which is like nectar and sustains all. The Name in almost all belief systems is employed as referring to the creator Himself. In Sikhism, it certainly is so and since the Lord sustains all existence, the Name of the Lord is rightly the support on which we all depend, on which the entire space-time continuum is resting. In other words, the visible universe and the apparent flow of time around us is nothing but the Lord Himself manifest in His immanent form.

He then says in the third line, *jay ko khāvai jay ko bhunchai tis ka hoye udhāro*–if one eats or partakes he is saved. The Guru is telling us that in front of us is laid a rich repast where we have the opportunity to feast on the divine, soul sustaining food in the form of truth, contentment, mediation. Further, we have the chance to drink down this highly nutritious intake with the divine nectar in the form of the Lord's Name. The reference is of course to the SGGS, which is the platter containing these offerings for the soul. If we have the good sense enough to partake of these, we will be uplifted. The term *udhāro* means freedom, liberation, lifting up and is here intended to indicate salvation, freedom from the cycle of birth and death.

The Guru then, in the fourth line, adds to this lesson with the advice, *eh vasat taji nah jāyi nit nit rakh ur dhāro*–this precious gift must never be renounced; bear it ever in the mind. This is to underline the message elsewhere given, that we must constantly focus our minds on the Lord, recite His name with every breath. In the Japji Sahib the Guru says, in the 32nd *pauṛi*, *ik doo jībho lakh hoye*–if we had hundreds of thousands of tongues, *lakh lakh geṛa ākhiye ek nām jagdis*–with each we must recite the name of the Lord hundreds of thousands times. In the same vein, we are told here never to let slip the awareness of that divine presence from within us.

The Guru says in the concluding line, *tamm sansār charan lag tarīai sabh Nanak brahm pasāro*–the journey from this dark world will be accomplished by focusing on the Lord's feet, and this vast expanse we see is His creation. The term *tamm* means intense dark. It is the belief in the Sikhism that we are a soul separated from the *Paramatma*, the Lord, because of our own actions and mistakes. We have been placed in this world to give us the opportunity to win our way back to the Lord, and unite and merge into Him. This world is full of false attractions and many dark things. The path to the Lord leads across a dark gulf called the *bhavsāgar*–meaning literally the ocean of dread. This unknown chasm is dark and strange to us. From our present predicament and for the journey across this gap our only support is the Lord. Therefore, the lesson here says fix your mind on Him; keep His feet ever in your heart. This is another way of saying that we should live in total surrender to Him. This device will help us across. One who has imbibed this lesson from the heart will not only go smoothly across but will then be able to see the entire universe as the manifestation of the Supreme Being.

We now come to the last hymn in this *bāṇi* and in the SGGS, where it is placed at page 1429, before the *Rāg māla*. The Guru expresses his gratitude to the Lord. He says:

ਸਲੋਕ ਮਹਲਾ ੫ ॥	Slok Mahla 5
ਤੇਰਾ ਕੀਤਾ ਜਾਤੋ ਨਾਹੀ ਮੈਨੋ ਜੋਗੁ ਕੀਤੋਈ ॥	Tera kīta jāto nāhi maino jog kītoyi
ਮੈ ਨਿਰਗੁਣਿਆਰੇ ਕੋ ਗੁਣੁ ਨਾਹੀ ਆਪੇ ਤਰਸੁ ਪਇਓਈ ॥	Mai nirguṇiāray ko guṇ nahi āpay taras paioyi
ਤਰਸੁ ਪਇਆ ਮਿਹਰਾਮਤਿ ਹੋਈ ਸਤਿਗੁਰੁ ਸਜਣੁ ਮਿਲਿਆ ॥	taras paiya mehrāmat hoyi satgur sajaṇ miliya
ਨਾਨਕ ਨਾਮੁ ਮਿਲੈ ਤਾਂ ਜੀਵਾਂ ਤਨੁ ਮਨੁ ਥੀਵੈ ਹਰਿਆ ॥੧॥	Nanak nām milai ta(n) jiva(n) tann mann thhīvai haria

Glossary:

ਤੇਰਾ ਕੀਤਾ	Tera kīta	Thy doings and actions
ਜਾਤੋ	Jāto	Known
ਜੋਗੁ ਕੀਤੋਈ	Jog kītoyi	Enabled, made capable
ਨਿਰਗੁਣਿਆਰੇ	Nirguṇiāray	One without merit
ਮਿਹਰਾਮਤਿ	Mehrāmat	Mercy
ਥੀਵੈ ਹਰਿਆ	Thhīvai haria	Becomes green, blooms

In the first line, the Guru says, *tera kīta jāto nāhi maino jog kītoyi*–I did not even recognise your blessing, O Lord yet you made me capable of serving you. This hymn should be taken as a continuation of the previous hymn called the *Mundāvaṇi*. That hymn indicated the completion of the task of compilation of the *Sri Guru Granth Sahib* which has since then been revered as the holy book and has been formally installed by the tenth Nanak, in 1708, as the ever present Guru from whom the Sikh community was to seek guidance for the future. In this hymn, he expresses his gratitude to the Lord and says he was not even aware of the mysterious doings of the Lord, and yet the Lord had granted him the great gift of the capacity to serve Him. Our very birth on this earth in this human form is a huge gift, entirely unearned. Not only the gift of the human form, but also the greater gift of the *Gurbāṇi* enshrined in the SGGS, to be forever our guide as we seek to achieve life's most important goal. The Guru, in this hymn, expresses his gratitude by saying he was ignorant and yet the Lord had found him worthy of rendering this service.

In the second line he says, *Mai nirguṇiāray ko guṇ nāhi āpay taras paioyi*–I am worthless, without any good qualities, yet you have taken pity on me. The Guru has often stressed that the Lord is not to be reached through our efforts but will Himself decide when to grant us salvation. This is not to say that we, therefore, need not worry about our actions at all; that we are now free to indulge in any wrongdoing to which our ego driven mind leads us. Rather, the Guru is emphasising the vital importance of humility, telling us not to be overtaken by what Sikhism calls *haumai*. In common parlance this term is often understood to mean ego, hubris or excessive pride. In spiritual terms, *haumai* is considered as the biggest hurdle to God-realisation. Spiritually speaking, this term is used to describe a sense of selfness, a sense of duality, of seeing oneself as something different from the creator. Once we overcome it, God-realisation floods in; in a trice, we will see the reality that was always around us but to which we were blinded by our *haumai*. The Lord has taken pity, says the Guru, and overlooking my total lack of merit He has granted me the honour of completing this task; as he said in the first line *maino jog kītoyi*–has made me capable.

In the third line, the Guru says, *taras paiya mehrāmat hoyi satgur sajaṇ miliya*–you took pity, granted me your grace and I could meet the true Guru. The meeting with the true Guru is the most important event in the spiritual life of any person. It is the good luck of a Sikh; and great foresight by the tenth Nanak, that the Guru is available in the form of the SGGS from the very first breath a Sikh draws on this earth. It is by the Lord's grace that we encounter the true Guru, who is our *sajaṇ*, our truest friend. The Guru is saying that he has experienced this grace and it is a sign that the Lord ignored the lack of merit and took pity on His servant.

The Guru concludes this hymn with *Nanak nām milai ta(n) jiva(n) tann mann thhīvai haria*–Nanak says if I am blessed with the Name, I am spiritually alive and my body and mind is in bloom.

Life on this earth is lived at various levels. We live the worldly life in which we find livelihood; we may be householders or have position of responsibility or power in society. All those roles are important in the sense that without that aspect being on a solid base it may be difficult to embark on our true mission, the search for the way back to the Lord from whom we were parted by our own mistakes and from whom our *haumai* is keeping us separated. For that purpose, our only support is the Name, not power, nor wealth, nor learning. With humility in the heart and in a sense of total surrender to Him, we have to learn to imbibe His name so that we breathe it with each breath and consume it with each morsel. The Guru is telling us in this final summing up that we, meaning our spiritual selves, are truly alive only when the Name of the Almighty is within our hearts and this will happen only when the Lord grants us this gift. When it happens our minds and bodies will be truly in bloom, as the Guru assures us when he says *tann mann thhīvai haria.* The term *Haria* means 'becomes green', but is to be understood here as meaning a state of blossoming and growing. When we are granted the gift of the Name, we are truly alive. Alive, not in the mere sense of breathing and existing, but greatly thriving in body and mind, and above all in the spirit.

With this, we come to the end of the Rehrās Sahib as prescribed in the *Rehat Maryāda* for the Sikhs.

As we have discussed earlier, many well-respected Sikh organisations prescribe longer versions of the Rehrās Sahib. Many of us will have seen the *guttkās* where the Rehrās Sahib includes an additional hymn at the start, before the *so dar*, and many hymns after the last hymn prescribed in the *Rehat Maryāda*. The *slok* usually recited at the start of the evening prayers is by Guru Nanak. It begins with, *Dukh dāru sukh rog bhaya.* There are three additional hymns usually recited at the conclusion of the Rehrās Sahib. These are by the Fifth Nanak, a *pauṛi,* beginning with *tithhai tu samrath*, and two *sloks* beginning with *antar gur ārādhṇa, jihva jap gur nāo,* and *ṙakhay rakhaṇhār āp ubārayan.* For the convenience of the many who recite these as part of the daily routine, a discussion on the first hymn is included as Appendix 1, and the three concluding hymns as Appendix 2.

Similarly, we had noted that many of these *guttkās* include extra quatrains to be recited as part of the *Chaupayi*. Some of these are added at the beginning, and some at the conclusion of the officially approved *chaupayi*. There is also another issue emerging from the differing views among some scholars that not this *Chaupayi* but instead another *Chaupayi* beginning with, *praṇvo ād ekankāra, jal thhal mahiyal kiyo pasāra,* should have been part of the daily liturgy. However, that is not the subject of our discussion here. We will, perhaps, have occasion to consider these issues at another time, in another book.

APPENDIX

1

Of the hymns most usually recited by Sikhs everywhere, though not included in the prescription laid down in the *Rehat Maryāda*, the first one, recited before the *so dar*, begins with, *Dukh dāru sukh rog bhaya.* It is from the *Āsa di Vār*, *Mahla* 1, page 469, SGGS. The Guru says:

ਸਲੋਕ ਮਹਲਾ ੧	Slok Mahla 1
ਦੁਖੁ ਦਾਰੂ ਸੁਖੁ ਰੋਗ ਭਇਆ ਜਾ	Dukh dārū such rog bhaia ja
ਸੁਖੁ ਤਾਮਿ ਨ ਹੋਈ ॥	sukh tām na hoyi.
ਤੂੰ ਕਰਤਾ ਕਰਣਾ ਮੈਂ ਨਾਹੀ ਜਾ ਹਉ	Tu[n] karta karṇa mai nāhī ja
ਕਰੀ ਨ ਹੋਈ॥	hau karī na hoyi.
ਬਲਿਹਾਰੀ ਕੁਦਰਤਿ ਵਸਿਆ॥	Balihāri kudrat vasya.
ਤੇਰਾ ਅੰਤੁ ਨ ਜਾਈ ਲਖਿਆ॥ ਰਹਾਓ॥	Tera unt na jāyī lakhiya.Rahāo.
ਜਾਤਿ ਮਹਿ ਜੋਤਿ ਜੋਤਿ ਮਹਿ ਜਾਤਾ	Jāt maih jot(e) jot(e) maih jātā
ਅਕਲ ਕਲਾ ਭਰਪੂਰਿ ਰਹਿਆ॥	akal kala bharpūr rahiya.
ਤੂੰ ਸਚਾ ਸਾਹਿਬ ਸਿਫਤਿ ਸੁਆਲਿਓ	Tu[n] sachā sahib sipht suāliyo
ਜਿਨਿ ਕੀਤੀ ਸੋ ਪਾਰਿ ਪਇਆ॥	jinn keeti so pār paiya.
ਕਹੁ ਨਾਨਕ ਕਰਤੇ ਕੀਆ ਬਾਤਾ ਜੋ	Kahu Nanak kartay kīya bāta jo
ਕਿਛੁ ਕਰਣਾ ਸੋ ਕਰਿ ਰਹਿਆ॥	kichh karṇa so karr rahiya.

Glossary:

ਤਾਮਿ	Tām	Then
ਕਰਣਾ	Karṇa	The doer
ਜਾਤਿ	Jāt	Creation, beings
ਜੋਤਿ	Jot(e)	The Lord's light
ਜਾਤਾ	Jāta	Can be seen
ਅਕਲ	Akal	Complete
ਕਲਾ	Kala	Portion
ਸੁਆਲਿਓ	Suālio	Beautiful

Simply translated this *slok* says that worldly pleasure is a disease because it causes us to forget the Lord, and pain is the cure for this disease. The Lord is the Doer, and I (human beings) can control nothing and whatever happens is because of His *hukam*, His ordinance. The Guru says he is a sacrifice to that Lord who resides in all nature, and is thus immanent, and whose limits we cannot measure. The Lord is manifest in all that exists and all beings are part of Him. The Lord is the only reality, His qualities are splendid and those who laud Him find salvation. Praise the Lord who, at His will, does that which is required to be done. Let us now look at it in more detail.

In line one, the Guru says the pleasures of the world become a disease when there is no devotion for the Lord and then pain becomes the medicine. We all see in real life how excess pleasure manifests as a disease for which pain is then the cure. Where there is overindulgence in pandering to the senses, devotion to the Lord will be absent. Humans sunk in self-indulgence will rarely remember the Lord, but the moment tragedy strikes, thoughts turn promptly enough to God. Then people will undertake acts of piety and offer more worship, only to revert to old habits the moment the troubles go away. The phrase *tām na hoyī* means 'then is not'. What is not? Learned ones interpret this varyingly. Some say it means the 'desire for devotion' is missing. Others say it refers to the Lord, that where sensual pleasures dominate, the Lord is not. Some even put it as meaning that "where, spiritual peace is there trouble is not". Some view *tām* as derived from *tamha* (avarice, greed). Some explain this phrase as, "the malady of rebirths is cured by the medicine of *Nām Simran.*" Prof. Sahib Singh renders it as, "when man gets spiritual peace, troubles go away". The more convincing, and the more commonly used interpretation, however, is that when pleasures overtake us, devotion to God vanishes. Bhai Vir Singh uses it in this sense as do Prof. Talib, Macauliffe, Dada Chellaram and Prof. Teja Singh.

In the second line, the omnipotence of the Lord is stressed. The Guru says that all power is with the Lord Creator *–karta*, and the Doer*–karṇā.* Whatever happens is because of Him and not by human volition. It is an oft-experienced reality that even when we strive hard, the results that ensue are often not as we wished. We must always remember that making the best effort is our duty and within our hands, but that the end results are entirely in the hands of the Lord.

In lines three and four, the theme is the vast mystery of the Lord. The Guru says, *balihāri kudrat vasya. Tera unt na jāyī lakhiya.* The Guru is saying he is a sacrifice to the Lord, who is manifest in the entire universe, whose limits we cannot delineate, who is unknowable and inscrutable. The term *lakhiya* is explained as 'understood', 'seen', 'measured' or 'comprehended'. The Guru conveys here the sense of a God who is totally beyond the human capacity to measure Him in any way.

Bhai Vir Singh's comments on these four lines are interesting. He explains it as saying that amazing are the Lord's ways. When we think something will give us *sukh* (joy), and we accumulate it we find it gives not pleasure but rather manifests as a disease of our inner selves. When the Lord sends us *dukh* (pain and troubles), we react with panic and revulsion, but it turns out to be the remedy for the disease we had acquired from our pursuit of pleasure. Therefore, the *sukh* that will give us real spiritual *sukh* can come only from the Lord who is the *karta*, the *karṇā*–the giver of such *sukh*. For whenever we try to get such *sukh* it does not come. The point is that we must not make worldly pleasures our aim in life because these will only damage our inner selves. Nor must we cry out when pain or trouble comes, because it may bring the spiritual cure for our diseased inner self. We must stop running after empty illusions and seek the true and lasting joy–*sukh*–from the Lord alone.

In line five, the Guru speaks of the immanence of the Lord. He says the Lord is manifest in His creation and all beings are in Him. He permeates every bit that exists. The term *kala* is explained by Dada Chellaram as 'Powers', by Prof. Teja Singh as 'Art', which is a Sanskrit meaning of the word, by Dr. Gopal Singh as 'Attributes', by Macauliffe as 'Animate', and by Prof. Talib as 'Might'. The *Shabdarth* renders it as 'Art' and translates *Akal kala* as meaning the 'art that is artless'–or 'comes without effort'; which, says the *Shabdarth,* is the highest art. Prof. Sahib Singh and Bhai Vir Singh have a more appealing interpretation. They construe *kala* to mean a portion, and *Akal* to mean entire, unbroken. Prof. Sahib Singh then interprets this line as saying that the Lord is *Akal kala*–not broken but manifest in all creation. Bhai Vir Singh renders it to say that the Lord in His *kala* form is manifest in

His beings. However, he is also *Akal*, entire and complete. So even while being part of each created being and thus divided, yet He is whole, one and unique in the entire universe. The explanation by these two great scholars is the more appealing, that the Lord cannot be seen as other than One, and that He is manifest in all creation.

In line six, the Guru says praise the Lord who is the only reality. His qualities are splendid and whosoever has worshipped Him has found salvation. The term *pār paiya* means 'crossed over'. This comes from the concept of the passage of the soul to the Lord from this world as leading across an ocean of dread that we have to cross, which can only be done with the Lord's grace. The other thought in this line is of *sipht suālio*, which means 'beautiful is thy praise'. The Lord has all splendid attributes, and there is no way anyone can overstate these qualities. The singing of praises of the Lord is the prescribed path to salvation in Sikhism. So the Guru is saying splendid and beautiful are the qualities–*sipht*–of the Lord; and now using *sipht* in its other sense as 'praising', he adds that whosoever has sung these praises has 'gone across' this ocean that separated us from Him.

In the last line, the Lord's omnipotence is the theme. The Guru says, praise the Lord who at His own will does whatever is required. Most learned ones have rendered it on the lines Bhai Vir Singh renders it. He says, "Talk of the Lord, sing His praises but don't start probing into His acts; for He does what He has to do". The Guru is telling us to sing His praises and, implicitly instructs as to surrender to Him unquestioningly, to accept His will, for what He wishes to happen will come about and there is no way we can alter it by demurring or raising questions.

APPENDIX

2

We now come to the additional hymns that are commonly recited at the conclusion of the Rehrās Sahib. The officially prescribed Rehrās Sahib ends with the hymn beginning with, *Tera kita jāto nāhi maino jog kītoyi.* However, it has become a common practice to recite after this hymn, three more hymns by the fifth Nanak. These are one *pauṛi*, and two *sloks.*

The *pauṛi* is from the *Vār* in *Rāg Rāmkali, Mahla* 5, page 962, SGGS. The Guru says:

ਪੌੜੀ	Pauṛi:
ਤਿਥੈ ਤੂ ਸਮਰਥੁ ਜਿਥੈ ਕੋਇ ਨਾਹਿ॥	Tithhai tu samrath jithhai koye nāhe.
ਓਥੈ ਤੇਰੀ ਰਖ ਅਗਨੀ ਉਦਰ ਮਾਹਿ॥	Othhai teri rakh agni udar māhe.
ਸੁਣਿ ਕੈ ਜਮ ਕੇ ਦੂਤ ਨਾਇ ਤੇਰੈ ਛਡਿ ਜਾਹਿ॥	Suṇ kai jum kay dut nāye terai chhadd jāhe.
ਭਉਜਲੁ ਬਿਖਮੁ ਅਸਗਾਹੁ ਗੁਰ ਸਬਦੀ ਪਾਰਿ ਪਾਹਿ॥	Bhaujal bikham asgāh gur sabdi pār pāhe.
ਜਿਨ ਕਉ ਲਗੀ ਪਿਆਸ ਅਮ੍ਰਿਤੁ ਸੇਇ ਖਾਹਿ॥	Jin kau lagi pyās amrit sey khāhe.

ਕਲ ਮਹਿ ਏਹੋ ਪੁੰਨੁ ਗੁਣ ਗੋਵਿੰਦ ਗਾਹਿ॥	Kal meh eho pun guṇ govind gāhe.
ਸਭਸੈ ਨੋ ਕਿਰਪਾਲੁ ਸਮ੍ਹਾਲੇ ਸਾਹਿ ਸਾਹਿ॥	Sabhsai no kirpāl samhālay sāhe sāhe.
ਬਿਰਥਾ ਕੋਇ ਨ ਜਾਇ ਜਿ ਆਵੈ ਤੁਧੁ ਆਹਿ॥	Birthha koye na jāye je āvai tudh āhe.

Glossary:

ਸਮਰਥ	Samrath	Capable
ਰਖ	Rakh	Protection
ਅਗਨੀ ਉਦਰ	Agni udar	Fire of the womb
ਅਸਗਾਹ	Asgāh	Ocean
ਸਮ੍ਹਾਲੇ	Samhālay	Protects, takes care

The Guru says in the first line that the Lord's power extends where no other power can reach. This is a reference to the omnipotence of the Creator. Then he adds in the second line, *othai teri rakh agni udar māhe*–in those inaccessible places, the Lord's protection is available. Even as we lie helpless in the womb, the Lord protects us from that fire. This refers to what is popularly called *jatthar Agni*–the fire in the womb and it is often used as an example of a place where we are totally helpless and hence entirely dependent on the Lord's protection.

In the third line, the Guru says, *suṇ kai jum kay dut nāye terai chhadd jāhe.* This literally means 'hearing your name, the messengers of death leave'. It is meant to be a statement of faith, that those who are imbued in the Name of the Lord will never die a spiritual death. This body is programmed to decay and die, and it will do so. However, those who live according to the way of the Lord as outlined by the Guru need never fear this event. This is because they are already living at a plane where the body's presence or absence is not of prime importance. For such devotees the passage to the Lord is easy, as the Guru says, *bhaujal bikham asgāh gur sabdi pār pāhe.* This means that we can navigate the dreadful and difficult ocean and cross it with the help of the Lord's Name.

The Guru tells us who will be the ones to benefit. He says, *jin kau lagi pyās amrit sey khāhe.* This means that this nectar like food will be partaken only by those lucky ones who are hungry for it. The Lord comes to us but we have to crave His presencc. We have to live the righteous life and surrender ourselves to the will of the Lord. When we are yearning for Him, we can hope to perhaps have our pleading answered. Then he says, *kal meh eho pun guṇ govind gāhe.*This means that in this age and time the proper path is to sing the praises of the Lord. This is in the context of the belief that in each *Yuga* the approach to worship changes. In the *Kalyug* through which we are passing, the right path is to sing His praises. This is not to say that the Lord is partial to sycophancy. No, the purpose is to cleanse our own inner selves through this constant exercise.

Finally, in the last two lines the Guru says, *sabhsai no kirpāl samhālay sāhe sāhe*. This means the Lord's blessing is available to all and with each breath, we take His care and protection is with us. The Guru emphasises this with the next line as he says, *birthha koye na jāye je āvai tudh āhe*. This means that none is denied His help and protection if someone comes under His aegis. In other words, one has the choice to live the life of the *manmukh*–the ego centred man, and to refuse to come to the Lord. His love will still be available to such as these because He is love personified and it is in

His nature to love His creation. However, if one seeks His protection then one must ask for it, for which total surrender to His will is necessary.

There follow two *sloks* which are from the *Vār* in *Rāg Gūjri* by the fifth Nanak and are placed at page 517 of the SGGS attached with the first *pauṛi* of that *Vār*. In the first of these two *sloks*, the Guru says:

ਸਲੋਕ	Slok
ਅੰਤਰਿ ਗੁਰੁ ਆਰਾਧਣਾ, ਜਿਹਵਾ ਜਪਿ ਗੁਰ ਨਾਉ॥	Antar gur ārādḥṇa, jihva jap gur nāo
ਨੇਤ੍ਰੀ ਸਤਿਗੁਰੁ ਪੇਖਣਾ, ਸ੍ਰਵਣੀ ਸੁਨਣਾ ਗੁਰ ਨਾਉ॥	Netri satgur pekhṇa sravaṇi sunaṇa gur nāo
ਸਤਿਗੁਰ ਸੇਤੀ ਰਤਿਆ, ਦਰਗਹ ਪਾਈਐ ਠਾਉ॥	Satgur seti ratiya, dargah paīai tthāo
ਕਹੁ ਨਾਨ ਕਿਰਪਾ ਕਰੇ, ਜਿਸ ਨੋ ਏਹ ਵਥੁ ਦੇਇ॥	Kahu Nanak kirpa karay, jis no eh vathh dey
ਜਗ ਮਹਿ ਉਤਮ ਕਾਢੀਅਹਿ, ਵਿਰਲੇ ਕੇਈ ਕੇਇ॥	Jug mah utam kāddhīeh, virlay kayi kay.

Glossary:

ਸ੍ਰਵਣੀ	Sravaṇi	With the ears, through listening
ਠਾਉ	Tthāo	Place, support
ਵਥ	Vathh	Thing, here the Lord's name
ਕੇਈ ਕੇਇ	Kayi kay	Few, only some

In this *slok,* the Guru speaks to us of what we need to do, of what the drill should be for our everyday living. What he is laying down is a prescription that the seeker needs to note carefully, and imbibe deeply.

He says in the first line, *antar gur ārādhṇa*–within the heart contemplate on the Guru; and then *jihva jup gur nāo*–with the tongue recite the Name that the Guru has taught. This is the Guru's way of telling us that we should always keep the Lord ever in our mind, so that when we act we do so in full awareness that He is watching us. Once this awareness comes, wrongdoing will automatically vanish. We will be on the path to the Lord.

The Guru then says, *netri satgur pekhṇa*–with your eyes see only the true Guru in everything; and, *sravaṇi sunaṇa gur nāo*–with your ears listen only to the Name. Thus, we are enjoined to be always aware of the Lord, with our ears, with the eyes, with the tongue as we speak, and within our hearts as we live. In other words, imbibe Him, and His message, completely.

The Guru, in the third line, then tells us what will accrue if we follow this path. He says, *satgur seti ratiya*–by immersing ourselves totally in the true Guru, by imbuing his message in our hearts; we will *dargah paīai tthāo*–gain acceptance before the Lord. This is, in other words, the path to God-realisation.

The Guru sums up the lesson in the last two lines. He says, *kahu Nanak kirpa karay, jis no eh vathh day*–Nanak says that those whom the Lord has granted this thing, the boon of His name; and then adds, *jug mah utam kāddhīeh, virlay kayi kay*–are the superior ones in this world but there are only a very few of these. The stress here is again on the concept that worship of the Lord is also a gift from Him. We acquire the great boon of seeing Him in everything, of keeping Him ever in our hearts, of always singing His praise, only when He chooses to grant it to us. The Guru puts in a caveat here as he says that this grace is granted only to a very few, such fortunate ones are *virlay kayi kay*–rare indeed.

The second *slok*, also by the fifth Nanak, says:

ਮਹਲਾ ੫	Mahla 5
ਰਖੇ ਰਖਣਹਾਰਿ, ਆਪਿ ਉਬਾਰਿਅਨੁ॥	Rakhay rakhaṇhār, āp ubārian.
ਗੁਰ ਕੀ ਪੈਰੀ ਪਾਇ, ਕਾਜ ਸਵਾਰਿਅਨੁ॥	Gur ki pairi pāye, kāj sawārian.
ਹੋਆ ਆਪਿ ਦਇਆਲੁ, ਮਨਹੁ ਨ ਵਿਸਾਰਿਅਨੁ॥	Hoa āp dayāl, manhu na visārian.
ਸਾਧ ਜਨਾ ਕੈ ਸੰਗਿ, ਭਵਜਲੁ ਤਾਰਿਅਨੁ॥	Sādh jana kay sung, bhavjal tārian.
ਸਾਕਤ ਨਿੰਦਕ ਦੁਸਟ, ਖਿਨ ਮਾਹਿ ਬਿਦਾਰਿਅਨੁ॥	Sākat nindak dusatt, khin māhe bidārian.
ਤਿਸੁ ਸਾਹਿਬ ਕੀ ਟੇਕ ਨਾਨਕ ਮਨੈ ਮਾਹਿ॥	Tis sahib ki teik Nanak manai māhe.
ਜਿਸ ਸਿਮਰਤ ਸੁਖੁ ਹੋਇ, ਸਗਲੇ ਦੂਖ ਜਾਹਿ॥	Jis simrat sukh hoye, saglay dūkh jāhe.

Glossary:

ਉਬਾਰਿਅਨ	Ubārian	Redeemed
ਭਵਜਲ	Bhavjal	Ocean of dread, this world
ਸਾਕਤ	Sākat	Worshippers of *Maya* and power
ਬਿਦਾਰਿਅਨੁ	Bidārian	Destroyed

The Guru says in the first line here, *rakhay rakhaṇhār, āp ubārian*–the Lord is our preserver and He redeems us. The inability of mortal humans to achieve salvation on their own has been a repeated theme in *Gurbāṇi*. It is in the Lord's hands, and no one else, to redeem us from this cycle of births and deaths, and it is only through total surrender to Him that we can hope to be worthy of His grace. The Guru is stressing this aspect here. The Lord preserves us from sinking into the iniquity of ego-centred thinking, keeps us on the right path and He Himself redeems us when it pleases Him. We cannot dictate any of these outcomes.

In the second line, he elaborates the process by telling us that for ensuring our salvation the Lord leads us to the true Guru. He says, *gur ki pairi pāye*–the Lord brings us to the feet of the true master, which is the SGGS in the case of the Sikh. What happens when we surrender to the Lord through the true Guru? The Guru says our *kāj sawārian*, which literally means that our tasks are easily performed, implying here that our desire for salvation is fructified. The term *kāj* literally means task, but is to be construed herein the sense of that which we were seeking to achieve. That purpose is *sawārian*, meaning that it is made easy.

In the third line, the Guru says, *hoa āp dayāl, manhu na visārian*–the Lord has bestowed on us His divine compassion and retained our spiritual link with Him. The term *manhu na visārian* can be rendered in two ways. It can mean the Lord does not forget us, or it can mean He resides ever in our hearts. In both interpretations the common factor is that, the Lord's link with us remains ever alive and this is the sign of His magnanimity, His kindness.

In the fourth line, the Guru says the Lord puts us in the company of godly men and thus we are enabled to cross this terrible ocean. The comparison of the journey to the Lord with the crossing of an ocean of dread is commonly employed. This journey takes us into the realm of the unknown and is thus fearsome. Also, we are, at least subconsciously aware of our numerous sins and shortcomings and therefore view with much dread the inevitable moment of truth when we will have to face the Lord. This journey is therefore like crossing a parlous ocean filled with dread. We will however cross it successfully when we are *sādh jana kay sung*–in the company of the godly. The Lord, as our savior puts us into such elevating company.

The Guru next says in line 5, that the despicable ones who worship *Maya*, the slanderers and the evil-minded ones will be destroyed in a trice. *Sākat, nindak and dusatt* are three categories often used by the Guru to describe those on the wrong path, away from the Lord and focused on material success and egocentric living. *Sākat* literally means the worshiper of the goddess *Shakti*, but is also often used in the SGGS to describe him who worships the material things of the world and is averse to pursuits spiritual. *Nindak* means he who slanders. This is another trait the Guru repeatedly condemns. The word *dusatt* is generic covering all types of evil doers and transgressors. All these wrong tendencies within us will disappear when the Lord bestows His glance of grace on us and in His infinite compassion decides to uplift us, as was said in the previous lines here. Learned ones have also rendered this to mean that those who are on these wrong paths will be destroyed. However, we have to remember that thc Lord is an ocean of Love and compassion and bears no ill will to any of His children. The mislead wrong doer is also His concern as much as the godly one. He cannot, therefore, be seen as destroying those whom He has created and who have been sent to this *karmabhūmi*–this field of action–to try to find their way back to Him. Our sojourn on this earth is an opportunity for redeeming ourselves and re-uniting with the Lord from whom we have been separated by our ignorance, our *haumai*. So, it is the evil within us that the Lord will destroy and not our very selves, however mislead we may be in our thinking and actions. He will grant us this boon when it so pleases Him. Till then such misguided souls will keep getting reincarnated and be given repeated chances to come to the right path.

In the concluding lines of this *slok,* the Guru says keep the Lord ever in the mind and seek succour from Him because by remembering Him peace shall prevail in the mind and all troubles will vanish. In other words, do not fall into the error of seeking help from those who are themselves dependent on the mercy of the Lord. Seek support and help from Him alone, because He is the One remembering whom all troubles will end. He is the saviour, the redeemer and peace ultimately comes only from Him.

ਸੋਹਿਲਾ

SOHILA

INTRODUCTION

We now come to the next *bāṇi*, the Sohila, which is the last one prescribed for the *Nitnem* to be read just before bedtime. It is to be found at pages 12 and 13 of the SGGS.

The term Sohila literally means a song of praise, a paean. The Guru is singing the praises of the Lord in this *bāṇi* in the SGGS, called the 'Sohila'. Since it is usually sung to music, it is, in common parlance, often called Kirtan Sohila. Some also call it Ārti Sohila, perhaps because it contains the beautiful hymn, by Guru Nanak, known as *Ārti*. Apart from being the last among the *bāṇis* prescribed in the *Nitnem* for daily recitation, it is also customary to recite this *bāṇi*, in the form of *kirtan,* to mark the conclusion of the last rites involving cremation of the mortal remains of the departed soul.

The Sohila is a compilation of different hymns, on the pattern of the Rehrās Sahib. It comprises five hymns in all, three by Guru Nanak, and one each by the fourth and the fifth Nanak. The *bāṇi* begins with the title and the invocation as below:

ਰਾਗੁ ਗਉੜੀ ਦੀਪਕੀ ਮਹਲਾ ੧	Rāg Gauṛi Dīpki Mahla 1
ੴ ਸਤਿਗੁਰ ਪ੍ਰਸਾਦਿ ॥	Ekonkār Satgur prasād

The title of the hymn is here specifying *Rāg Gauṛi Dīpki* as the musical metre to which it has been set, and informing us that the author is *Mahla* 1, meaning Guru Nanak.

The Guru begins with the usual invocation to the Lord to seek His blessings for its unimpeded completion of the task. The most usual invocation in Hinduism is to Lord Ganesha, also called *Vighneshwara* or Remover of obstacles. In the *Gurbāṇi*, however the Creator Himself is always invoked. The Guru here uses the shortest version of the *Mool Mantra*. This term, as we have discussed earlier, means the 'basic creed' and has been used by the Guru throughout the SGGS in various forms–full or shortened–as an invocation to the Lord.

The full form, to be found at the very beginning of the SGGS, of the *Mool Mantra* is *Ik Onkār Satnām Karta purakh Nirbhau Nirvair Akāl mūrat Ajūni Saibhang Gurprasād*. It is then repeated at the beginning of many compositions, usually in its full form but also at some places in shortened form. As we discussed earlier, scholars tell us that the full form of the invocation has been used 33 times in the *SGGS*; and that 26 of the 31 *rāgs* open with this. A somewhat shorter form, *Ik Onkār Satnām Karta purakh Gur prasād*, occurs nine times in the SGGS. A much shorter form–*Ik Onkār Sat Gur Prasād*–has been most frequently employed, nearly 520 times. The briefest form–*Ik Onkār*–has also been used a few times, in the concluding hymns.

We can say that the *Mool Mantra* is an effort by a realised soul, a master, to communicate to us a vision of the Eternal One, trying to put into words a mystical insight that he has personally experienced. The task is obviously daunting, and akin to describing colour to the blind. So, he attempts to do it by stressing some of the main attributes we humans can ascribe to the One Lord.

We can now look at this shortened version of the invocation. The Guru is referring here to the foremost attribute of the Lord; that He is *Ik Onkār*. This literally means that there is but One God. The Guru is saying that He is 'One', and He is the 'Word'. The concept of the 'Word' as Creator is prevalent in many belief systems. There is the word or incantation, *Aum* or *Om* in Hinduism. Then there is the ancient Greek concept of 'Logos', the creative word. Guru Nanak modified the Hindu incantation Om by affixing the word *Ik* with the term *Onkār*, which is a modified form of Om. The Guru in this way annunciated his new philosophy, postulating a Lord Creator who is over and above the various Trinities and powers that it was customary at that time to worship. Implicit in the term *Ik Onkār, also written as Ekonkār,* is a Creator who is one, unique by Himself, and permeates His creation as the immanent Lord. The Lord is thus not merely the prime cause, but is also Himself within that creation. The Guru, in short, is telling us that the Lord is transcendently the Creator, the sole Reality; but He is also the immanent presence within that creation.

The term *Gur Parsād* means by the grace of the Guru. The Guru says that the Lord is to be realised through the guidance of the Guru, through his grace. *Gurbāṇi* lays great stress on the importance of the Guru as the guide who will show us the way to the Lord. Because of this there are many for whom it has become convenient to present themselves as the Guru and use it more for their own material gains than spiritual guidance to the follower. In Sikhism, this Guru is none else but the *Sri Guru Granth Sahib*, as was prescribed by the tenth Nanak in 1708 AD before he passed from this world.

The Guru in this invocation says that there is but one God, the Creator immanent within His creation. He is to be found through the grace of the Guru. Let us now consider the first hymn of the Sohila.

1

SING HIS PRAISES

The first hymn of this Bāṇi titled Sohila is by Guru Nanak. This hymn occurs again at page 157, SGGS, where the title of the *rāg* is changed from *Rāg Gauṛi Dīpki* to *Rāg Pūrbi Gauṛi Dīpki.* Also, the word *bīchāro* is written as *bīchār(u)*. Again, in line four the line *hau vāri jit sohilai* one word has been added and the line becomes *hau vāri jāo jit sohilai.* These minor changes do not at all alter the message. The Guru says:

ਜੈ ਘਰਿ ਕੀਰਤਿ ਆਖੀਐ ਕਰਤੇ ਕਾ ਹੋਇ ਬੀਚਾਰੋ ॥	Jai ghar kīrat ākhīai kartay ka hoye bīchāro.
ਤਿਤੁ ਘਰਿ ਗਾਵਹੁ ਸੋਹਿਲਾ ਸਿਵਰਿਹੁ ਸਿਰਜਣਹਾਰੋ ॥੧॥	Tit ghar gāvho Sohila sivroh sirjaṇhāro. 1.
ਤੁਮ ਗਾਵਹੁ ਮੇਰੇ ਨਿਰਭਉ ਕਾ ਸੋਹਿਲਾ ॥	Tum gāvho meray nirbhau ka Sohila.
ਹਉ ਵਾਰੀ ਜਿਤੁ ਸੋਹਿਲੈ ਸਦਾ ਸੁਖੁ ਹੋਇ ॥੧॥ ਰਹਾਉ ॥	Hau vāri jit sohilai sada sukh hoye.1. Rahāo.
ਨਿਤ ਨਿਤ ਜੀਅੜੇ ਸਮਾਲੀਅਨਿ ਦੇਖੈਗਾ ਦੇਵਣਹਾਰੁ ॥	Nit nit jīaṛay samāliyan dekhaiga devaṇhār.
ਤੇਰੇ ਦਾਨੈ ਕੀਮਤਿ ਨਾ ਪਵੈ ਤਿਸੁ ਦਾਤੇ ਕਵਣੁ ਸੁਮਾਰੁ ॥੨॥	Teray dānai kīmat na pavai tis dātay kavaṇ sumār. 2.

ਸੰਬਤਿ ਸਾਹਾ ਲਿਖਿਆ ਮਿਲਿ	Sambat sāha likhia mil kar
ਕਰਿ ਪਾਵਹੁ ਤੇਲੁ ॥	pāvho teil.
ਦੇਹੁ ਸਜਣ ਅਸੀਸੜੀਆ ਜਿਉ ਹੋਵੈ	Deh sajaṇ asīsṛīya jio hovai
ਸਾਹਿਬ ਸਿਉ ਮੇਲੁ॥੩॥	sahib siu meil.3.
ਘਰਿ ਘਰਿ ਏਹੋ ਪਾਹੁਚਾ ਸਦੜੇ	Ghar ghar eho pāhucha sadṛay
ਨਿਤ ਪਵੰਨਿ ॥	nit pavann.
ਸਦਣਹਾਰਾ ਸਿਮਰੀਐ ਨਾਨਕ ਸੇ	Sadaṇhāra simrīai Nanak sey
ਦਿਹ ਆਵੰਨਿ॥੪॥੧॥	deh āvann.4.1

Glossary:

ਕੀਰਤਿ	Kīrat	Praise
ਸਿਰਜਣਹਾਰੁ	Sirjaṇhār	Creator
ਸਮਾਲੀਅਨਿ	Samāliyan	Are cared for
ਦਾਨੈ	Dānai	Grain
ਸੰਬਤਿ ਸਾਹਾ	Sambat sāha	Auspicious time
ਪਾਹੁਚਾ	Pāhucha	Invitation
ਆਵੰਨਿ	Āvann	Come, become available

In the first two lines, the Guru evokes the image of an abode that blessed house where the *gurmukhs*, the Guru oriented ones, sing the praises of the Lord. He says, *jai ghar kīrat ākhīai kartay ka hoye bīchāro*–the house, where the Lord is extolled and where the devotees sit, discuss and ponder over the mysteries of the Creator. He, then, instructs us to profit from that house–*tit ghar.* What is it that we should do? The Guru says, sing paeans to the Lord and ponder on the grand mysteries of the Creator, our Lord–*gāvho Sohila sivroh sirjaṇhār*. Remember that we are supposed to read this *bāṇi* at the end of the day. Having begun with the Japji Sahib singing His praises, we then wind up the day on the same note, singing paeans to the Lord.

In the next two lines, the third and the fourth, the Guru speaks of the benefits that would ensue. In the third line, he says, *tum gāvho meray nirbhau ka Sohila.* The Guru is telling us to sing the praises of the *nirbhau* Lord, the fearless one. The description of the Lord has necessarily to be in the form of negatory terminology. The vast, unknowable Lord is to the human only to be recognised by what He is not. The *neti-neti* method is the most appropriate and the Guru employs it here by referring to the Lord as not having fear, calling Him *Nirbhau*, the one without fear. This epithet is, of course, part of the *Mool Mantra*, and is to be seen in the very first *bāṇi* in the SGGS. In using the phrase *meray nirbhau*–my fearless one, the Guru is stressing also his own intimate and deep connection to the eternal Lord. He is saying he belongs to the Lord, and by the same measure, the Lord is His. In the next line, he says, *hau vāri jit sohilai sada sukh hoye*, meaning that he would be a sacrifice to the paean of praise that brings complete and lasting peace to him who sings the praises of the Lord.

In the fifth and the sixth lines, the Guru speaks of the infinite gifts of the Lord who sustains us all. He says in the fifth line, *nit nit jīaṛay samāliyan dekhaiga devaṇhār,* meaning that the Lord sustains His beings on a daily basis and the eternal giver will look after us. This is a theme often stressed in the SGGS. We need however, to understand that this is not a prescription for inaction. He is not saying you sit back and do nothing and the *devaṇhār* will perform your daily tasks and grant you your daily sustenance. No, the message of *Gurbāṇi*, and the basic spirit of the Sikh faith is to actively participate in the activities of this world, always to strive and while doing so continue to practice a conscious discipline to stay on the Guru's path. Within the parameters of this essential activity is this prescription to be understood, that in the overall context it is the Lord who sustains us, and not our own efforts. It is another way of stressing the omnipotence of the Lord and the fact that the universe moves as per His wishes and not by the puny efforts of any other power. In addition, the stress is on the Lord as the ever-loving Creator who sustains each one of us. In the sixth line, the Guru underlines these aspects more directly as he says, *teray dānai kīmat na pavai tis dātay kavaṇ sumār.* He says, *teray dānai–* your single grain, your petty philanthropy is deemed as something big, *kīmat na pavai.* Just think then of the vastness of that great giver, whose munificence is the support of all created beings. He is here stressing the vastness of that divine philanthropy to make the point that the Lord is vast beyond human reckoning.

The seventh and the eigth lines, the Guru speaks of the inevitable day when we will meet our maker. He says, *sambat sāha likhia mil kar pāvho teil*, meaning that the precise time of that moment when we are to meet Him is pre-ordained, and by implication inexorable. So, let us welcome it gladly. The phrase, *mil kar pāvho teil* derives from the custom where householders will sprinkle oil on the threshold of the house before ushering in some very special guest, such as a bride or a newborn child; in other words anyone who is most welcome. This ritc is supposed to be an especially auspicious way of welcome. Here, the Guru says perform this rite by pouring the welcoming oil, meaning that we must gladly welcome that moment. This is because for a *Gurmukh* no other moment can be as auspicious. This is the time when the time of our travail upon this world of mortals is over and the fruit of a life righteously lived will come to us. In the eighth line, the Guru highlights this by seeking from friends the blessings that we may meet the Lord. He says, *deh sajaṇ asīsṛīya jio hovai sahib siu meil,* meaning 'oh my dear well-wishers and friends bless me so that I may meet my Lord'. The grant of salvation is in the exclusive domain of the Lord and no effort by us can guarantee us such a consummation. All that a *Gurmukh* can really aspire for is at the very least to have a glimpse of that Glory that is the Lord.

In the concluding lines, the ninth and the tenth, the Guru sums up his message of not being afraid of that decisive moment when the Lord's summons come. He says, *ghar ghar eho pāhucha sadṛay nit pavann,* meaning that the invitation, the summons from the Lord comes to each house and regular is this invitation from the Lord. The term *pāhucha* is used normally for the invitation to a wedding. Here, the Guru has deliberately used it to keep up the picture of our departure from this world, our meeting with our maker, being a happy event. He concludes in the tenth line with the lesson, *sadaṇhāra simrīai Nanak sey deh āvann*, meaning let us fix our minds on the one who has sent us the invitation because that fateful day is nigh indeed.

The inevitability of the day of our departure from this mortal world is an *a priori* assumption here. The argument proceeds from there and the Guru tries to make us understand that this event is nothing fearsome or dreadful; it is a routine occurrence in our existence. This very thought has been expressed by the Guru in the Āsa di Vār, page 474, SGGS, when he says, ਜੋ ਆਇਆ ਸੋ ਚਲਸੀ ਸਭੁ ਕਈ ਆਈ ਵਾਰੀਐ॥–*Jo aya so chalsi sabh ko āyi vārīai*, meaning that he who is born shall depart this world when his turn has come. It is a routine event. So, the Guru is telling us that it is no different from the invitation to a wedding in our neighborhood that we might receive. As we would attend to that function so should we treat the invitation to return to the Lord. We need not dread it or even give it any great thought. Instead, we should constantly focus our minds on the power that controls our comings and goings. Therefore, the Guru tells us to fix our minds on the Lord, sing paeans to Him and hope and pray that we will be able to meet our maker with joy and confidence.

2

THE LORD IS ONE

The second hymn in this *bāṇi* is also by Guru Nanak. The same hymn occurs at page 357, SGGS but with small differences. For instance in the third line, the word *baba* is omitted at page 357. Similarly, in line four, the word *toye* becomes *tohe*. In line five, the last word changes from *hoa* to *bhaya.* These, of course, do not change the message in any way.

While referring again to the abode where the glory of Lord is extolled, the Guru tells us about the unique oneness of the Creator. He says:

ਰਾਗੁ ਆਸਾ ਮਹਲਾ ੧ ॥	Rāg Āsa Mahla 1
ਛਿਅ ਘਰ ਛਿਅ ਗੁਰ ਛਿਅ ਉਪਦੇਸ ॥	Chhay ghar chhay gur chhay updeis
ਗੁਰੁ ਗੁਰੁ ਏਕੋ ਵੇਸ ਅਨੇਕ ॥੧॥	Gur gur eko veis aneik
ਬਾਬਾ ਜੈ ਘਰਿ ਕਰਤੇ ਕੀਰਤਿ ਹੋਇ ॥	Baba jai ghar kartay kīrat hoye.
ਸੋ ਘਰੁ ਰਾਖੁ ਵਡਾਈ ਤੋਇ ॥੧॥	So ghar rākh vaddāyi toye. 1.
ਰਹਾਉ ॥	Rahāo.
ਵਿਸੁਏ ਚਸਿਆ ਘੜੀਆ ਪਹਰਾ ਥਿਤੀ ਵਾਰੀ ਮਾਹੁ ਹੋਆ ॥	Visoye chasya ghaṛīya pahra thiti vāri māh hoa.

ਸੂਰਜੁ ਏਕੋ ਰੁਤਿ ਅਨੇਕ ॥	Sūraj eko rut aneik.
ਨਾਨਕ ਕਰਤੇ ਕੇ ਕੇਤੇ ਵੇਸ॥੨॥੨॥	Nanak kartay kay ketay veis. 2.2.

Glossary:

ਛਿਅ ਘਰ	Chhay ghar	Six schools of philosophy.
ਵੇਸ	Veis	Form.
ਰਾਖੁ	Rākh	Adopt, follow.
ਵਡਾਈ	Vaddāyi	Benefit, elevation.
ਵਿਸੁਏ	Visoye	Very brief moment, equal to 15 blinks of the eye.
ਚਸਿਆ	Chasya	Brief moment equal to 15 visoye.

The Guru here speaks of the unique oneness of the Lord. He says there are apparently different formulations and ways of thinking, each viewing Him in different ways. In the first line, he says there are six houses, six Gurus and six different teachings. The reference is to the six schools of Hindu philososphy. These have evolved over the ages and while essentially upholding the oneness of the Creator, these seek to present different ways of approaching Him.

These six schools are 1) the Sānkhya of Kapil Muni, 2) Niyāye of Rishi Gautam, 3) Vaisheshik of Kaṇād Muni, 4) Mimānsa of Rishi Jaimini, 5) Yoga of Rishi Pātanjli, and 6) Vedanta of Rishi Vyās, also called Ved Vyās, because he is believed to be the compiler of the Vedas and the great epic, the Mahabharata. The Guru refers to these six schools and the *chhay gur*–six masters or teachers referring to the authors of these schools. These six masters have given us *chhay updeis*–six different lessons.

In the second line, the Guru says, *gur gur eko*, that the enlightener of these masters is but one, though there are *veis aneik*–multiple forms. In other words, the apparent diffences in interpretation are but superficial and all these derive from the same source. The essential lesson is the same. This lesson is that we must adopt the school where the the Lord is extolled and His praises are sung.

He says in the third line, *baba jai ghar kartay kīrat hoye*–that house where the praises of the Creator are sung, are spoken. Of these various *ghar*–schools of thought, the one worthy of being adopted is that which teaches you to sing the Lord's praise. The right path is the one where the way of worship is through constant recitation of the Lord's greatness and His myriad virtues.

Having told us how to identify that school, the Guru then tells us in the fourth line, *so ghar rākh vaddāyi toye*–adopt that house and you will achieve success and will flourish. The Guru has prescribed a pause after this line indicating that this was the centre point of the lesson. Forget about the finer points of religious thought or the niceties of theological arguments. Just focus on the path of constant recitation of His name, of ever singing His praises, because the Lord from whom all these schools spring is one. Cut through the rigmarole of rites or esoteric practices, and choose only the singing of His praises as the philosophy to follow. If you do this, you will grow and flourish.

In the concluding three lines, the Guru restresses the theme of all knowledge springing from that one source, the Lord. In the fifth line he says, *visoye chasya ghaṛīya pahra thiti vāri māh hoa.* He is describing the measures of time that we humans have devised. He says there are *visoye*–the briefest time measure taken to be equal to 15 blinks of the human eye.

Then there are the *chasay*, which are 15 times of the *visoye.* The next larger measure on this scale is the *gharīya*–equal to 60 *pal.* Here, the Guru has not mentioned the *pal*, but in this system it is equal to 30 *chasay.* The next measure after the *gharī* is the *pahar* equal to seven and a half times the *gharī.* Then we come to the larger measures called *thiti, vār, māh.* The *thiti* refers to the lunar method of reckoning and relates to the waxing and waning moon. The *vār* refers to the day of the week of which there are seven in a week. *Māh* means months. All these terms, thus, refer to the different ways of measuring the divisions of the year. The Guru is saying that the stream of time flows inexorably and these various divisions of time rapidly elapse.

In the sixth line, the Guru connects this recitation to the theme of this hymn. He says all these various measures seem distinct and separate but remember that all these derive from the one sun. There are varying seasons and we sense time as divided into various parts, but the essential source is one. Similarly, he implies that there are many schools of thought but the only source is the Lord.

The last line, the seventh, sums it up. He says, *Nanak kartay kay ketay veis*–the Creator is one though the forms be many. Just as the one sun gives rise to such seemingly diverse ways of looking at time, we perceive the one Lord in varying and seemingly diverse ways. Yet, all that exists, all that we see is nothing but the Lord incarnate in diverse forms and shapes.

3

THE COSMOS WORSHIPS THEE

We now come to that magnificent hymn by Guru Nanak, known popularly as *Ārti*. This term is used for the ritualistic prayer where lit lamps, placed in a metal plate are used to pay homage or accord worship to a deity. The Mahan Kosh tells us that this is an elaborate rite performed with lit lamps numbering anywhere between one and a hundred placed in a flat metal plate. The worshipper then moves the plate around in front of the deity or person being welcomed or worshipped. It is customary to do so four times around the feet, twice at the level of the navel, once before the face and finally seven times around the entire torso. The Guru here debunks this ritualistic worship and evokes for us a cosmic picture of the *ārti* performed by the entire creation for its Creator. This hymn is at page 13, SGGS and occurs again at page 663, where the title is *Dhanāsri Mahla 1 Ārti*. And there is one small difference in the last line where instead of *terai nāye vāsa,* the phrase *terai nām vāsa* has been used. This, of course, has the exact same meaning, so the message does not change in any way. Let us now look at what the Guru says:

ਰਾਗੁ ਧਨਾਸਰੀ ਮਹਲਾ ੧ ॥	Rāg Dhanāsri Mahla 1
ਗਗਨ ਮੈ ਥਾਲੁ ਰਵਿ ਚੰਦੁ ਦੀਪਕ ਬਨੇ ਤਾਰਿਕਾ ਮੰਡਲ ਜਨਕ ਮੋਤੀ ॥	Gagan mai thhāl rav chand dipak banay tārika manddal janak moti.
ਧੂਪੁ ਮਲਆਨਲੋ ਪਵਣੁ ਚਵਰੋ ਕਰੇ ਸਗਲ ਬਨਰਾਇ ਫੂਲੰਤ ਜੋਤੀ ॥੧॥	Dhūp malyānlo pavaṇ chavro karay sagal banrāye phūlant joti.1.
ਕੈਸੀ ਆਰਤੀ ਹੋਇ ॥ ਭਵ ਖੰਡਨਾ ਤੇਰੀ ਆਰਤੀ ॥	Kaisi ārti hoye. Bhav khanddna teri ārti
ਅਨਹਤਾ ਸਬਦ ਵਾਜੰਤ ਭੇਰੀ ॥੧॥ਰਹਾਉ॥	Anhata sabad vājant bheri. 1.Rahao.
ਸਹਸ ਤਵ ਨੈਨ ਨਨ ਨੈਨ ਹਹਿ ਤੋਹਿ ਕਉ ਸਹਸ ਮੂਰਤਿ ਨਨਾ ਏਕ ਤੁੋਹੀ ॥	Sahas tav nain nan nain hai tohe kao sahas murat nana ek tohi
ਸਹਸ ਪਦ ਬਿਮਲ ਨਨ ਏਕ ਪਦ ਗੰਧ ਬਿਨੁ ਸਹਸ ਤਵ ਗੰਧ ਇਵ ਚਲਤ ਮੋਹੀ ॥੨॥	Sahas pad bimal nan ek pad gandh bin sahas tav gandh iv chalat mohi.2.
ਸਭ ਮਹਿ ਜੋਤਿ ਜੋਤਿ ਹੈ ਸੋਇ ॥	Sabh meh jot jot hai soye
ਤਿਸ ਦੈ ਚਾਨਣਿ ਸਭ ਮਹਿ ਚਾਨਣੁ ਹੋਇ ॥	Tis dai chānaṇ sabh meh chānaṇ hoye.
ਗੁਰ ਸਾਖੀ ਜੋਤਿ ਪਰਗਟੁ ਹੋਇ ॥	Gur sākhi jot pargatt hoye.
ਜੋ ਤਿਸੁ ਭਾਵੈ ਸੁ ਆਰਤੀ ਹੋਇ ॥੩॥	Jo tis bhāvai so ārti hoye.3.
ਹਰਿ ਚਰਣ ਕਵਲ ਮਕਰੰਦ ਲੋਭਿਤ ਮਨੋ ਅਨਦਿਨੋ ਮੋਹਿ ਆਹੀ ਪਿਆਸਾ ॥	Har charaṇ kaval makrand lobhit mano andino moh āhi pyāsa.
ਕ੍ਰਿਪਾ ਜਲੁ ਦੇਹਿ ਨਾਨਕ ਸਾਰਿੰਗ ਕਉ ਹੋਇ ਜਾ ਤੇ ਤੇਰੈ ਨਾਇ ਵਾਸਾ ॥੪॥੩॥	Kripa jal deh Nanak sārang kao hoye ja tay terai nāye vāsa.4.3.

Glossary:

ਰਵਿ ਚੰਦੁ	Rav chand	The sun and the moon
ਧੂਪੁ	Dhūp	Offering of Incense
ਮਲਆਨਲੋ	Malyānlo	Fragrant breezes
ਬਨਰਾਇ	Banrāye	Plants, all flora
ਫੂਲੰਤ ਜੋਤੀ	Phūlant joti	Refulgent glow
ਭਵ ਖੰਡਨਾ	Bhav khanddna	Dispeller of fear, redeemer
ਅਨਹਤਾ	Anhata	Unstruck note, the divine music
ਵਾਜੰਤ ਭੇਰੀ	Vājant bheri	Plays the musical instruments
ਸਹਸ ਪਦ	Sahas pad	Thousand feet
ਬਿਮਲ	Bimal	Pure, stainless
ਕਵਲ ਮਕਰੰਦ	Kaval makrand	The essence of the lotus
ਲੋਭਿਤ ਮਨੋ	Lobhit mano	The mind craves
ਸਾਰਿੰਗ	Sārang	Papeeha bird, also called Chatrik.

In the first line of this magnificent piece of devotional poetry, the Guru compares the divine worship that all creation accords to its Creator. He is implicitly decrying the ritualistic *ārti* practiced as part of the Hindu rituals. The Guru has repeatedly taken on such ritualistic practices, as we can most prominently see in the *Āsa di Vār.* This was intended to bring people back to the essence of worship–which, he teaches us, needs to be done with the heart and the mind and not through superficial rituals. He has, therefore, referred to various such practices of the Hindus who adopt more such rituals, but also, often similarly referring to the Muslim practices. In the first line here, he says, *gagan mai thhāl rav chand dipak banay tārika manddal janak moti*, the firmament itself is the offering plate, and the Sun and the Moon are the lamps refulgent in that plate and the stars are the studded jewels. He is telling us to forget about our puny offerings and petty worship that we are offering to that vast and mysterious power. He says the true *ārti* to some one as great as the Lord can only be offered on a divine, cosmic scale, and it is in fact constantly being offered by the entire creation. For that divine *ārti,* the offering plate is the entire firmament itself. He implies that the worship to Him cannot be offered by using mere human artifacts however ornately and richly decorated these may be. The offering plate for the divine *ārti* to the Lord has the stars as decoration; so what human gems or jewels could dare to compare?

The Guru continues then to juxtapose the human ritual of *ārti* with the cosmic worship he spoke of in the first line. In the second line, therefore, he refers to the other items used in this ritual and then tells us of to focus our minds instead on the Lord for whom vast creation is offering the cosmic *ārti*. The practice during the *ārti* was to burn fragrant incenses, offer flowers, with someone standing and fanning the idol with the *chawar*–a ceremonial whisk. The Guru now evokes the image of the cosmic worship and says, *dhūp malyānlo pavaṇ chavro karay sagal banrāye phūlant joti*–the temple incense is the fragrant breezes, and the winds themselves provide the fanning *chawar*. All flora, the created plants are an offering to the Lord, like the offering of the flowers in a temple *ārti*.

The term *malyānlo* derives from the hills known as the Mallya range located in the south of India, where Sandalwood trees grow in abundance. The breeze coming off that range is therefore often fragrant with the scent of Sandal. The term is, therefore, synonymous with any pleasant and welcome breeze. This *malyānlo* is, says the Guru, the fragrant incense in that cosmic worship. The natural breezes that blow are the ceremonial whisk *–chawar–*constantly fanning His grand presence. The floral offering is not limited to a few ritual flowers; rather the entire world of flora is the offering in this divine *ārti*. Bhai Vir Singh, and most learned ones, render the term *joti-* refulgent light–at the end of this line as referring to the Lord, that all these offerings are being made to that *joti*. The other view could be that these flora are the *joti*–the light. The first is the more appealing rendering.

The Guru sums up the thought in the third line when he says, *kaisi ārti hoye. Bhav khanddna teri ārti*–what a wondrous *ārti* this is, O dispeller of fear. He underlines the grandeur of this cosmic worship that all creation is constantly offering to the Lord. How magnificent is this worship that creation offers to its maker. It is wondrous indeed, and by implication the human ritual is petty and not worthy of that great Lord. The Guru addresses the Lord here as the *bhav khanddna. Bhav* means fear, and the reference here is to the fear of death and rebirth, which afflicts us all; and *khandann* means to dispel, to break. As the Guru says in the Rehrās Sahib, *saranjam lāg bhavjal taran kay*–get busy in the effort to swim across the dreadful water. The *bhavjal* here is the ocean of dread we perceive when we see the end of our lives here on this world, forgetting that this is a mere stop in a very long journey that the soul has to undertake from the time it separated from the Lord till it achieves re-union. For this, we will keep coming to this world, our *karmabhūmi*, to earn the merit that would make us fit for that divine presence. This dread, this terrible fear is dispelled when we follow the true Guru and live a life of total surrender to the Lord. Living the right life, we can hope to be fit for His glance of grace, which will dispel this dread. Thus, the Lord is the dispeller of fear, the *bhav khanddan*, to whom the entire creation is offering this wondrous cosmic *ārti*, says the Guru.

In the fourh line, the Guru says, *anhata sabad vājant bheri*–the musical accompaniment in that cosmic *ārti* is the *anhat shabad* itself. This concept of the *anhat shabad* is an inherent part of the eastern belief systems. Literally, it means the 'unstruck chord'. This chord is in terms of faith believed to be the echo of the Word, often called *Om* or *Aum*, with which the Creator brought this universe into existence. The concept of creation with a word is not exclusive to Hinduism. Even the Semitic religions hold to this view. The Lord said the word and the universe came into existence. That chord reverberates through the cosmos eternally and is the marker of the Lord Creator. Mystics also call it the music of the spheres, or the song celestial. That, says the Guru, is the music that accompanies the worship that the entire creation is offering to Him. Learned ones often render the word *bheri* as flute. However, it actually refers to a conical two-faced drum that is very commonly used during worship in temples. The Mahan Kosh tells us that a *nafīri*, which is like a *shehnāyi* or a trombone, usually accompanies it. The sense in which the Guru uses it here is not to stress a particular instrument or music but to evoke the picture of the musical accompaniment always used in the worship.

In the fifth line, the Guru makes an effort to describe the Lord who is beyond all description. He says, *sahas tav nain nan nain hai tohe kao*–thousands of eyes are Yours, yet You have no eyes. Then he adds, *sahas murat nana ek tohi*–Yours are all these thousands of forms, yet You have no form. The allusion here is to the Lord having no specific form, shape, colour or sign to identify Him. This picture we see drawn thoughout *Gurbāṇi,* in the SGGS as also in the *bāṇi* of the tenth Nanak. The lesson here is that all we see is but the Lord incarnate. He permeates all existence and all creation is, thus, but a reflection of that Reality. In this sense, all eyes that created beings are endowed with are really the eyes of the Lord. Yet, there is no eye we can say is His eye. Similarly, all shapes that exist are the Lord incarnate, yet none of these shapes can be identified as exclusively being Him. He is, in this manner, all shapes yet can have no shape. The Lord's omnipresence is juxtaposed here with our inability to ascribe to Him any shape, sign or form.

The Guru continues in the same vein as he says in the sixth line, *sahas pad bimal nan ek pad*–You have thousands of feet and yet You do not have a single foot. The word *bimal* derives from *vi* and *mal*, meaning free from taint. Thus, it means pure, chaste. The feet of His creation are pure and chaste, because these are in reality His own feet. Similarly, he says, *gandh bin sahas tav gandh*–You have no olefactory organ, yet You have thousands of such organs, such noses. He then concludes this recitation of the Lord's wonders with, *iv chalat mohi*–I am enchanted with this play of Yours. The picture the Guru is painting here is a continuation of the thought in the previous line. He says the Lord has thousands, meaning uncounted, feet yet no foot is exclusively His. He has the sense of smell of thousands but none is exclusively His alone. This wondrous image, where the Lord permeates everything that exists but has no identifiable shape, has the Guru in ecstasy; this playful display of the Almighty's divine mystery enchants him.

In the eighth line, the Guru says *sabh meh jot jot hai soye*–You are the light within everyone. The Lord that permeates all creation and therefore all beings are but His reflection. The light that shines within us and gives us existence is the Lord.

The Guru is telling us that there can be no hierarchies in human beings and we all are exactly the same–visible manifestations of the Lord's life giving light. The same thought continues in the ninth line. The Guru says, *tis dai chānaṇ sabh meh chānaṇ hoye*–that Light is the light that engenders the life, the awareness within all. It is, incidentally also a reminder to us that all created beings are equal in His eyes and none can claim to be superior on any grounds of wealth, power, caste or creed.

In the 10th line, the Guru says, *gur sākhi jot pargatt hoye*–this light is attained through the Guru's teachings. The term *sākhi* literally means witnessed or seen. In other words, the knowledge of the Lord's existence is revealed, made known, to us through the sight granted to us by the Guru's teachings. The importance of the Guru has always been held to be paramount in *Gurbāṇi* and, therefore, this gift will come to us only through the Guru.

The 11th line makes another important lesson clear; that, we must fully accept the Lord's will. The Guru says, *jo tis bhāvai so ārti hoye*–His *ārti* means total acceptance of His divine will. He is here returning to the concept of the *ārti* that humans perform. He is saying that the mere ritual of moving a lamp before the image of the deity is but supreficial homage. Real worship comes from the heart and the mind. It means living your life in accordance with the Lord's will, in total surrender to Him. Such complete acceptance of Him and His will is the true worship.

The Guru concludes this lesson with the last two lines of this magnificent hymn. In the second last, the 12th line, he says, *har charaṇ kaval makrand lobhit mano andino moh āhi pyāsa*–my mind thirsts day and night for the lotus-feet of the Lord. Devotees, to express their great love for the Lord often use similar phraseology. *Makrand* means the essence of the flower, prepared by treating the flower petals to derive a honey like sweet concoction. It is often of medicinal value and it is highly valued for its delicious taste. The Guru says the Lord's feet are to him as desirable as the *kaval makrand,* the sweet essence of the lotus flower. The worship he was talking about is this constant hunger for the Lord, not the ceremonial waving of a plate with lit lamps.

Then, in the last, the thirteenth, line he adds, *kripa jal deh Nanak sārang kao hoye ja tay terai nāye vāsa*–bestow Your mercy on Nanak, who thirsts for it as the *sarang*. This bird is also called the *papīha.* What is the gift the Guru is seeking from the Lord? That he may ever stay attached to the Name. The *papīha* is a popular name for the weaverbird. Since this vociferous bird is most commonly heard before the rainy season, the popular belief is that it yearns for the rains to fall. This is viewed romantically as a burning desire for a drop of water to fall into its mouth. The Guru compares his own burning hunger for the Lord to such a bird thirsting for water.

The essence of the lesson is that do not try to trivialise your worship by merely going through the motions of rituals such as the ritual of what we call *ārti*. Instead, remember that the Lord is vast and mysterious and there is a multitude of created things offering a divine cosmic *ārti* to Him. Your true *ārti* would be fixing of your mind on Him, living the life on His path as instructed by the Guru, and carrying in your heart a constant desire to be near Him.

4

KEEP THE COMPANY OF THE GODLY

The next hymn is by the fourth Nanak, Guru Ram Das. He speaks of the evils that beset humans constantly, and the device for ridding ourselves of these. The same hymn occurs again at page 171, SGGS, in the same form. The Guru says:

ਰਾਗੁ ਗਉੜੀ ਪੂਰਬੀ ਮਹਲਾ ੪ ॥	Rāg Gauṛi Pūrabi Mahla 4
ਕਾਮਿ ਕਰੋਧਿ ਨਗਰੁ ਬਹੁ ਭਰਿਆ ਮਿਲਿ ਸਾਧੂ ਖੰਡਲ ਖੰਡਾ ਹੇ ॥	Kām krodh nagar bahu bhariya mil sādhu khanddal khandda hay
ਪੂਰਬਿ ਲਿਖਤ ਲਿਖੇ ਗੁਰੁ ਪਾਇਆ ਮਨਿ ਹਰਿ ਲਿਵ ਮੰਡਲ ਮੰਡਾ ਹੇ ॥੧॥	Pūrab likhat likhay gur pāia mann har liv manddal mandda hay.1.
ਕਰਿ ਸਾਧੂ ਅੰਜੁਲੀ ਪੁਨੁ ਵਡਾ ਹੇ ॥	Kar sādhu anjuli pun vadda hay.
ਕਰਿ ਡੰਡਉਤ ਪੁਨੁ ਵਡਾ ਹੇ ॥੧॥ ਰਹਾਉ ॥	Kar ddanddaut pun vadda hay.1. Rahāo.
ਸਾਕਤ ਹਰਿ ਰਸ ਸਾਦੁ ਨ ਜਾਣਿਆ ਤਿਨ ਅੰਤਰਿ ਹਉਮੈ ਕੰਡਾ ਹੇ ॥	Sākat har ras sād na jāṇiya tin antar haumai kandda hay.
ਜਿਉ ਜਿਉ ਚਲਹਿ ਚੁਭੈ ਦੁਖੁ ਪਾਵਹਿ	Jiu jiu chaleh chubhai dukh

ਜਮਕਾਲੁ ਸਹਹਿ ਸਿਰਿ ਡੰਡਾ ਹੇ ॥੨॥	pāveh jamkāl saheh sir(i) ddanddda hay.2.
ਹਰਿ ਜਨ ਹਰਿ ਹਰਿ ਨਾਮਿ ਸਮਾਣੇ ਦੁਖੁ ਜਨਮ ਮਰਣ ਭਵ ਖੰਡਾ ਹੇ ॥	Har jan har har nām samāṇay dukh janam maraṇ bhav khandda hay.
ਅਬਿਨਾਸੀ ਪੁਰਖੁ ਪਾਇਆ ਪਰਮੇਸਰੁ ਬਹੁ ਸੋਭ ਖੰਡ ਬ੍ਰਹਮੰਡਾ ਹੇ ॥੩॥	Abināsi purakh pāia parmesar bahu sobh khandd brahmandda hay.3.
ਹਮ ਗਰੀਬ ਮਸਕੀਨ ਪ੍ਰਭ ਤੇਰੇ ਹਰਿ ਰਾਖੁ ਰਾਖੁ ਵਡ ਵਡਾ ਹੇ ॥	Ham garīb maskīn prabh teray har rākh rākh vadd vadda hay.
ਜਨ ਨਾਨਕ ਨਾਮੁ ਅਧਾਰੁ ਟੇਕ ਹੈ ਹਰਿ ਨਾਮੇ ਹੀ ਸੁਖੁ ਮੰਡਾ ਹੇ ॥੪॥੪॥	Jan Nanak nām adhar teik hai har nāmay hee sukh mandda hay.4.4.

Glossary:

ਖੰਡਲ ਖੰਡਾ	Khanddal khandda	Broken into pieces, dispelled
ਮੰਡਲ ਮੰਡਾ	Manddal mandda	Decorated and installed
ਅੰਜੁਲੀ	Anjuli	Ceremonial obeisance
ਸਾਕਤ	Sākat	Worshipper of power, godless one
ਚੁਭੈ	Chubhai	Pierces, rankles
ਮਸਕੀਨ	Maskīn	Humble one
ਅਧਾਰੁ ਟੇਕ	Adhar teik	Support

In the first line, the Guru says, *kām krodh nagar bahu bhariya mil sādhu khanddal khandda hay*–anger and sensual concerns prevail in this town, meaning this human body, and these will be overcome in the company of the godly. The term *nagar* literally means habitation or town, but is here used for the human body. This vessel, in which the divine soul separated from the Lord dwells on this mortal abode, is filled with the baser emotions. The Guru is referring to the natural weakness that afflicts all flesh; propensity to great anger and constant pandering to the senses. We are overwhelmed by these base emotions and are therefore prevented from achieving our true goal; re-union with the Lord. Because we are so full of these destructive traits, we are unable follow the right path and become condemned to repeating the cycle of death and rebirth. Salvation from this fate comes through the company of the godly. When we start to be with them all these evil traits will be *khanddal khandda.* The term *khandd* means, inter alia, to break up into pieces, and it is here used in that sense. The Guru is saying the evils will be totally cut to pieces, be excised and expelled from within us, by the benign company of the godly. Learned ones interpret the term *sadhu* here to refer to the Guru, meaning that the riddance from these evils will come through the right Guru, because the Guru puts us on the path to God-realisation.

In the second line, the Guru makes this aspect clearer. He says, *pūrab likhat likhay gur pāia mann har liv manddal mandda hay*–the Lord had ordained that we meet the Guru and now, through him, the Lord resides in our hearts. The stress on the Guru as the one who will put us on the right path will be found throughout *Gurbāṇi*. It is the belief that the Guru will show us the right path so that we could make ourselves worthy of the Lord's glance of grace. It is a greatly fortunate event, therefore, when we do find that Guru, and it comes about only if the Lord so ordains.

The concept of *pūrab likhat* needs to be understood here. The term literally means 'written before', but refers here to the effects of our actions in our past births. The Guru has touched on this issue when he told us in *pauṛi* 20 of the Japji Sahib, ਪੁੰਨੀ ਪਾਪੀ ਆਖਣੁ ਨਾਹਿ॥ ਕਰਿ ਕਰਿ ਕਰਣਾ ਲਿਖਿ ਲੈ ਜਾਹੁ]–*Puni pāpi ākhaṇ nāhe. Kar kar karṇa likh lai jāhu.* This means do not think good or evil deeds are mere talk. Whatever actions we perform will be indelibly written on our souls and the consequences thereof we will carry with us into the future, into new incarnations. Good deeds, and living in accordance with the Lord's way will earn us merit. Equally, we will accumulate the onerous load of our evil deeds. Actions leave their inevitable mark on the soul; bad actions slide us down the ladder and good actions uplift the soul on the path towards the Lord. The actions of the man are the determinants of his fate in this sense. The Guru says in the Āsa di Vār, *Slok Mahla* 1, page 470, *SGGS*:

ਮੰਦਾ ਚੰਗਾ ਆਪਣਾ ਆਪੇ ਹੀ ਕੀਤਾ ਪਾਵਣਾ॥
Manda changa āpṇa āpay hee kīta pāvṇa.

This means that the good and the bad of our actions we will ourselves have to face. The responsibility for the uplift of our soul is here squarely cast upon our own selves.

Again, the Guru says in *Rāg Āsa Mahla* 1, page 433, SGGS,
ਦਦੈ ਦੋਸੁ ਨ ਦੇਊ ਕਿਸੈ ਦੋਸੁ ਕਰੰਮਾ ਆਪਣਿਆ॥ ਜੋ ਮੈ ਕੀਆ ਸੋ ਮੈ ਪਾਇਆ ਦੋਸੁ ਨ ਦੀਜੈ ਅਵਰ ਜਨਾ॥
Dadai dos na deu kisay dos karamma āpṇia.
Jo mai kīya so mai pāiya dos na dījay avar jana.

This broadly translates as, "Seek not to lay the blame at another's door; the fault lies in our own actions. Whatever I did so was I rewarded." In other words, the good and the bad of our actions will be visited on our own heads. This theme runs continuously throughout the *SGGS*. Hence, Sikhism is not a religion for the quietist; it requires of us constant action with scrupulous attention to the propriety of what we do. The effects of these actions are the *pūrab likhat*–pre-ordained destiny that we bring with us. Learned ones speak of three types of these fate-determining actions. The Mahan Kosh says that the first is the ਕ੍ਰਿਆਮਾਨ–*Kriyāmān,* referring to actions currently being performed. The second type is ਪ੍ਰਾਲਬਧ–*Prārabdh, or prālabdh* referring to the earned merit that has given us this particular body. The third type is ਸੰਚਿਤ–*Sanchit*, that merit which still stands in our credit, to which we could add through the *Kriyamān*.

The *purab likhat* will then determine if we will find the Guru. The Guru tells us in *Rāg Gauṛi Pūrbi Mahla* 5, page 204, SGGS, ਪੂਰਬ ਕਰਮ ਅੰਕੁਰ ਜਬ ਪ੍ਰਗਟੇ ਭੇਟਿਓ ਪੁਰਖੁ ਰਸਿਕ ਬੈਰਾਗੀ॥–*Pūrab karam ankur jab pragattay bhettiyo purakh rasik bairagi.* This means when our past actions bear fruit we will meet the loving one who is yet without any attachments, meaning the Lord Himself. This will happen through the Guru. Here in this *bāṇi* the same thought is stated as *purab likhat likhay gur pāia*–due to our destiny we found the Guru.

When we do have the good luck to find that Guru, he will remove the evils from within us and will, instead, install therein the Lord Himself. The term *mandda* has many meanings, but is used here in the sense of decorated, ornamented. The Guru is saying that the mind is now immersed in the Lord, or as he puts it *mann har liv*–the mind is fixed on the Lord. The Guru has used the terms *khanddal khandda* and *manddal mandda* here in juxtaposition not merely for the rhyming poetic resonance of these. He is, in fact, through this delineating a very uplifting picture of the process of evil being totally destroyed from within us and the Lord's name being ornamented and installed instead.

In the third line, he tells us, *kar sādhu anjuli pun vadda hay*–to offer obeisance to the saint, meaning here the Guru, is an act of great merit. The term *anjuli* describes a gesture in which the two hands are cupped together as we offer obeisance. This is done to show great reverence. The Guru is saying do *anjuli* to the saintly ones and you will earn great merit. This is another way of telling us to keep the company of the men of god and to show them all respect.

In the fourth line he adds to the same thought when he says, *kar ddanddaut pun vadda hay*–prostrating completely is a deed of virtue. The term *ddanddaut* describes a particular form of prostrating respectfully. It is customary everywhere, and especially in India, to show deep respect for someone by bowing. The deeper the bow the higher is supposed to be the intensity of one's devotion. This is true, of course, only when it is meant from the heart. Some times men bow for the wrong reasons also. As the Guru told us in Āsa di Vār, *Slok Mahla* 1, page 470, SGGS, ਸੀਸਿ ਨਿਵਾਈਐ ਕਿਆ ਥੀਐ ਜਾ ਰਿਦੈ ਕੁਸੁਧੇ ਜਾਹਿ॥–*sīs nivaīai kia thhīai jay ridai kusudhay jāhe.* This means what avails it to bow your body if there is evil in the heart.

To bow oneself is a sign of respect for a superior. When extreme respect is to be exhibited people will lie down completely, hands stretched over the head and the body fully prostrate on the ground. The Guru is saying here that it earns us great merit when we show such respect to the saintly. The Guru has given great importance to this thought as is indicated by the *rahāo*–pause, marked at the end of this line. This is the Guru's direction for us to stop a bit and ponder on the thought enunciated, the lesson imparted. To recapitulate, the Guru has till here told us that this body of ours is overwhelmed by the forces of worldly attractions and that these will be dispelled only through the Guru and through the company of the saintly ones. Show utmost respect to these, he is telling us.

In the fifth line he says, *sākat har ras sād na jāṇiya tin antar haumai kandda hay*–those obsessed with power and with the worldly attractions will never taste the blissful joy of the Lord's name, because within them is the thorn of their ego. The term *sākat* literally means worshippers of *Shakti*–power. Learned ones also render it as a worshipper of *Maya*. It is used generally to describe those who are not on the right path to the Lord. The sense in which the Guru uses it here is probably derives from the Arabic sense of the word where, the Mahan Kosh tells us, it means apostate or the fallen one. Such ungodly ones will never experience that bliss of being immersed in the name of the Lord, because they are prevented from doing so by the thorn of the *haumai* within them. This thorn is so constantly an irritation and a distraction that bliss just cannot enter their souls. Learned ones often render the term *haumai* as ego, which interpretation is also correct in its own way. However, more accurately the term has to be seen as referring to a sense of selfness, of duality, of being apart from the Lord. This alienation from that sole Reality is what causes these various evils, like pride, anger, an inflated ego to fester within us.

In the sixth line, the Guru explains the problem that this *haumai* causes. He says, *jiu jiu chaleh chubhai dukh pāveh jamkāl saheh sir(i) ddanddda hay*–such people suffer throughout their existence because this thorn *(haumai)* continues to bite painfully into their soul. They will, therefore, continue to suffer the agonies of existence and the terror of death. The continuing pain of the thorn of *haumai* rankles within them each passing moment of their existence. Not only this, they also suffer the fatal blows from the messengers of the death god. The allusion here is to the fear of death that marks our daily existence. The human body is destined to deteriorate and one day ends. The soul, however, is immortal, a part of the divine light separated from its creator by the *haumai* within. Once we recognise the reality this fear will vanish; we will know that the body may perish but we will not be dead. There will, then be no scope for fear of the god of death. No messenger of that god can then touch us. For that, we have but to lose our *haumai*.

In the seventh line this issue is further clairified as the Guru says, *har jan har har nām samāṇay dukh janam maraṇ bhav khandda hay*–the devotees of the Lord are totally absorbed in His Name, and therefore do not suffer the pain and the dread of birth and death in this world. This is an elaboration of the lesson of the previous line. Those immersed in the Lord will have lost their *haumai*; will have recognised the Lord as the sole reality. The pain, and fear, of *janam maraṇ* - death and rebirth–will vanish for such devotees.

The Guru stresses the same thought in the eighth line and says, *abināsi purakh pāia parmesar bahu sobh khandd brahmandda hay*–they have realised the Immortal one and earn honours throughout the world. The term *khandd brahmandda* is here used to refer to the entire created universe. Throughout this creation, such devotees of the Lord will gain honour and renown, says the Guru. Those who have attained the *abināsi purakh*–the deathless one, the *parmesar*–the Almighty Lord, will deserve such accolades. These fortunate ones will have honour and success in this world, but beyond that, and more importantly, they will be honoured in the presence of the Lord.

In the ninth line he says, *ham garīb maskīn prabh teray har rākh rākh vadd vadda hay*–I am weak and helpless but preserve me because I belong to the Lord who is the greatest of the great. The lesson here is to recognise ones own puny stature compared to the Lord Creator. The Lord is the greater than any power we can imagine, He is the greatest of the great. Compared to Him what are we? The Guru says we are the *garīb* and we are *maskīn.* The term *maskīn,* according to the Mahan Kosh, denotes one who is humble and very patient; one who can suffer silently. It denotes a sense of meekness and humility. *Garīb* means poor. The Guru says we are *garīb* and *maskīn.* We lack all greatness, but yet, the Guru says, we have one claim to the Lord's glance of grace; we are *teray*. We belong to Him. Thus the pre-requisite for His grace is to own Him, to surrender ones own self totally to Him. In other words, get rid of out *haumai,* our sense of selfness which leads to our ego-centric way of life. Because we are His, He will preserve us from the coils of *Maya*, of illusion and ignorance. This is the prayer and the hope to which the Guru wants us to hold.

In the last line, the tenth, the Guru sums it up with, *jan Nanak nām adhar tteik hai har nāmay hee sukh mandda hay.* This translates as, "the Lord's Name is Nanak's sustenance and support and the Name gives great peace and comfort." The Mahan Kosh tells us that the term *mandda*, which has different connotations, is to be construed here as meaning achieved or experienced. The Guru is saying that he is the Lord's creature and for him the only support is the Lord's name. He has experienced, reached, a state of peace only through meditation on the Lord's name.

We have now seen how the Guru has shown us the path from, as he said in the first line of this hymn, the *nagar* full of *kām and krodh* to the state of *sukh,* by surrendering to the Lord and focusing on Him as your sole support.

We now come to the last hymn of this *bāṇi*, which is by the fifth Nanak. The same hymn is placed also at page 205, SGGS, with some small differences. Firstly, the order of lines has been altered, with the third and fourth lines being shifted to the beginning. Accordingly, the *rahāo*–the pause, occurs at line two instead of line four. Then, in line five, the word *sansa* has been changed to *sahsa*, both having the same meaning. In line six, the spelling of *piāvai* has been spelled as *piāye*, and in line seven, *bihājho* is spelled as *vihājho*. All these are minor changes and make no difference to the message of this hymn. The Guru says:

ਰਾਗੁ ਗਉੜੀ ਪੂਰਬੀ ਮਹਲਾ ੫ ॥	Rāg Gauṛi Pūrabi Mahla 5
ਕਰਉ ਬੇਨੰਤੀ ਸੁਣਹੁ ਮੇਰੇ ਮੀਤਾ ਸੰਤ ਟਹਲ ਕੀ ਬੇਲਾ ॥	Karo(n) benanti suṇho meray mīta sant ttehal ki bela
ਈਹਾ ਖਾਟਿ ਚਲਹੁ ਹਰਿ ਲਾਹਾ ਆਗੈ ਬਸਨੁ ਸੁਹੇਲਾ ॥੧॥	Īha khātt chalo har lāha āgai basan suhela.1.
ਅਉਧ ਘਟੈ ਦਿਨਸੁ ਰੈਣਾਰੇ ॥	Audh ghattai dinas raiṇaray.
ਮਨ ਗੁਰ ਮਿਲਿ ਕਾਜ ਸਵਾਰੇ ॥੧॥ ਰਹਾਉ ॥	Mann gur mil kāj sawāray.1. rahāo.
ਇਹੁ ਸੰਸਾਰੁ ਬਿਕਾਰੁ ਸੰਸੇ ਮਹਿ ਤਰਿਓ ਬ੍ਰਹਮ ਗਿਆਨੀ ॥	Eh sansār bikār sansay meh taryo brahm giāni.
ਜਿਸਹਿ ਜਗਾਇ ਪੀਆਵੈ ਇਹੁ ਰਸੁ ਅਕਥ ਕਥਾ ਤਿਨਿ ਜਾਨੀ ॥੨॥	Jiseh jagāye piāvai eh ras akathh kathha tin jāni.2.
ਜਾ ਕਉ ਆਏ ਸੋਈ ਬਿਹਾਝਹੁ ਹਰਿ ਗੁਰ ਤੇ ਮਨਹਿ ਬਸੇਰਾ ॥	Ja kao aye soyi bihājho har gur tay maneh basera.
ਨਿਜ ਘਰਿ ਮਹਲੁ ਪਾਵਹੁ ਸੁਖ ਸਹਜੇ ਬਹੁਰਿ ਨ ਹੋਇਗੋ ਫੇਰਾ ॥੩॥	Nij ghar mahal pāvho sukh sahjay bahur na hoyego phera.3.
ਅੰਤਰਜਾਮੀ ਪੁਰਖ ਬਿਧਾਤੇ ਸਰਧਾ ਮਨ ਕੀ ਪੂਰੇ॥	Antarjami purakh bidhātay sardha mann ki pūray.

ਨਾਨਕ ਦਾਸੁ ਇਹੈ ਸੁਖੁ ਮਾਗੈ ਮੋ ਕਉ ਕਰਿ ਸੰਤਨ ਕੀ ਧੂਰੇ ॥੪॥੫॥	Nanak dās ehai sukh māngai mo kao kar santan ki dhūray.4.5.

Glossary:

ਬੇਲਾ	Bela	Occasion, opportunity, time
ਲਾਹਾ	Lāha	Gain, profit, advantage
ਅਉਧ	Audh	Alloted span of time
ਸੰਸਾਰੁ ਬਿਕਾਰੁ	Sansār bikār	Worldly attractions, evils
ਸੰਸੇ	Sansay	Doubts,
ਬਿਹਾਝਹੁ	Bihājho	Trade, deal in
ਧੂਰੇ	Dhūray	Dust

In the first line, the Guru says, *karo(n) benanti suṇho meray mīta sant ttehal ki bela*–heed my words, friend, this lifetime is your opportunity to serve the saints, the godly ones.(The term krau though written as *karo* in Gurmukhi is to be pronounced as *karo(n),* with a nasal sound). The message contained in this line is a basic tenet of the Sikh faith. The Guru has told us throughout the SGGS that this human birth is an excellent opportunity to win our way back to reunion with the Lord, from whom we were separated by our own actions and from whom our *haumai* continues to keep us separated. This hymn is an almost exact restatement of the thought the Guru had expressed in *Rāg Āsa, Mahla 5,* page 378 SGGS; there he told us*, bhayi parāpat mānukh dehuriya, gobind milaṇ ki eh teri bariya*–you have been gifted this human form, this is your turn, your opportunity to reunite with the Creator. Here, the Guru is also saying that this task of achieving reunion with the Lord will be made easier if we serve and keep the company of those immersed in the Lord. That right company will make it easier for us to tread the correct path ourselves. By serving the saintly, we will acquire the right frame of mind, will always have the right example before us and, therefore, will ultimately learn to overcome our *haumai*.

In the second line, the Guru makes his lesson clearer as he says *īha khātt chalo har lāha āgai basan suhela*–recite the name of the Lord and you will earn great profit from this opportunity in this world. If you do so, you will ensure a pleasant existence in the next world. This is another way of telling us that salvation awaits us when we live in accordance with the path shown by the Guru. Of course, salvation is not ours to claim but is for the Lord to grant when He so deems fit. However, as the Guru said in the fourth *pauṛi* of the Japji Sahib, *karmi āvai kapṛa nadri mokh duār*. The assured reward to the follower of the right path is to be blessed with a deserving *kapṛa*. This word translates literally as apparel, cloth or dress. Here it is used for the human body, which indeed is the attire for the soul in this world. Therefore, even if we are not yet worthy of salvation, of being in His presence, we can surely hope for a more comfortable existence. Seek to earn the maximum merit through the right company. The Guru is comparing our dealings here to the actions of the wise trader who strives always for higher profits. He is exhorting us here to do this holy trade and earn profits for our soul. He had used a similar analogy in the Japji Sahib, in *pauṛi* 26, first two lines when he told us, *amul guṇ amul vāpār;* and then, *amul vāpārīye amul bhanddār.* He is saying, 'priceless are His qualities'. He implies that no human mind can put a value on these. There are, however, many who seek after Him and try to learn of these qualities. They exchange this knowledge; they talk of it; they learn and they teach. This dealing is the *vāpār*–the trading to which the Guru is referring. He says not only are the Lord's qualities invaluable, but *amul*–invaluable is this trade. Not only the trade but also the fortunate ones who do this trade are beyond value. Trade usually entails profit taking, greed and material considerations. However, here the dealers, the traders are involved in a holy commerce. This is commerce we must wholeheartedly ply and earn from it as much profit as possible. This is the only asset we will be able to carry beyond this mortal world. This asset will make our existence comfortable beyond this life.

In the third line he says, *audh ghattai dinas raiṇaray*–by the moment your allotted span is passing away. We come to this world, this *karmabhūmi*, this arena with a pre-ordained time allotted to us. With the first breath we draw, that span starts eroding. As we celebrate birthdays and with each passing year, this invaluable commodity, this span is eroding. The Guru wants us to be aware of this harsh reality. When we are conscious of this mortality, we will also remember the Lord, and will be loath to waste our time in petty enjoyment of worldly pleasures. Elsewhere, the ninth Nanak tells us, in *Rāg Tilang Mahla* 9, page 726, SGGS, *chetna hai tau cheit lay nis din may prāni, chhin chhin audh bihāt hai phūttay ghatt jiu pāni.* The Guru is asking us to fix our minds on Him now if we ever intend to do so, because with each moment our allotted span is leaking away like water from a broken earthen container. Here the Guru says that the *audh*–the allotted span, is elapsing each night and each day, meaning with each passing moment.

In the fourth line he says, *mann gur mil kāj sawāray*–My mind, come to the Guru and set right your affairs. The concept here is that the Guru will teach you how to live the right life and how to keep your mind fixed on the Lord. At the end of the line, the Guru has prescribed a *rahāo*, meaning pause. This is a device the Guru uses throughout the SGGS and it is meant to highlight the main point, the thrust of the lesson. Here, lines three and four constitute that thrust. Our lifespan is fast eroding, hurry and put this time to proper use; come to the Guru and follow his path to the Lord.

In the fifth line, the Guru says, *eh(o) sansār bikār sansay meh taryo brahm giāni*–This world is sorely beset by doubts and misgivings, but those whom he grants understanding achieve salvation. The concept of crossing an ocean of dread is found in many belief systems. The transition from this world of the mortals to the divine presence is like crossing an ocean, sometimes called the *bhavsāgar*–ocean of dread. This refers to our massive fear of the phenomenon of this mortal body's demise. This dread will vanish when we know our reality; that we are really part of that divine entity, the creator Lord. When we realise it, we become *brahm giāni*, possessors of the knowledge of the universe. No doubts remain in that state and we will have become as one with Him; would have achieved salvation. Learned ones have rendered this phrase to mean that people are immersed in *vikār* because they have material bodies and their minds are in *sansay*–doubts. *Vikār* means evils, wrongdoing, and bad habits. In this sense, the phrase would mean that the world is lost in *bikār* and suffers from doubts and misgivings. In the midst of all this chaos, only the *brahm giāni* will be saved.

In the sixth line, the Guru says, *jiseh jagāye piāvai eh ras akathh kathha tin jāni*–only he can know the unknowable mysteries of the Lord whom the Lord awakens and gives the boon of the His name. The theme of salvation being a gift from the Lord is continued here. We cannot claim to be able to achieve that blessed state on our own strength. It will come only when the Lord decides to bestow on us His glance of grace. He will awaken us and will bestow on us the blissful taste of His name; and thus will the unknowable mysteries of life and death become clear to us.

In the seventh line, the Guru tells us, *ja kao āye soyi bihājho har gur tay maneh basera*–trade in the commodity for which you have come to the world and through the grace of the Guru the Lord will settle in your mind. The purpose of our birth is one, and only one; to strive to win our way back to the Lord from whom we have been separated. It is a different matter, and a hard reality that while we are still alive, myriad worldly dealings seem to acquire prime importance for us. Family, society, material possessions, worldly power and generally pandering to the senses become our first priorities and we forget the real reason for our sojourn here. The Guru is gently reminding us that these were not our real aims, the reason we were sent here was different. Focus the mind on that real purpose and deal only in that commodity. Follow the path your Guru has delineated and the Lord will surely dwell in your heart. The implicit message is that once He does that we will be on the right course to salvation. It is also important to note here that for the Sikh the ever-present Guru is the Sri Guru Granth Sahib (SGGS) from where this right counsel is ever available to us.

In the eighth line, the Guru says, *nij ghar mahal pāvho sukh sahjay bahur na hoyego phera*–within your heart the Lord will reside without effort, and you will never again have to suffer birth or death. In the seventh line we were told, *har gur tay maneh basera*–through the Guru the Lord will within us make His residence. Now the Guru stresses that point again and says that *nij ghar*–within you, the *mahal*

–Lord's abode will be created *sukh sahjay*–with ease and comfort. Once that happens a very happy consequence will ensue, says the Guru. We will be blessed with *bahur na hoyego phera*–never again will we suffer the cycle of death and rebirth.

In the last two lines, the Guru concludes this lesson with the ninth line saying, *antarjami purakh bidhātay sardha mann ki pūray*–o all-knowing, omniscient one, the Lord who determines our fates please fulfill our desires. Then he says in the final, the tenth line, *Nanak dās ehai sukh māngai mo kao kar santan ki dhūray*–Your devotee Nanak, begs for your blessings to make him the dust of the feet of the saints. The Guru's prayer to the Lord is to grant him the dust of His devotees. It is the only boon he seeks, and why does he do that? Because once you are in the company of the godly, you will automatically be on the right path, the path to salvation.

KEY TO PRONUNCIATION

	Gurmukhi Script	Roman script	Pronunciation
1	ਅ	a	short 'a', as in 'normal', except at the end when it is long as in 'war'
2	ਆ	ā	long a, as in 'war'
3	ਇ, ਿ	i	short 'i' as in 'fit'
4	ਈ, ੀ	ī	long 'i' as in 'meet
5	ਉ, ੁ	u	short 'u' as in 'put'
6	ਊ, ੂ	ū	long 'u' as in 'boot'
7	ਏ, ੇ	e	sharp 'a' as in 'grey'
8	ਐ, ੈ	ai	broad 'a' as in 'fat'
9	ਅੰ, ੰ	[ng]	nasal, short sound, as in sing
10	ਆਂ, ਂ	ā[n]	nasal, long sound as in brand
11	ਸ	s	as in sad
12	ਸ਼	sh	as in sharp, shut
13	ਕ	k	as in kit
14	ਖ	kh	as in *khālsa*, or silk hat (uttered quickly together)
15	ਗ	g	as in good
16	ਘ	gh	as in ghost, or log-hut (uttered quickly together)
17	ਚ	ch	as in chat
18	ਛ	chh	as in Chhatisgarh, or church-hill uttered quickly together

19	ਜ	j	as in just
20	ਝ	jh	as in *jhang*, or hedgehog
21	ਟ	tt	hard sound, as in talk, or curt
22	ਠ	tth	hard sound, as in thakur, or hot-house
23	ਡ	dd	as in dark, or card
24	ਢ	ddh	as in *dholak*, or in red-hot (uttered quickly together)
25	ਣ	ṇ	as in *madhāṇī*
26	ਤ	t	soft 't', as in *talwandī*
27	ਥ	thh	as in thick
28	ਦ	d	soft 'd', as in then
29	ਧ	dh	as in *dhobi*, or breathe hard
30	ਨ	n	as in nun
31	ਪ	p	as in pup
32	ਫ	ph or f	as in phone or fix
33	ਬ	b	as in but, or tube
34	ਭ	bh	as in *Bhagat*, or abhor
35	ਮ	m	as in mat, or time
36	ਯ	y	as in yet
37	ਰ	r	as in rat
38	ਲ	l	as in love
39	ਵ	v,w	as in vent, with
40	ੜ	ṛ	as in *pahāṛ*
41	ਜ਼	z	as in zero

SELECT BIBLIOGRAPHY

1. Sri Dasam Granth Sahib
Bhai Chatar Singh,
Jiwan Singh

2. Sri Guru Granth Sahib Darpan
Prof. Sahib Singh
(Raj Publishers, 1972)

3. Shabdarth Sri Guru Granth Sahib Ji
Sharomani GurdwaraParbandhak Committee, 1995

4. Sri Guru Granth Sahib (English)
Prof. Gurbachan Singh Talib
Publication Translation Bureau, Punjabi University, Patiala, 1988)

5. Pajgranthi Steek
Bhai Vir Singh
(Bhai Vir Singh Sahit Sadan, New Delhi, 2005)

6. Gurshabad Ratnakar (Mahan Kosh)
Bhai Kahan Singh
(Punjab Languages Dept., 1974)

7. Adi Sri Guru Granth Sahib Steek (Faridkot wala teeka)
Reprint Bhasha Vibhag Punjab, 1989 (Punjabi), Vol. I

8. The Encyclopaedia of Sikhism
Editor in Chief: Harbans Singh (Punjabi University, Patiala, 1998)

9. Santhya, Sri Guru Granth Sahib Ji
Bhai Vir Singh
(Khalsa Samachar, Hall Bazar, Amritsar, 4th reprint, 1981)

10. Sacred Nitnem (English)
Harbans Singh Doabia
(Singh Brothers Mai Sewan Bazar, Amritsar, Edition 1995)

11. Rehras, Evensong, The Sikh Evening Prayer
Translated by Reema Anand and Khushwant Singh
Viking, 2002

12. A Popular Dictionary of Sikhism
W. Owen Cole and Prem Singh Sambhi
(Rupa & Co., 1990)

13. Sri Guru Granth Sahib (English)
Dr. Gopal Singh
(World Book Centre, Asaf Ali Road, New Delhi, International Edition, 1989)

14. Nitnem, Daily Prayer of the Sikhs
Gurcharan Singh Talib
(Guru Nanak Foundation, New Delhi, 1983

15. Sikh Rehat Maryada
Dharam Parchar Committee
(SGPC, Amritsar, July 1997)

16. Panj Granthi Steek
Bhai Vir Singh
(Bhai Vir Singh Sahit Sadan, New Delhi, 9th Print, July 2005.)

17. Sri Guru Granth Sahib (English)
Prof. G. S. Talib
(Punjabi University, Patiala, 1988)

18. Gurshabad Ratnakar (Mahan Kosh)
Bhai Sahib Bhai Kahan Singh (Punjab Languages Dept., 1974)

19.Nitnem Steek
Prof. Sahib Singh
(Singh Brothers, Amritsar, 2005)

20. Sri Guru Granth Sahib
Bhai Manmohan Singh

21. The Sikh Religion
Max Arthur Macauliffe
Singh Brothers, Amritsar

22. Nitnem Saral Steek
Bhai Joginder Singh Talwara
Singh Brothers, Amritsar, 2005

23. Gurbani Nitnem Steek
Bhai Harnam Singh
Gurmat Prakashan House, New Delhi, 2007

24. A History of Sikh People
Dr. Gopal Singh
World Book Centre,
New Delhi, 1988

25. A History of the Sikhs
J. D. Cunningham
SChand & Co., 1966

26. A Treasury of Mystic Terms
Science of Soul
Research Centre
Radha Swami Satsang, Beas

27. **Guru Granth Vishwakosh**
Editor, Dr. Ratan
Singh Jaggi
Punjabi University,
Patiala, 2002

28. Nitnem, Daily Prayer of the Sikhs
Guru Nanak Foundation
New Delhi, 1983

29. The Koran
Translated by J. M. Rodwell
Phoenix, London, 1909
(reissued in 1992 and 1994)

30. The Illustrious Qur'an
Abdullah Yusuf Ali
Adam Publishers, Chitli
Qabar, Delhi, 1997

31. Rehatnamay
Ed. Piara Singh Padam
Singh Brothers, Amritsar

32. Guru Granth Vichar Kosh
Piara Singh Padam
Publication Bureau, Punjabi
University, Patiala

33. Early Sikh Tradition
W. H. Mcleod
Clarendon Press, Oxford,
1980

34. The Sikh Gurus
K. S. Duggal
Himalyan International
Institute of Yoga Science
Honesdale, Pennsylvania,
USA

Maneshwar S. Chahal has an honours degree in English Literature, a degree in Engineering and a Masters in Public Administration. He has been an army officer, a senior bureaucrat in the IAS, CMD of the Punjab & Sind Bank, and a member of the State Human Rights Commission in Punjab. In the midst of these multifarious roles, he has continued to be a deeply devoted student of Spirituality, especially of the intensely humanistic Sikh Religion.

His series 'Way to God in Sikhism' offers a lucid and easy-to-understand delineation of the Spiritual path in the context of the Sikh belief system. Starting with the *Japji Sahib*, it has been warmly welcomed and much appreciated by scholars and lay readers alike.

Chahal lives in Chandigarh and can be reached at
chahal37@hotmail.com.